2016 Dissertation
   Exile + the Rec  rmation

# STRANGE BRETHREN

# Studies in Early Modern German History

H. C. Erik Midelfort, Editor

# Strange Brethren

## REFUGEES, RELIGIOUS BONDS, AND
## REFORMATION IN FRANKFURT, 1554–1608

Maximilian Miguel Scholz

UNIVERSITY OF VIRGINIA PRESS

CHARLOTTESVILLE AND LONDON

University of Virginia Press
© 2022 by the Rector and Visitors of the University of Virginia
All rights reserved
Printed in the United States of America on acid-free paper

*First published 2022*
1 3 5 7 9 8 6 4 2

Library of Congress Cataloging-in-Publication Data

Names: Scholz, Maximilian Miguel, author.
Title: Strange brethren : refugees, religious bonds, and reformation in Frankfurt, 1554–1608 / Maximilian Miguel Scholz.
Description: Charlottesville : University of Virginia Press, 2021. | Series: Studies in early modern German history | Includes bibliographical references and index.
Identifiers: LCCN 2021023496 (print) | LCCN 2021023497 (ebook) | ISBN 9780813946757 (hardcover) | ISBN 9780813946764 (ebook)
Subjects: LCHS: Frankfurt am Main (Germany)—Church history—16th century. | Religious refugees—Germany—Frankfurt am Main—History—16th century.
Classification: LCC BR858.F7 S36 2021 (print) | LCC BR858.F7 (ebook) | DDC 261.8/328—dc23
LC record available at https://lccn.loc.gov/2021023496
LC ebook record available at https://lccn.loc.gov/2021023497

Cover art: "Römer or City Hall." From Caspar Merian's *Beschreibung und Abbildung aller königl. und churfürstl. Ein-Züge, Wahl und Crönungs Acta*. Frankfurt am Main: Merian, 1658.

To Lauren, with all my love

# CONTENTS

# ACKNOWLEDGMENTS

T HIS BOOK REPRESENTS the time and sweat of many brilliant and generous people. I want to thank Carlos Eire first. Carlos inspired my interest in Reformation history when I was a college student, and he nurtured my love of historical research in graduate school. He taught me to appreciate the real impact of religion on history. (He also convinced me that refugees may see the world in a more honest way than others.)

I am also indebted to my other professors at Yale who helped me develop as a scholar of early modern Europe. Bruce Gordon spent countless hours reading the pages of this book, and I cannot believe my good luck in having the global expert on Calvinism as a friend and mentor. Francesca Trivellato read hundreds of pages of my work in meticulous detail and helped make it all readable. Paul Kennedy encouraged me when I was flagging, and I am truly grateful to him, Amanda Behm, and everyone else at International Security Studies at Yale, which funded my years of research and writing. My research was also supported by the MacMillan Center at Yale and the Yale Program for the Study of Antisemitism.

Ayelet Shachar gave me the opportunity to start my career within a dynamic interdisciplinary department, and I thank her—and the entire Max Planck Institute for the Study of Religious and Ethnic Diversity—for making this book possible. I also want to thank my colleagues at Max Planck who helped me with my work, especially Stefan Schlegel.

The raw material for this book was mined at the Institut für Stadtgeschichte in Frankfurt am Main. Roman Fischer at the Institut deserves special thanks for the hours he spent answering my questions about Frankfurt's history and about the intricacies of Frankfurt's archives. This book would not exist without Dr. Fischer's *Gutachten*. Luise Schorn-Schütte at the Goethe Universität helped develop my ideas. Karl Murk at the Hessisches Staatsarchiv Marburg helped expand this project outside the bounds of Frankfurt. I want to thank the Fulbright Commission for supporting my research in Frankfurt. I also want to thank Daniel Kunkel for improving (and vernacularizing) my German.

A staggering number of people read and improved pages of this book. Nazanin Sullivan and Justine Walden, my fellow early modernists, deserve special thanks. Ryan Hall, David Petrucelli, Caitlin Verboon, and Christopher Bonner all spent a great deal of time helping me. These are true friends.

I want to thank my colleagues at Florida State University for supporting me and my research. I also want to thank the many early modernists who helped me. I am indebted to Jesse Spohnholz, who spent hours pruning and improving this book. Christopher Close, Marc Forster, Duncan Hardy, Ward Holder, Benjamin Kaplan, David Luebke, Nicholas Must, Mirjam van Veen, and Kenneth Woo all shared their time and expertise in ways that helped me tremendously. I am fortunate to be part of a field with such supportive colleagues and mentors.

This book would not have developed as it did without the tireless support of the experts at the University of Virginia Press. I want to thank Erik Midelfort, Dick Holway, and especially Nadine Zimmerli for fashioning my research into a publishable form. Nadine's expertise as a historian and writer helped me realize this work.

Most importantly, I want to thank my family for making this book possible and for inspiring me in every way. My mother, Dr. Rachel Acosta Scholz from East Los Angeles, and my father, Dr. Joachim Josef Scholz from Neisse in Upper Silesia, inspired me to work hard and care about (and for) other people. They proofread countless pages of this book. My sister Bettina continues to be my role model. Her book *The Cosmopolitan Potential of Exclusive Associations* sits in front of me as I write this. My sister Antonia proofread pages of this book. Toni proves that in a family of academics, the nonacademic may be the most intelligent.

Finally, I want to thank my wife, Lauren Henry Scholz, who supported me throughout this book project and daily inspires me with her brilliance as an academic and as a person. Any insight or creative energy existing in this book resulted from my love of Lauren, and I therefore dedicate this book to her.

# NOTES ON NAMES AND TERMINOLOGY

THE INDIVIDUALS IN THIS BOOK spelled their names in many ways and often used multiple names. I have used only one name for each individual and privileged the name in the individual's native language—thus Elector Friedrich instead of Elector Frederick and Sebastian Matte instead of Sebastian Storea. I make exceptions for famous figures widely known in English by a different name—thus John a Lasco instead of Jan Łaski and Philip Melanchthon instead of Philipp Schwartzerdt. Place-names are given in their English form.

Several terms that appear throughout this book—Protestant, Reformed, Lutheran, Low Countries, Dutch, French, and refugee—require explanation. The first three in particular deserve justification because the supporters of the Reformation, including the main characters in this book, usually referred to themselves simply as Christian. But since this is a book about the splintering of the Reformation, I need to be able to speak about a starting point before that splintering took place, and I have therefore used the term "Protestant" to refer broadly to Western Christians who accepted Martin Luther's call for church reform and rejected the authority of the papacy. This kaleidoscopic group of people divided into competing confessional camps over the course of the story here. To refer to those Protestants who embraced the religious tradition emerging in Swiss cities under the guidance of John Calvin, I have used the term "Reformed" instead of the term "Calvinist," which was a pejorative word in the sixteenth century. To refer to those Protestants who identified with the religious tradition emerging from Wittenberg under the guidance of Luther and his successors, I have used the term "Lutheran."

The "Low Countries," in this book, refers to the Habsburg Netherlands, a collection of territories—usually numbered at seventeen—ruled by the Habsburg family since 1482 and nominally part of the Holy Roman Empire. The political position of these territories within the empire shifted over the course of the sixteenth century.[1] The Low Countries comprised an area roughly coterminous with the present-day Netherlands, Belgium, Luxembourg, and the French departments of Nord and Pas-de-Calais. The Dutch language dominated in the northern parts of the Low Countries, while French and French dialects were common in the south. The language divide between the Dutch north and the French south was fluid. German was spoken in parts of the east.

The terms "Dutch" and "French" appear frequently in this book and denote language groups rather than ethnic or national identities. Thus, Dutch refugees in Frankfurt were refugees who used Dutch as their language of worship. The majority of the Dutch people in this book came from Flanders and Brabant, leading some Frankfurters to call them Flemish. But many also came from the cities of the northern Low Countries, rendering the term "Flemish" too narrow. The Dutch in Frankfurt referred to themselves with either the Dutch adjective *Nederlands* or the German equivalent *Niederländisch*, words that I have translated as Dutch rather than Netherlandish to capture their linguistic denotation and avoid reference to the entire multilingual area of the Low Countries. The French refugees in Frankfurt mostly came from cities in the southern Low Countries, such as Arras, Lille, Mons, Tourcoing, Tournai, and Valenciennes. Frankfurters sometimes called these people Walloons, but they called themselves French to distinguish themselves from their Dutch brethren. Their religious services were in French, and some of them came from cities within France like Bourges. I have therefore used the term "French" to refer to these French-speaking refugees.

Finally, it may surprise readers to see the label "refugee" applied to individuals displaced before the year 1572, when the term first appeared.[2] The displaced men and women who asked Frankfurt for refuge in 1554 referred to themselves as expellees or simply as foreigners.[3] I contend that the term "refugee" best captures the experience of the displaced Christians entering Frankfurt in 1554 and helps illuminate the massive displacement in the aftermath of the Reformation, when, after all, the term "refugee" first appeared in French specifically to describe the type of people discussed in this book: persecuted Christians receiving accommodation abroad.[4] Here the term applies to those individuals who settled outside of their communities of origin due to a well-founded fear of violence. This definition bears a clear resemblance to the 1951 United Nations definition but differs from it by not relying on delimited national boundaries or the international obligation of *non-refoulement*, neither of which existed in the sixteenth century.[5]

My definition of "refugee" draws no distinction between ordered expulsion and supposedly voluntary relocation. While certain cases of sixteenth-century displacement were incontestably involuntary, as when the Catholic

Duke George of Saxony recorded the names of Protestants in Leipzig and escorted them out of his duchy in 1532, most cases defy easy categorization.[6] For example, the Spanish Duke of Alba arrived in the Low Countries in 1567 carrying pardons for any Protestants who would return to the Catholic Church; recalcitrant Protestants would be executed.[7] Should we then consider Protestants who fled from this ultimatum refugees by choice? In the case of Frankfurt, several groups of refugees arrived in 1554, some having been expelled by formal order and others not. Frankfurt's authorities acknowledged no distinction between these groups and treated all of the newcomers as one community of refugees.

In using the term "refugee," I seek to capture the experience of physical displacement from one's homeland. Therefore, my definition of "refugee" excludes the notion of "inner exile," a concept that usually describes alienation or dissimulation.[8] Sixteenth-century refugees did not understand their predicament as a state of alienation but rather as a state of exteriority resulting from physical dislocation from their hometowns.[9] Dislocation caused intense suffering, but this does not mean that refugees were poor and helpless victims.[10] On the contrary, many of the refugees entering Frankfurt were wealthy merchants with many options for resettlement. Some would quickly join the Frankfurt citizenry whereas others refused. What bound all these displaced people together was not feelings of alienation or estrangement but rather a shared inability to return safely to their homelands.

It is highly doubtful that Calvin would have considered inner exile anything akin to life physically removed from one's homeland. He famously denounced Protestants who dissimulated in Catholic countries, so-called Nicodemites, who behaved like the biblical Pharisee Nicodemus, who would only meet Jesus at night.[11] Calvin insisted that such people should relocate or else endure martyrdom. The men and women whose stories are told in the following pages acted upon this directive— they fled their homes rather than accept the Catholicism of their rulers. Exile offered them the opportunity to preserve their physical and spiritual lives together, or so they hoped.

# STRANGE BRETHREN

Map 1. The Holy Roman Empire

# Introduction

❧

IN EARLY 1554, a small community of refugees approached the imperial city of Frankfurt am Main and asked for shelter. These refugees—just twenty-four families in total—were led by their minister, a man named Valérand Poullain. Minister Poullain and his flock had fled their homes in the Low Countries because their renunciation of the Catholic Mass had aroused the fury of their Catholic lord. Fearing persecution for their religious beliefs, they had fled to England, but the ascension of the Catholic Queen Mary Tudor in 1553 left them homeless once more. Desperate for a new place to rebuild their lives, Poullain and his followers petitioned the German city of Frankfurt for admission. "[We] do not want to overburden you or the citizenry," Poullain assured the city council.[1] Frankfurt had never before sheltered a community of refugees, but in March 1554, the city agreed to do so. Frankfurt granted the refugees housing, work space, and a place to worship. This act of hospitality heralded a new era—one still ongoing—during which refugee accommodation became a regular affair in Frankfurt.

Why did Frankfurt decide to experiment with refugee accommodation? To be precise, it was the city's ruling council, an oligarchy of forty-three men, that decided to admit the refugees. The citizenry and other residents had no say in the matter. The councilmen gathered together in the city hall on 18 March and decreed that the refugees "should be welcomed in the name of God."[2] It was men like Claus Bromm, the city's junior mayor and richest citizen, and his brother Hans, also a councilman, who first supported the refugees. In an early modern city like Frankfurt, the admission of refugees depended on the patronage of specific, powerful figures like the Bromms. But what, exactly, had Poullain said to the Bromms and their peers to elicit such unprecedented support for displaced people? And how would the citizenry react to these new-comers? This book begins with these two questions before addressing a larger one: What were the consequences—for both the refugees and their hosts—of Frankfurt's early modern accommodation of refugees?

Frankfurt's early modern encounter with displaced people paralleled hundreds of similar cases across Europe. Unbeknownst to Poullain, the Bromms, and the other individuals living in Frankfurt, they were partic-ipating in a historic and far-reaching shift in Europe's social geography as hundreds of thousands of religious minorities resettled in cities and territories across Europe.[3] The Reformation had fractured Europe's reli-gious landscape and left thousands stranded on the wrong side of newly drawn religious borders. And religious borders could realign suddenly. For instance, on 6 July 1553, the Protestant King Edward VI of England died, and his Catholic half sister, Mary, inherited the throne. Imagine the fear of English Protestants like Anne Hooper, who had married the Protestant bishop of Gloucester under Edward VI. Anne now faced the wrath of a queen who rejected clerical marriage. Like Poullain and his followers, Anne fled to Frankfurt. Over the course of the sixteenth century, thousands of vulnerable religious minorities fled their home-lands rather than face the prospect persecution. By 1572, so many peo-ple had fled their homes and settled abroad that Antoine Perrenot de Granvelle—archbishop of Mechelen-Brussels and chief minister to the Spanish Habsburgs—began using the term *refugees* (*réfugiés*) to describe displaced persons deserving of shelter and protection.[4] The human dis-placement arising from the Reformation gave birth to the refugee and in-augurated a new era in which Europeans began to articulate, define, and debate their ethical obligations to displaced foreigners. This book takes Frankfurt as a case study of Reformation refugees and their impact on European society. As the story of Frankfurt demonstrates, early modern refugee accommodation transformed the religion of refugees and hosts alike. Several prominent features of modern Protestantism in Frank-furt—its division into competing confessional camps, its intramural in-stitutions of conflict arbitration, and its liturgical exactitudes—resulted from the city's early modern experience of refugee accommodation.

## REMEMBERING REFORMATION REFUGEES

Historians have long acknowledged the economic impact of early mod-ern refugees. In an era of stagnant populations and limited economic growth, the resettlement of thousands of people transformed the economic landscape of the continent while also vitalizing Europe's colonies overseas.[5] In the case of Frankfurt, historians have ascribed economic motives to both the decision to admit refugees and the later hostility directed at the newcomers.[6] Such economic interpretations neglect the prominence of personal bonds and personal feuds in determining the fate of refugee accommodation. For example, in 1555 a rivalry between two English clergymen in Frankfurt convinced a substantial portion of the English refugees in Frankfurt to abandon the city and relocate to Geneva.[7] Still, it cannot be denied that the movement of Reformation refugees transformed economies, as was the case in Frankfurt. Refugees from Antwerp, like the banker Johann von Bodeck, established a currency exchange in Frankfurt that would grow to become the Deutsche Börse, one of the world's largest stock exchanges, still headquartered in the city.[8] Displaced people had a similarly momentous impact on Frankfurt's political landscape and religious constitution.

Across Europe, refugees played pivotal roles in the ongoing religious changes of the era, a fact suggested by their ubiquity and confirmed by their prominence as leading reformers. Martin Bucer, the influential leader of ecclesiastical reforms in Strasbourg, died a refugee in England. The Genevan reformer Marie Dentière fled persecution in her native Tournai. John Calvin, John Knox, and John a Lasco were all refugees. The last Catholic archbishop of Canterbury, Reginald Pole, learned of his family's execution from his safety in exile. Another Englishman, William Allen, organized Catholic publications and founded Counter-Reformation seminaries, all while in exile. Less famous refugees could likewise reshape the religious institutions around them. Refugees like Poullain and his followers—through their activities, writings, and mere presence—helped steer the course of the Reformation in Frankfurt. As is the case today, refugees were not only the victims of epochal change; they were also shapers of ongoing changes.[9]

Studying memoirs and religious texts authored by refugees, historians have identified the marks left by displacement upon the Reformed religious tradition, a tradition to which most of the refugees in Frankfurt belonged.[10] Exile became part of their narrative and institutional identity.[11] Displacement became a sure sign that a person was one of God's elect.[12] Moreover, life in exile could provide a Reformed community with the fresh start necessary for systematic church building. Displacement spread the Reformed tradition, introducing it into German lands, among many other places.[13]

By examining one German city hosting Reformed refugees, it is possible to see beyond the confines of the refugee community itself and understand how the city as a whole—Reformed and non-Reformed—changed as a result of refugee accommodation. It is important to consider the position of the native Frankfurters, especially those who became staunch opponents of the refugees and their religious practices. The prevailing characterization of those who opposed the refugees remains the one crafted by the refugees themselves, and it is wholly unsympathetic.[14]

Recent scholarship has reminded us that displacement afflicted Christians of every confession, and indeed Jews and Muslims too.[15] Refugees of all religions were forced to defend the boundaries of their religious communities in foreign lands, necessitating the creation of poor-relief systems and disciplinary tools like consistories and catechisms.[16] This proved the case in Frankfurt as well. In Frankfurt, hardened confessional boundaries did not precede but rather followed the experience of refugee accommodation. The story of refugees in Frankfurt demonstrates how these displaced people provoked the creation of confessional boundaries. In this way, refugees bridge the chronological divide, constructed by historians, between the first part of the sixteenth century—when Martin Luther and other reformers set Europe ablaze with their criticisms of the Catholic Church—and the second part—when European rulers calmed the flames and began the systematic and sustained institutionalization of reforms.[17]

Increasingly, early modern historians have looked at episodes of refugee accommodation and asked how rulers managed to accommodate competing religious communities in a supposedly intolerant era.[18] Thus, refugees fit into a growing literature on coexistence, one that shifts the focus away from philosophical texts toward institutional sources that allow for an investigation of ordinary society, the "whole milieu" in which new modes of coexistence emerged.[19] Even before the emergence of modern, liberal notions of toleration—premised on individual freedom of conscience as a positive good—early modern Europeans still managed to accommodate religious heterodoxy via "negotiated demarcation," "fictions of privacy," "tactics of toleration," "pragmatic toleration," or simply by exhibiting "an accommodating stance."[20] The historians who have identified such informal arrangements insist that they are not identical to the modern legal protections usually associated with the word "toleration" today. As one historian studying refugees in the German city of Wesel explains, early modern coexistence did not necessarily entail "legal protection of religious minorities nor principled defenses of their toleration."[21]

Another historian, looking at religious plurality in early modern Antwerp, notes that the city's rulers did not "intend their tolerant practices to be applied universally. . . . They sought to actively defend only those heterodox inhabitants whose presence benefited the municipality."[22] In the sixteenth century, toleration carried the sense of a body's capacity to endure pain.[23] Still, these caveats notwithstanding, the recent reassessment of religious plurality in early modern Europe has been largely positive, demonstrating the possibility of peaceful coexistence, even in a world rife with regimes and philosophies of intolerance.[24] Early modern people found nonviolent, informal ways to manage religious heterodoxy.

How did sixteenth-century religious minorities perceive the various modes of formal and informal toleration that have been described by historians? The story of refugees in Frankfurt helps to answer this question. In Frankfurt, refugees experienced both formal religious toleration—by which I mean formal legal sanction for their community's religious services, which other historians have called "freedom of worship"—and informal arrangements like private worship that facilitated coexistence after the Frankfurt Council withdrew its formal sanction in 1561.[25] In the writings of refugees like Poullain, a clear dissatisfaction with informal modes of coexistence emerges. Furtive worship did not satisfy. One of the leaders of the Dutch refugees in Frankfurt, a twenty-four-year-old preacher named Pieter Datheen, so resented Frankfurt's 1561 insistence on private household worship that he wrote a scathing account of Frankfurt's intolerance toward his community. Datheen sought public recognition of his community's religious services. Indeed, the demands of early modern refugees seem remarkably like those of refugees today: admission to citizenship, economic opportunity, and formal legal protection of religious services. The possibility of worship mattered, naturally, but so did the right to worship "publicly" (öffentlich in German and publico in Latin), by which they meant worship in a church building with the same number of steeples as the other city churches.[26] Limitations on public worship—however small they seem compared to the violent persecution occurring in other parts of Europe—were viewed as repressive acts aimed at expelling refugees from Frankfurt.[27] Refugees sought formal toleration, whether at the local, regional, or imperial level. And while the refugees in Frankfurt would take advantage of informal modes or sentiments of acceptance, these would not suffice. They wanted the city authorities to grant them a church and formally protect their services.

Although the leaders of the refugees in Frankfurt sought legal protection of their services, they did not support universal freedom of worship or freedom of conscience. Instead, they sought acknowledgment from Frankfurt's rulers that refugee services, like the city's, constituted an expression of God's one truth. Men like Datheen, who fought for his community's rights, utterly rejected religious accommodation for Anabaptists, Protestants who believed Christians should be baptized as adults. Decades later in Ghent, when the Reformed community seized power, Datheen became a leading voice for suppressing alternative faiths.[28] While in Frankfurt, he and other refugees insisted that the city tolerate their independent religious services not out of dedication to the principle of religious freedom but because the religion of the refugees was right and true.

While the story of Frankfurt's refugees speaks to scholars of economics, Reformed religiosity, confessionalism, and toleration in early modern Europe, the characters and events in the story do not fit perfectly into the paradigms of any one of these subfields. The stories of these people challenge each paradigm by showing how the experience of refugee accommodation transformed the religion of guest and host alike while forcing both newcomer and native to confront the challenge of living alongside people of another faith. This is a book about the twin winding paths of a displaced religious community and a host city, as both worked to define and defend a new religious order.

## FRANKFURT: A CITY BOTH TYPICAL AND UNIQUE

Frankfurt straddled the Main River near the geographic center of the Holy Roman Empire—a collection of principalities, ecclesiastically controlled territories, knightly castles, and free cities. In 1512, the empire had officially assumed the suffix "of the German Nation" in recognition of the overwhelmingly German population living within its kaleidoscopic borders.[29] Within the empire, Frankfurt enjoyed the distinction of being an imperial city, legally able to govern its own affairs. Imperial cities—including the so-called free cities like Strasbourg and Cologne, which had originally been under the authority of an episcopal lord—enjoyed imperial immediacy (*Reichsunmittelbarkeit*), meaning they enjoyed the same free station as the most powerful lords of the empire, answering to no ruler but the emperor himself.[30] Frankfurt cherished its political autonomy within the empire.

The independence enjoyed by imperial cities like Frankfurt allowed them to embrace Luther and his reforms, and a vast majority of these cities did so in the first half of the sixteenth century. But while they embraced Luther's reforms, imperial cities remained beholden to the emperor and the institutions of the empire, which were in turn beholden to the Catholic Church.[31] Imperial cities became battlegrounds of the Reformation, where Luther's urban supporters challenged the bond between the empire and the Catholic Church. Protestant imperial cities became popular destinations for Protestant refugees fleeing France, the Low Countries, and other areas under Catholic princely authority in the late sixteenth century. In two important respects, then, Frankfurt was a typical self-governing city: it embraced Luther's message in the 1530s, and it opened its doors to refugees in the 1550s. Frankfurt, like Aachen, Cologne, Hamburg, and Strasbourg, took part in the massive early modern accommodation of religious refugees.

Yet Frankfurt was also uniquely important as the geographic, commercial, and symbolic heart of the entire empire.[32] Frankfurt lay at a nexus of several vital trade routes, including ones connecting Paris to Vienna and Hamburg to Switzerland.[33] Twice a year—during Lent and then in August—Frankfurt hosted an international trade fair that drew merchants from across Europe and facilitated long-distance commerce, especially in cloth, luxury goods, and books.[34] In fact, Poullain explained to the council that he had selected Frankfurt as a refuge for his flock specifically because of the city's commerce and fairs: "I was initially attracted because of the wide praise of the city of Frankfurt and reasons like its business and two fairs, and I could not invent a more charming place than Frankfurt."[35] The city's role as a commercial hub had not escaped the notice of Luther, who (ever the miner's son) lamented the loss of German metals through international trade: "Frankfurt is the hole through which all the gold and silver flows out of Germany."[36]

Frankfurt's bridge over the Main River was an asset of enormous value to merchants and other travelers, as the Main cut from east to west across the middle of the empire. The city derived its name from its position as a river crossing (a Frankish ford), and this geographic position lent the city major military significance too. Armies hoping to move north or south on the east side of the Rhine River had to use the bridge in Frankfurt or else ferry troops across the Main.[37] By the sixteenth century, Frankfurt had also become an important site of military recruitment, where commanders from various countries met and hired the German and Swiss mercenaries who filled the ranks of early modern armies.[38]

Finally, Frankfurt enjoyed symbolic importance within the empire as the location of imperial elections. The Golden Bull of 1356, the fundamental legal constitution of the empire, had established seven princes as imperial electors and designated Frankfurt as the site of elections.[39] The seven electors were to gather in St. Bartholomew's Church (which still bears the sobriquet "Imperial Cathedral") to elect the next emperor.[40] In 1562, Frankfurt gained further prestige when it replaced Aachen as the site of imperial coronations. When Frankfurt decided to welcome and shelter refugees, other cities noticed.

## STUDYING FRANKFURT: A MATTER OF SOURCES

Despite its centrality in early modern Europe, its prominence as a destination for displaced people, and its similarity to more-studied cases of refugee accommodation, Frankfurt remains on the fringes of most scholarship on the Reformation and Reformation refugees. This neglect by scholars is not accidental but rather traces back to 29 January 1944, when the United States bombed Frankfurt's city archive and thus destroyed most of its early modern records, including those documenting the Reformation in the city.[41] A study of Reformation refugees in Frankfurt must, therefore, scrutinize a compilation of fragmentary texts, documents that had not been housed at the archive, and documents that had been reproduced before the destruction of the archive.

This book emerges from a broad source base that can be divided into six types of documents: refugee petitions; civic and princely edicts and treaties; citizenship lists; consistory minutes; refugee letters (both printed and unprinted); and memoirs by refugees reflecting on their experience of exile. The first category is especially rich because the refugees from the Low Countries established themselves as an independent congregation apart from the city's civic church, thereby provoking conflict that resulted in numerous petitions addressed to the council from the city ministers, from the refugees, and eventually from succeeding generations, who continued to litigate the religious conflicts emerging from Frankfurt's first experiment with refugee accommodation. Put simply, refugee accommodation provoked religious animosity, eliciting competing sets of petitions to the Frankfurt council. These written appeals became important evidence during an eighteenth-century court case when

the community founded by refugees—which now called itself Reformed
to distinguish itself from Frankfurt's Lutheran majority—sued the city
before the Imperial Aulic Council (Reichshofrat), alleging that the city
authorities unjustly suppressed the public practice of the Reformed faith
in Frankfurt.[42] The city council had refused permission for them to build
a place of worship, so the Reformed now petitioned the empire's central judiciary in Vienna. The court collected evidence submitted by both
the Reformed community and the city's authorities, printing dozens
of sixteenth-century petitions, edicts, and letters (in French, German,
and Latin) in two volumes under the title *Franckfurtische Religions-
Handlungen* (1735).

The petitions printed in 1735 reveal the desires of the refugees in the
city, though not directly.[43] Petitions of this kind—authored by the initial group of French-speaking refugees as well as later communities of
English- and Dutch-speaking newcomers—comprise rhetorical strategies
and should not be understood as transparent representations of the desires of an entire community. Such petitions were written by the religious
leaders of the refugee community, men who naturally represented the religious aspirations of the refugees as paramount. Additionally, the petitions
of the refugees in Frankfurt, like all early modern religious supplications,
employ what one historian has labeled a "strategic calculus, ... so that the
more the argumentation specifies, the less of a religious legal basis exists
for the petitioner to call upon."[44] In short, excessive argumentation in a
petition is a clear indication of a weak legal claim.

Although the sources in *Franckfurtische Religions-Handlungen* illuminate the relationship between the refugee community and Frankfurt,
these sources cast only weak light on the inner life of the refugee community itself. Published memoirs along with unpublished consistory
records from the French and Dutch communities help tremendously.
The memoirs of William Whittingham, Jan Utenhove, and Pieter Datheen describe the travails of displaced people in Frankfurt. These texts
became prominent testimonials of religious fortitude, cherished by Reformed communities across Europe and reprinted many times. Decidedly partisan in nature, these memoirs prove most useful when coupled
with unprinted consistory records never intended for publication. Consistory records from the French and Dutch refugees in Frankfurt and
their descendants are now kept in the city archive (they were housed
elsewhere in 1944, fortunately), and these records include formal reso-
lutions and discussion minutes. They also contain membership lists and

many letters to other refugee communities outside of Frankfurt and to nearby princes.

It is important to consider the position of the Frankfurters like Minister Hartmann Beyer, who preached against the accommodation of refugee religious services.[45] And while the records of Frankfurt's city church, the *Acta Ecclesiastica*, were destroyed in 1944, letters between Beyer and the refugees do still exist, though not in the city archive. They can be found in the archive of Frankfurt's Goethe University.

Finally, several invaluable documents were collected and printed before 1944, either as appendices to histories or as stand-alone primary source collections rich with chronicles, letters, and even songs from sixteenth-century Frankfurt.[46] Letters from Frankfurters and refugees found their way into printed collections of Calvin's correspondence.[47] Such letters are especially important for understanding Poullain, the intrepid, if quarrelsome, leader of the refugees in Frankfurt. Poullain's letters and letters about him written by his opponents and successors are published in the *Corpus Reformatorum* and appear throughout this account.

## The Story of Frankfurt's Refugees

This book proceeds chronologically, starting in the decades before the 1554 admission of refugees in Frankfurt. By tracing the roots of accommodation in one particular city, we begin to see why mass displacement became a wider phenomenon in the mid-sixteenth century. As chapter 1 demonstrates, the Reformation created new affinities alongside new animosities, such that the refugee community and Frankfurt saw each other as allies because both had rejected the Catholic Mass. Protestants in the Low Countries could realistically hope for support from coreligionists abroad whom they had never met. They acted on this hope in 1554 and approached Frankfurt seeking shelter. Frankfurt, too, sought allies and support and saw in the refugees a potential path forward in the new and dangerous world of post-Reformation Europe.

Soon after the arrival of these people from the Low Countries in Frankfurt, the relationship between them and the city soured dramatically. Chapter 2 explains why this souring occurred and what it heralded. Frankfurt's seven official city ministers had initially welcomed the refugees in the name of Protestant solidarity, but upon witnessing the liturgy of the newcomers, the city ministers labeled them heretical. And while only the ruling council had the power to expel the refugees, the city's ministers could still stoke popular anger toward them. Beyer, the city's chief minister, did his best to turn the citizenry against the newcomers via a series of fiery sermons that portrayed the refugees as dangerous outsiders.

Within a year of their arrival the refugees had, by their very presence, forced the city's religious leaders to redefine the boundaries of their own congregation. Moreover, the dogmatism of Beyer and Frankfurt's other ministers threatened the irenic disposition of the ruling councilmen, who considered liturgical differences insufficient cause for action against the refugee community. The city's ministers worked tirelessly to establish a new confessional boundary between the citizenry and the refugees. In Frankfurt, refugee accommodation sparked confessionalism.

Eventually, Frankfurt's political rulers also turned against the displaced community and outlawed its religious services. The city councilmen did so in 1561 in the name of conflict prevention. They had grown frustrated by ceaseless internal disputes emerging from within the refugee community, as chapter 3 shows. It was made clear to the refugees that they were no longer welcome in Frankfurt. The refugees now faced the bitter choice of either leaving the city or finding a way to survive in its increasingly intolerant climate.

Chapter 4 follows the refugees who chose to leave Frankfurt after the city banned the public practice of their religious services in 1561. Hundreds left the city to establish new communities in small villages outside of the city's jurisdiction. Under the protection of nearby princes, these once-again exiled individuals wrote tracts criticizing Frankfurt and bemoaning the ephemeral nature of civic protection. They especially criticized Frankfurt's ministers, who had campaigned against the refugee services. Datheen and others who abandoned the city were not satisfied by private worship in households and resettled in places where they could publicly practice their faith. Datheen's writings reveal the deeply held aspirations of displaced Christians in early modern Europe.

The fifth and final chapter focuses on the refugees who remained in Frankfurt and the institutional mechanisms that allowed them and their descendants to survive in this hostile city for centuries. Realizing that messy internal disputes attracted the attention of Frankfurt's authorities, the refugee community repurposed its central religious institution, the consistory, in order to better arbitrate conflicts. The consistory as an institution remains a hallmark of Reformed religiosity and continues to attract scorn as a symbol of puritanical oppression. Yet as chapter 5 shows, the consistory was a respected court of arbitration that responded to the needs and desires of the Reformed community in Frankfurt. It helped prevent intramural conflicts from reaching the ears of Frankfurt's rulers and thereby helped preserve the position of the Reformed in the city.

In the conclusion, after summarizing the book's central claims, I offer a new perspective on the events occurring in Frankfurt between 1554 and 1608. The story of Frankfurt's welcome and eventual rejection of refugees is not a purely pessimistic one, for it led, indirectly, to the development of new institutions and traditions that helped the refugees' Reformed faith to thrive. Frankfurt's religious intolerance may have persisted into the eighteenth century, as made evident by the failed suit before the Imperial Aulic Council, yet Reformed Christianity survived in Frankfurt, and indeed members of the Reformed community became some of the richest and most prominent residents of the city. This story of refugees in Frankfurt shows how Protestant fraternity dissolved into two competing confessional communities that, ultimately, were able to survive side by side for centuries. A brief epilogue traces the story of the Reformed community in Frankfurt through the next four centuries. Today, the Reformed still maintain churches in Frankfurt, buildings that testify to the centrality of refugees in the story of the Reformation.

# 1

# New Dangers, New Allies, and the Emergence of Refugee Accommodation in Frankfurt

❧

It was because of our Christian religion alone, and no other reason, that we were made foreigners.

—Valérand Poullain's petition to the Frankfurt Council, 1554

THE ARRIVAL OF REFUGEES in Frankfurt in March 1554 was a momentous event but not a spontaneous one. Over the course of the early sixteenth century, a series of provocative, dangerous, and profoundly unsettling events had led Frankfurt's leaders and the refugees from the Low Countries to see each other as potential allies. They discovered that they shared similar goals and faced similar dangers. Both groups had embraced the Reformation, abandoned the Catholic Mass, and worked to reform their churches. And in their quests for religious reform, the refugees and Frankfurt's leaders faced a common enemy: Charles V, the Holy Roman emperor and lord of the Low Countries. Charles posed a double threat as he pursued religious and political goals at once. While executing supporters of the Reformation in cities like Bruges and Ghent, Charles also endeavored to consolidate the Low Countries into a single country and restructure the empire as a whole.[1] His machinations sent western Europe into religious and political convulsions. Protestants in the Low Countries fled their homelands in fear for their lives while Frankfurt suffered a serious military siege resulting from the struggle between Charles and the princes of the Holy Roman Empire.

13

Upon their meeting in 1554, refugees from the Low Countries and Frankfurt's leaders realized they could help each other. Frankfurt, thanks to its influential position within the empire, could house and protect the refugees, while the refugees—many among them weavers using state-of-the-art techniques—could bring an important new industry and tax base to the city. Yet refugee accommodation involved more than financial designs. The imperial instabilities and dangers threatening both Frankfurt and the refugees resulted in a new affinity between them. The two saw each other not only as potential sources of economic stability but also as kindred spirits, brethren pursuing the same religious vision in an increasingly hostile world.

To understand the origins of refugee accommodation in Frankfurt, one must appreciate the winding paths that had led the city and the refugees to the year 1554. This chapter begins with Frankfurt's story, focusing on the city's patricians, who dominated the city and its roughly twelve thousand residents.[2] In the early sixteenth century, the long-standing bond between the patricians and the imperial throne became distorted in new ways as a result of the Reformation and the violence it unleashed. This chapter then traces the path of the first twenty-four refugee families who came to Frankfurt, with their leader, Valérand Poullain, acting as a lens into their experience. Weaving together the story of Frankfurt with that of Minister Poullain brings us to the city's decision to admit the refugees, a decision that the final portion of this chapter dissects. How did Poullain secure such generous terms of accommodation for his community? Council minutes and written petitions demonstrate how he appealed directly to Frankfurt's most powerful patrician families, reminding them of their religious and economic ambitions and arguing that his community fit into both. The interplay of economic and religious goals thus explains how the refugees and Frankfurt's rulers came to help each other, seeking to preserve their livelihoods and their recent religious reforms. In facing the aggressive and destructive acts of Charles V, they needed each other as allies.

## FRANKFURT WITHIN THE EMPIRE AND UNDER THE EMPEROR

In the late fourteenth and early fifteenth centuries, Frankfurt had enjoyed a period of sustained prosperity, a "period of blossoming," according to the standard economic history of the city.[3] Frankfurt's population and wealth increased in this era thanks to the city's privileged position within the empire and its close relationship to the emperor.[4] The emperor granted Frankfurt the right to host a biannual trade fair and guaranteed protection for merchants traveling to Frankfurt. The emperor also granted Frankfurt control over an important timber forest south of the city, and the right to govern and tax the city's Jewish population, the largest in the German-speaking lands of Europe.[5] Most importantly, the emperor guaranteed Frankfurt the right of self-governance as an imperial city.[6] Imperial cities like Frankfurt swore allegiance to the emperor. And in exchange for protection from the interference and taxation of secular and spiritual princes, imperial cities—including the so-called free cities, which had formerly been under the authority of a spiritual lord—agreed to pay an imperial tax, especially in times of military crisis, although the city often neglected or resisted this financial commitment.[7]

An imperial tax list from 1521 lists eighty-five imperial cities, and within this number Frankfurt belonged to a very small elite—along with Nuremberg and Ulm—whose independence traced back to time immemorial.[8] Frankfurt had purchased a confirmation of its ancient independence from the emperor in the fourteenth century.[9] At the end of the fifteenth century the city's importance within the empire grew further when imperial cities—led by Augsburg, Frankfurt, Nuremberg, Strasbourg, and Ulm—formed the Urban Diet (Städtetag) to represent their interests at the imperial level.[10] Frankfurt became responsible for coordinating all cities in central and northern Germany.[11]

The emperor allowed Frankfurt and other imperial cities to govern their day-to-day affairs, which Frankfurt did through an oligarchical city council of forty-three men. The council consisted of three benches, with the first and highest bench consisting of fourteen judges (Schöffen) drawn from the city's most influential patrician families.[12] In addition to acting as councilmen, these judges formed the city's judiciary. The second bench of the council included fourteen seats, also reserved for patricians. The third and least important bench consisted of fifteen guild representatives, selected not by the guilds themselves but by the patricians on the first two benches. Put simply, Frankfurt's council was one of the least democratic in the empire, effectively controlled by a few patrician families, like the Bromms, Glauburgs, Holzhausens, and Lambs. These families were divided into two clubs (Stubengesellschaften): a senior club called Alten Limpurg, whose members were eligible for the first two benches of the council, and a junior club called Frauenstein, whose members were

Figure 1. Frankfurt's city hall (marked as #1) between the Alten Limpurg Lodge (#2) and the Frauenstein Lodge (#3), from Caspar Merian's *Beschreibung und Abbildung Aller Königl. und Churfürstl. Ein-Züge, Wahl und Crönungs Acta* (1658).

eligible for the second bench.[13] Only the members of these clubs exercised any real political power in sixteenth-century Frankfurt. In a sense, these early modern patricians still overshadow the city—their names mark the most important streets and subway stops in Frankfurt.[14] In the sixteenth century, the patricians exhibited their power over Frankfurt via two ornate, members-only lodges constructed on either side of the city hall—the Alten Limpurg lodge to the left of the city hall and the Frauenstein lodge to the right.[15] Frankfurt's government sat sandwiched between the patricians' two clubhouses.

The patricians' governance over Frankfurt (and thus their ability to admit refugees) stemmed from the city's imperial immediacy—they controlled Frankfurt and answered only to the emperor. The patricians treasured this status and conscientiously cultivated a close bond with the imperial throne.[16] The emperor was the guarantor of Frankfurt's independence. The city patricians relied on the emperor's military support since the incorporation of gunpowder into European military strategy had rendered the city's walls vulnerable.[17] While some fourteenth-century

Figure 2. *The Imperial Diet of Augsburg* (1530), by Georg Köler. (Courtesy of University of Arizona, Special Collections)

emperors had attempted to sell jurisdiction over Frankfurt, in the early sixteenth century the powerful Emperor Maximilian granted imperial cities a place of prominence within the newly reformed imperial diet.[18] During meetings of the diet, representatives of the imperial cities sat together on benches, facing the emperor, flanked on either side by the empire's spiritual and secular princes. Frankfurt's patricians elected one of their own number to represent Frankfurt at these diets, and thus the patriciate as a whole enjoyed a cultural and political significance within the empire at large [19] Throughout the sixteenth century, the patricians worked to retain their prominence within the empire, under only the jurisdiction of the emperor himself. Under Maximilian, Frankfurt's leaders enjoyed their close bond to the imperial throne.

The death of Emperor Maximilian in January 1519 afforded Frankfurt an opportunity to shine on the imperial stage. After Maximilian died, Albrecht von Brandenburg—the twenty-eight-year-old archbishop-elector of Mainz, imperial chancellor, and enthusiastic indulgence seller—summoned the six other imperial electors to Frankfurt to elect a new emperor. The Golden Bull of 1356, one of the empire's foundational ordinances, had designated Frankfurt as the site of imperial elections.[20] Elections were to take place in St. Bartholomew's Cathedral in the center of the city. Although St. Bartholomew's was not an episcopal seat, it enjoyed the status of a cathedral thanks to the Golden Bull. Albrecht also sent a deputy to Frankfurt to meet with Hamman von Holzhausen, one of the city's most powerful patrician judges, who served four times as senior mayor (Frankfurt had two mayors) including the previous year.[21] Holzhausen and his patrician peers were to organize the election for Maximilian's successor.

Frankfurt's status as site of imperial elections came with serious costs. The city paid a large contribution to newly crowned emperors and was also responsible for keeping the peace during elections, a complicated task considering that each elector was entitled to bring a guard of two hundred mounted men.[22] Yet despite the complications and costs, Holzhausen and the other patricians relished their status as hosts of imperial elections, and the council maintained a sizeable reserve fund for the occasion and for accompanying festivities.

That June, the seven electors met in St. Bartholomew's, and after celebrating mass they gathered in the Electoral Chapel adjacent to the high altar. The chief candidate to succeed Maximilian was his grandson Charles, the king of Spain. Charles was a native of the Low Countries and, since 1516, comonarch of Spain with his mother, Joanna.[23] Charles was in Barcelona, but his specter loomed large over Frankfurt during the election.[24] As the king of Spain, Archduke of Austria, Lord of the Low Countries, and ruler of the Spanish lands in the Americas, Charles was the most powerful man in Europe, and he paid a huge sum to secure his election. Moreover, he had stationed a small army outside of Frankfurt to improve his odds of winning the 1519 election.[25] The electors unanimously chose him to be the next Holy Roman emperor on 28 June.[26]

Thus, Charles became the next guarantor of Frankfurt's status as imperial city. Holzhausen and his fellow patricians sought a close relationship with the new emperor, especially after Holzhausen and his son-in-law Arnold von Glauburg learned in August 1519 that sizeable armies of knights from nearby territories had begun to mass around the city.[27] Now more than ever, allegiance to the emperor seemed key to maintaining peace and prosperity in Frankfurt. Holzhausen, Glauburg, and the other patricians cherished their imperial status and connection to the emperor, and they could not have predicted how fraught the city's relationship with Emperor Charles would soon become. Over the coming decades, Frankfurt's long-standing goal of maintaining accord with the emperor confronted a new obstacle: a profound desire for church reform, shared by Frankfurters of all types.

## The Reformation in Frankfurt

The patricians and citizens of Frankfurt had long bemoaned the practices of the medieval Catholic Church and eagerly sought religious reforms, which was also the case in other imperial cities.[28] The church's acquisition of houses in exchange for the saying of Masses infuriated Frankfurters, because the church could then charge rents on the properties in perpetuity (while often neglecting to say the Masses as promised).[29] By the first decade of the sixteenth century, Frankfurt's citizens had developed a robust tradition of mocking and deriding the clergy of the city, whom they resented for consuming but not contributing to the city's wealth.[30] The council and its patricians also despised church control over houses, as this frequently caused urban blight when citizens abandoned buildings with expensive rents charged by the church.[31]

Matters came to a head once Frankfurters began to read and hear the message of Martin Luther, the Augustinian monk and professor of theology at the University of Wittenberg. During the August trade fair of 1520, thousands of copies of Luther's texts filled the stalls reserved for booksellers near the Main River.[32] Luther's message appealed to Frankfurt on two important levels. His attack on clerical corruption and the church's theological fixation on works-based salvation (the latter responsible for the former, in his thinking) captivated citizens tired of church entitlements and abuse.[33] Luther also appealed to the city's rulers by calling on the German nobility to ignore the prerogatives of the church hierarchy, and to set about reforming religion on their own. Luther derided the idea that secular rulers should have no control over church matters: "Now, how Christian is the rule that says that secular authorities are not above the clergy and also may not punish them. That is like saying the hand should not help if the eye suffers severely. Is it not unnatural, not to say unchristian, for one member not to help the other, not to guard it against harm?"[34] Luther justified the nobility's right to reform religion thusly: "Since the secular authority has been baptized like the rest of us and has the same faith and the same gospel, we must allow it to be priest and bishop."[35] Frankfurt's patricians sought to answer Luther's call. In

1520, Holzhausen and the patricians of the Alten Limpurg Club established a new Latin school for Frankfurt's young men and hired Wilhelm Nesen, a religious reformer and humanist in the mold of Desiderius Erasmus, as rector for the new school.[36] The earliest histories of the Reformation in Frankfurt label Nesen "the first stimulator of the Reformation."[37] Yet, as a recent study of Frankfurt's Catholic clergy has shown, it was not Nesen's arrival that sparked the Reformation in Frankfurt, but rather the arrival in Frankfurt of Luther himself.[38]

In April 1521 Luther entered Frankfurt on his way to Worms, where Charles had summoned him to account for his writings.[39] Luther arrived in Frankfurt on a Sunday wearing his Augustinian habit and preceded by an imperial herald.[40] The city's residents went out to see him, and he was quickly surrounded by Frankfurters eager to greet the man whose message of reform had begun to resonate in the city.[41] Later that month, Luther passed through Frankfurt again on his way back from Worms, where he had refused to recant his writings. The popularity of his writings and his tenacious refusal to renounce them led Frankfurters to write songs of support for Luther, at least according to Johann Cochlaeus, dean of the Church of Our Lady in Frankfurt and adamant opponent of Luther.[42] Luther's mysterious disappearance soon after leaving Frankfurt cooled support for reform in the city. His reappearance in Wittenberg in 1522 inspired Frankfurt's patricians to bring his message to the city's pulpits.[43] Over the next decades, the patricians supported the Reformation in Frankfurt by appointing reforming pastors to preach in the city churches.

Frankfurt housed twenty-seven churches, administered by various collegiate chapters, mendicant orders, military orders, and the city's patricians themselves. The archbishop-elector of Mainz claimed spiritual jurisdiction over the most important of Frankfurt's churches—including St. Bartholomew's Cathedral—and he also served as the official censor for the city's book fairs.[44] But he did not control Frankfurt's churches directly. St. Catherine's Church in the center of the city answered to the city's patricians, who served as patrons of the church, a transferrable right. St. Catherine's was part of a convent founded by the patricians for their daughters.[45] It was in this patrician-controlled church that Reformation preaching first became a regular occurrence. In March 1522, a former Franciscan named Hartmann Ibach began to preach a message of reform at St. Catherine's that resonated in the city and enraged many of Frankfurt's priests.[46] We know the content of these sermons via the accounts of one Catholic priest who kept a journal. Ibach denounced perpetual rents, denounced veneration of saints, and advocated for poor relief and clerical marriage.[47]

The archbishop of Mainz confronted the limits of his episcopal authority when the Frankfurt Council ignored his demands to silence the Reformation preaching in St. Catherine's. The Reformation spread, and by 1525, denunciations of the Catholic Mass and the Catholic clergy could be heard in German coming from the pulpits of several of the city's churches. The patricians did their part to promote the Reformation by refusing to reprimand Ibach and other Reformation preachers.[48] Holzhausen even invited a fiery supporter of Luther's to preach in St. Bartholomew's Cathedral, though the archbishop of Mainz succeeded in eventually removing this man.[49] Holzhausen and the other patricians were content to see clerical celibacy, perpetual rents, the cult of the saints, and the Catholic Mass suffer under waves of denunciations.

The patricians were not alone in their support for church reform. In 1525, the guilds wrote to the council demanding evangelical preaching and denouncing Catholic opponents of such preaching.[50] Later that spring, in the midst of the Peasants' War, the citizens of the city marched in protest against the city's Catholic clergy—especially the Dominicans—and they presented the council with forty-six demands, starting with a demand that the citizenry have a say in the appointment of pastors.[51] Many of Frankfurt's clergy also supported Luther and his message. All but two of the city's Franciscans supported the new reforms, and the Franciscan church became the center of evangelical preaching.[52] One of the loudest reforming priests, Bernhard Algesheimer, inaugurated clerical marriage in Frankfurt when he married a woman from the city in May 1526.[53] The Reformation proved popular at every level of Frankfurt's society, and religious reform became a chief goal of the council in the late 1520s.

The patricians must have realized that implementing religious reforms went against Charles's Edict of Worms, which had condemned Luther. Holzhausen served as the city's deputy to imperial diets, where, over the coming years, Charles's brother and representative Ferdinand made clear the emperor's continued opposition to unsanctioned reforms.[54] Yet in the late 1520s, the emperor could not impose his will on the empire, as he was preoccupied by the threat of an Ottoman attack. Frankfurt's patricians pushed ahead with their effort to remodel the city's church along the lines advocated by Luther and Martin Bucer, the influential reformer and pastor in Strasbourg whose church order, the *Concordia Buceriana*, the Frankfurt Council would eventually adopt.[55] Inspired by Bucer, the council began to replace the Catholic Mass with a modified Lord's Supper.[56] The first Protestant Lord's Supper took place in 1528 with the distribution of both the bread and wine to the laity.[57] In 1529, the council insisted that preachers appointed by the council inspect all celebrations of the Eucharist.[58] In 1530—the same year that Charles returned to the empire after capturing much of northern Italy and receiving his imperial coronation from the pope—Frankfurt's council agreed to a new order of service for the Eucharist, which stressed singing and preaching.[59] On 23 April 1533, the council announced a ban on the Catholic Mass in Frankfurt, although certain religious houses were given a temporary reprieve.[60] In taking steps to reform the city's church, the council and the city's reforming ministers consulted with Bucer in Strasbourg, who helped guide reforms in several south German cities.[61]

Bucer proved the most influential reformer during Frankfurt's early Reformation, and his position on the Eucharist represented a compromise between the positions of Luther, who accepted the real presence of Jesus in the Eucharist, and the Swiss reformer Huldrych Zwingli, who insisted Jesus was only symbolically present. Bucer's understanding of Jesus's presence fell somewhere in between and emerged from "a friendly, brotherly discussion" with both parties, as he put it.[62] In 1542, the Frankfurt Council would adopt as the standard for the Eucharist Bucer's text, which begins with the following two articles:

> I. In the Lord's Supper, following the Words of Institution, the true body and the true blood of Christ are truly and essentially [*vere & essentialiter / wahrhafftig und wesentlich*] attained and received by those enjoying the Sacrament.

> II. But this puts forth no spatial or circumscribed presence of the Lord, wherefore one should not think here about the descent of God from heaven.[63]

With the first article, Bucer distinguished his understanding of the Eucharist from Zwingli's idea of symbolic presence. With the second article, Bucer distinguished his position from Luther's notion of real spatial presence.[64] Bucer's understanding of the Eucharist lay somewhere in between these two titans of the early Reformation, and it was Bucer's understanding that would eventually become normative in Frankfurt.[65]

By attacking the Mass in the early 1530s, Frankfurt's leaders positioned the city in direct opposition to the emperor's religious policy, which still insisted on adherence to the Edict of Worms.[66] They did so at an opportune time. During the 1530s and early 1540s, Charles could not easily impose his religious policy within the empire, even though his military forces were impressive. For one thing, he was rarely present in the empire and usually embroiled in wars with the Ottoman Sultan Suleiman I, the French King Francis I, or both monarchs at once. In 1535 and 1541, for example, he led campaigns to North Africa against Suleiman.[67] Moreover, Frankfurt was not the only imperial city charting a reforming course; many of the empire's largest territories and richest cities supported the Reformation, thereby limiting Charles's ability to reverse religious reforms at the imperial diets.[68] In early 1531, the representatives of seven powerful princes and eleven cities met in the town of Schmalkalden and agreed to a military alliance in defense of Protestantism and the right of imperial rulers and imperial cities to enact reforms in their territories.[69] Frankfurt did not immediately join this Schmalkaldic League, though it had been invited. At the time of the league's foundation, Charles confronted the Ottoman threat and suffered a serious health crisis; thus he was forced to negotiate a truce with the Schmalkaldic League in Nuremberg in 1532.[70]

However limited he was militarily, Charles still had ways of punishing Frankfurt for pursuing religious reforms unsanctioned by its bishop, Archbishop Albrecht of Mainz.[71] In 1531, Charles moved the site of imperial elections to Cologne, thus depriving Frankfurt of one of its chief distinctions.[72] Frankfurt would eventually regain the honor of hosting imperial elections, but not before the seven electors met in Cologne to elect Charles's brother Ferdinand next-in-line for the imperial throne.[73] Charles and his deputies reminded Frankfurt's patricians representatives of his displeasure at imperial diets and whenever the city pursued legal cases at one of the empire's two supreme courts. In 1534, Holzhausen and his son Justinian returned from Speyer to warn the city of the imperial court's determination to oppose unsanctioned reform with "violent and quick" action.[74] Alarmed by this news, Johann Fichard, another patrician and the city's attorney, assured Charles in writing of Frankfurt's loyalty.[75] At the same time, Fichard and the other city leaders looked for new allies.

Charles's opposition to religious reforms in Frankfurt forced the city's leaders to distinguish between loyalty to the empire and loyalty to the emperor. The council wrote letters to nearby rulers who, like Frankfurt's patricians, sought to enact religious reforms while preserving their high standing within the empire. Philipp, the landgrave of Hesse, a powerful Protestant prince to the north and a founding member of the Schmal-kaldic League, reached out to the council and even supported the city's religious reforms in opposition to the archbishop of Mainz.[76] But Frank-furt remained wary of Hesse, especially after Philipp stationed his army just north of the city in the spring of 1534.[77] Replacing the city's long-standing alliance with the imperial throne proved problematic.

Ultimately, the fear of Charles impelled Frankfurt to join the Schmal-kaldic League in 1536.[78] Three years later, the Nuremberg truce between Charles and the league was reaffirmed in Frankfurt.[79] Over the next decade, Charles defeated his many enemies abroad and redoubled his efforts to reverse unsanctioned religious changes within the empire. In 1541, Charles returned to Germany.[80] In 1546, he placed the leaders of the Schmalkaldic League under imperial ban, effectively declaring them outlaws.[81] Finally, in April 1547, Charles allied with the ambitious Prot-estant duke of Saxony, Moritz, and crushed the Schmalkaldic League at the Battle of Mühlberg, taking the league's leaders hostage. In doing so, Charles proved that he was more than the king of Spain and Holy Ro-man emperor; he was the undisputed master of Europe, a political reality captured by a celebratory image commissioned years later by Charles's son Philip.[82]

In the image pictured in figure 3, Charles's international adversaries (Suleiman, Pope Clement, and Francis) stand humbled on his right, while the recently defeated imperial princes (the Duke of Cleves, the Duke of Saxony, and the Landgrave of Hesse) submit on his left. Charles sits upon a black eagle whose beak holds the cords binding the emperor's adversaries. The eagle was the emblem of the empire and the insignia of the Habsburg family. In this image, the eagle is also an apt representa-tion of Frankfurt, whose symbol was and remains the eagle. As the poor bird struggles under the weight of the triumphant Charles, so the city of Frankfurt found itself crushed and at the mercy of the emperor, fol-lowing his victory at Mühlberg. Pastor Melchior Ambach of Frankfurt captured how Protestants felt toward the victorious Emperor Charles: "Now that the holy Gospel has richly risen up and illuminated a light of truth, gloriously first in Germany, in these our times, that same lord of darkness and father of lies has . . . never ceased to darken, if not kill, the same saving light . . . and has ultimately, though the pope and his gang,

Figure 3. Miniature from Simonzio Lupi's series *The Triumphs of Charles V* (1593). (The British Library, Illuminated Manuscripts, Additional 33733)

managed to persuade the mighty Emperor Charles V to be his vasal and sworn captain."[83]

After his military triumph, Charles summoned all the imperial estates, including the imperial cities, to a diet in Augsburg, where they assembled in May 1548. Charles issued a decree, titled the "Declaration of His Roman Imperial Majesty on the Observance of Religion within the Holy Empire until the Decision of the General Council," which mandated the return of seized Catholic properties, the resumption of the Catholic Mass, and the observance of holy days in the empire.[84] This decree came to be known as the Augsburg Interim, revealing the stopgap nature of Charles's intentions. The emperor still held out hope that an ecumenical council could induce Protestants to return to the Catholic fold. In the meantime, the Interim demanded that cities like Frankfurt allow the Catholic Mass within their walls.

In cities across Germany, Protestant clergymen decried the Interim and demanded that city councilors reject it. In Frankfurt, a tortuous, two-year religious and political debate over the imposition of the Interim began. The city's pastors insisted that Frankfurt could not in good conscience accede to "the devilish Interim against Christ and his word," as Pastor Ambrach put it.[85] Yet on 17 August 1548, the council summoned the ministers to the town hall and explained that Frankfurt would be accepting and implementing the Interim.[86] The guilds and the greater community were ordered to abide by the Interim.[87] The council permitted Catholic canons associated with the city's collegiate churches, including St. Bartholomew's Cathedral, to sing their hours, and slowly Masses resumed in the collegiate churches, though almost exclusively for the canons and their families.[88] (The Mass continues in the cathedral to this day.) St. Bartholomew's returned to its former masters, namely its canons and its provost, who represented the archbishop of Mainz. The citizenry of Frankfurt had largely abandoned Catholicism.[89]

The frosty reception of the Augsburg Interim in Frankfurt speaks to the larger issues of the Reformation's popularity and how Protestant pastors understood reform. And while the destruction of the city's ecclesiastical records obscures our view, the first historian of the Reformation in Frankfurt, Johann Balthasar Ritter, reproduced several fascinating church records in his 1726 history. According to Ritter, the city's ministers fought the ruling council over every measure of the Interim's implementation. They argued that a return of the old rituals would be unfair to the citizenry, who had become fully accustomed to Protestant ceremonies that used the vernacular and omitted incense.[90] Still, it seems one of the city's ministers, Peter Geltner, broke ranks from the others and accepted the Interim as a necessary evil. According to the diary of one of the city's Catholic priests: "In the year 1548 on the Sunday after the Assumption of Mary the honorable town council had Peter Geltner, a Lutheran preacher, declare and announce from the chancel that one must from now on abstain from meat on Friday and Saturday in the week . . . and further that one must fast on the eve of all of the moveable feasts from now on and should celebrate wholeheartedly on the following day."[91] Geltner reasoned that, as long as people were not "of the opinion that they thereby achieved the forgiveness of sins," such dietary regulations were of no harm.[92]

Geltner's pronouncement alarmed the other ministers and impelled Pastor Hartmann Beyer to denounce any accommodation with the Interim.[93] After dismissing Geltner's theological accommodation for Catholic fasting, Beyer attacked the council's new plan for conducting Protestant and Catholic ceremonies in the same churches. The council had sought to continue Protestant services in the city's collegiate churches—the city's largest and most opulent—which had now reintroduced the

Mass. The council maintained that Protestants and Catholics should share these impressive buildings. After all, the council reasoned, the city had just purchased and installed new seats for women attending Protestant services in St. Bartholomew's before the Interim, and it would be a waste to relinquish these to the Catholics.[94] Surely Protestants and Catholics could share churches. The council's plan to share church space prompted Beyer to pen a letter titled "The Question of Whether Both Religions, Evangelical and Papist Can Be Contained in One Church, under One Roof, Even Temporarily, in Good Conscience."[95] The answer to this question, according to Beyer, depended on the "circumstances and the occasion of the city."[96] In a "Papistical city," church sharing could be a healthy solution to confessional tensions, provided the Protestant preacher "punish [straffe], refute [wiederlege], and overthrow [umstosse] the false teachings, idolatry, and misuse of God's Word" intrinsic to Catholicism.[97] But in Protestant cities, no sharing of churches could be permitted. Thus in Frankfurt, "where the Interim violently reintroduced the Papistical atrocity [of the Mass] in purged churches," Protestants ought to retreat to churches that remained free of the Mass.[98] Beyer and his colleagues lamented that they had only saved eight city churches from the reintroduction of the Mass; they could not save the collegiate churches, including St. Bartholomew's Cathedral.[99]

Despite the opposition of the city's clergy, the council acceded to the emperor's religious demands, a not entirely surprising fact considering the city's long-standing goal of maintaining a close tie to the imperial throne. After the Schmalkaldic War the cities of the empire were at the mercy of the victorious emperor. Since the structures of the empire were profoundly feudal in their emphasis on loyalty and honor, any act of disloyalty dishonored the emperor and thus warranted punishment. Hence, the emperor could declare an entire city without rights and permit a nearby prince (sometimes the emperor himself) to capture it. In August 1548, Charles did just this to the city of Konstanz. When Konstanz refused the Interim, his army of Spanish and Austrian troops seized the city. Charles then stripped Konstanz of its independence and incorporated it into his brother Ferdinand's Austrian territories.[100] Konstanz lost its right to self-rule via a city council.[101] Charles's demonstration worked—imperial cities such as Frankfurt ignored the protestations of their clergy and accepted the Interim.

Resistance to Charles in the Schmalkaldic War proved costly. The war emptied Frankfurt's treasury. Indebtedness was a terrifying new reality, considering that Frankfurt often paid to avoid sieges. Before 1546, the city had amassed a sizable reserve fund of 30,000–40,000 gulden.[102] The war ate this savings. Loans extorted by the allied princes, coupled with a massive indemnity payment demanded by the victorious emperor, cost the city 185,000 gulden.[103] Charles demanded an additional 150,000 over the next six years, an amount Frankfurt simply had no resources to pay.[104] Charles also stationed a garrison of imperial troops within the city walls. With the arrival of these troops, Frankfurt's alliance with the Protestant princes of the empire died and its Schmalkaldic misadventure ended.[105] Not only had the city failed to preserve its religious reforms, it had incurred a huge war debt and, ultimately, failed to find a sustainable replacement for its centuries-old alliance with the emperor.

## THE SIEGE OF FRANKFURT IN 1552

If they found resistance to Charles expensive, Frankfurters soon realized that a renewal of their imperial loyalty incurred its own costs. In 1552, the Protestant princes of the empire—Frankfurt's recent allies—renewed hostilities against the emperor and targeted Frankfurt for its return to the imperial fold.[106] Barely recovered from a deadly winter flood, the city found itself besieged by the combined forces of the Protestant rulers of Saxony, Brandenburg, Hesse, Mecklenburg, and the Palatinate.[107] All of Protestant Germany seemed to be lobbing bombs into the city. The city's attorney, the patrician Hieronymus zum Lamb, calculated that "over 3,000 bombs and shots hit the city, although many people give a larger number."[108] Frankfurters recognized that the religious reforms of the Reformation had sparked this violence, though by 1552 the violence engulfing the city had moved beyond a simple Catholic-against-Protestant conflict. Pastor Ambach captured the complexity of the era in a chronicle from 1552. He described how the city was attacked first by the troops of "Count Reinhard of Solms, a defiant imperialist and enemy of the Gospel" and subsequently by an alliance of Protestant princes "who sought to preserve the pure and true teachings of the Gospel, which the Roman antichrist and his priests attacked via the emperor."[109] In this confusing new situation, Frankfurt had the unenviable choice of capitulating to attacking princes or making a deeper commitment to the emperor. The city's rulers chose the latter option. The council recognized that a renewed allegiance to the emperor could ensure the city's safety, which proved accurate.

The siege of Frankfurt came to an end on 2 August 1552 with the Peace of Passau. Frankfurt's twelve thousand residents cautiously ventured outside the city walls. The summer-long siege had confined Frankfurters and inflicted cannon fire, plague, and starvation on the entire city and its hinterland.[110] For the people in the city, a return to peace promised a chance to resume their lives and their commerce.

The council commissioned six songs expressing gratitude to the 6,500 imperial troops who defended the city during the siege.[111] The lyrics of the first song, "Of the Siege of the City of Frankfurt," begin by establishing that Frankfurt "had no guilt in the matter" that had led to the siege.[112] The song then asserts: "Emperor Charles held the city in his care, he gathered there a cohort good, of horsemen and troops, who were ever very generous, with their blood in the fight."[113] The lyrics also heap praise upon Colonel Conrad von Hanstein, the commander of the imperial garrison defending Frankfurt. Following the siege, Colonel Hanstein had helped provision the city with food, demanding that nearby territories supply the city with, among other things: "three thousand portions of corn, one thousand portions of flour, six thousand portions of oats, one thousand of sheep, five hundred heads of cattle and cows, [and] hay fodder."[114] The city's return to the emperor's fold had borne fruit. The council accepted the old order of allegiance to the emperor and credited imperial troops for saving the city.[115]

Yet Frankfurters could not consider the end of the siege a propitious moment heralding a period of calm. As Lamb recounted: "As the gates were opened again, and as our neighbors entered the city once more, it was possible to examine the perceptible damage done by the cannon fire to the adjacent areas."[116] Lamb lamented, "many had died," and "2000 sheep and cattle were taken by the enemies."[117] Nor did Frankfurt's Jews rejoice; instead they held fasts on Mondays and Thursdays to implore God to help the Jews in the still-besieged nearby imperial city of Schweinfurt, which would be destroyed by warring princes over the next two years.[118] Pastor Ambach, who had denounced the Interim, ended his chronicle of the siege of Frankfurt expressing apprehension that God might have "sharper rods" in store for the city.[119] After all, the siege constituted an attack on a Protestant city by Protestant armies. These armies had fought to preserve the right of imperial estates to enact religious reforms and to avoid the "eternal servitude that one sees in Spain."[120] The Reformation had disrupted the religious and political fabric of the empire and left Frankfurt—and indeed many other cities and territories of the empire—stranded in a new era, uncertain of the loyalties on which it depended for its safety and prosperity.

Desperate to repair its relationship with the emperor, the Frankfurt Council sent its junior mayor and richest patrician, Claus Bromm, to Brussels to seek a "reconciliation with the emperor" that would bring Frankfurt financial relief from its war debts.[121] Bromm beseeched the imperial court for a reduction in the city's indemnity payments and for permission to end rent payments for Catholic Church properties.[122] The court rejected both petitions. Having failed, Bromm began his journey home to Frankfurt in late 1553. He stopped in Cologne on his way, and there he crossed paths with another dejected fellow, Valérand Poullain of Lille, a pastor seeking a home for his refugee flock of twenty-four families. In Poullain, Bromm sensed a kindred spirit who faced the same dilemma that confronted the city of Frankfurt: a desire for church reform imperiled by Charles V. Bromm also detected in Poullain and his congregation a possible solution to Frankfurt's recent financial troubles.

## Valérand Poullain's Winding Path to Frankfurt (1520–1554)

We can only speculate about the meeting between Bromm and Poullain in wintery Cologne. Poullain regularly called his refugee community "the chased" or "the expelled," and perhaps this language elicited compassion from Bromm.[123] Like many of his followers, Poullain had spent his adult life in search of a stable home. Poullain's own path can be reconstructed, and his story illuminates the dangers of persecution and displacement in the wake of the Reformation.

"I am a gentleman, I am called Valerandus Polanus, and Lille in Flanders is my homeland," Poullain would later explain to the Frankfurt Council.[124] He identified as a citizen of Lille throughout his life, even as he spent most of it outside of Lille. In 1527, aged seven, his citizenship had been purchased for him by his father, Jacques Poullain, when the family had moved to Lille from Franche-Comté.[125] Lille lay in the Low Countries, a diverse collection of seventeen provinces roughly coterminous with all three Benelux countries. These provinces were highly urbanized and on the forefront of world commerce and industry.[126] Growing up in Lille in the 1530s, Valérand walked through the streets of a booming center of industry and commerce. Lille's wool weavers were busy revolutionizing their industry by combining wool with lighter materials to produce lighter clothes that became immensely popular.[127] A population boom accompanied this industrial success, and the city grew from around twenty thousand residents in 1500 to around thirty thousand by midcentury.[128] Lille dwarfed Frankfurt in size.[129]

In this urban environment, popular enthusiasm for religious reform clashed most directly with Charles V's political and religious aspirations. Charles was himself a native of the Low Countries, born in the city of Ghent. All seventeen provinces which comprised the Low Countries were his private estates—he had inherited them from his grandmother, Mary of Burgundy.[130] No intermediary prince, city council, or diet could impede his directives as they did in the German-speaking lands of the empire (and indeed in Spain itself).[131] Charles prized the Low Countries and worked to consolidate them under his direct rule.[132] Moreover he embraced the responsibility of protecting Christianity within these lands. Unfortunately, Charles and his subjects disagreed about the form of Christianity deserving of protection.

Already by the early 1520s, an affinity had developed between city-dwellers in the Low Countries, like Poullain, and the ideas of the Reformation. City-dwellers across Europe revered Luther, and by 1530 he had gained followers in a dozen cities in the Low Countries.[133] We do not know when Poullain himself embraced the call for reform because, like John Calvin, he wrote little about his conversion from medieval Christianity.[134] All we know stems from a single autobiographical passage, discovered by a twentieth-century biographer in a tract written by Poullain about the Lord's Supper sometime around 1550.[135] In it, Poullain described his conversion while recalling his childhood bafflement over the notion that a priest could transform bread and wine into God: "I have a passion now as I recollect having in my youth when I first heard joyfully that God was all powerful. I think that I had never been so confused; hearing [the priest convey] the absolute power which is the attribute of the Lord; which is against truth, against justice."[136] By the time he reached adulthood, Poullain's confusion over the words of consecration had transformed into revulsion. At some point between 1540 and 1543, he—like many other citizens of Lille—rejected transubstantiation as "against truth, against justice."[137]

Denouncing the Mass in Lille was a dangerous prospect. Charles quickly condemned any of his subjects in the Low Countries who abandoned Catholic orthodoxy. Starting in 1519, he issued a series of antiheresy decrees punishing both those who produced heretical literature and those who owned or even read such materials.[138] Poullain confronted the same question as the German reformer Wolfgang Musculus, whose treatise *Proskairos* asked, in its English translation, whether "it bee lawfull without offence of conscience to him that knoweth the veritie of the holy scriptures, to bee present at the papisticall supersticious services through the compulsion of his superiours?"[139] Musculus answered his own question with a firm "no," and Poullain must have agreed because he translated *Proskairos*, with its anti-Mass and anti-accommodationist message, into French.[140] The Mass was an abomination to reform-minded Christians like Poullain, and if Charles compelled residents of the Low Countries to attend, then those with a conscience ought to stand for their beliefs, even if it meant fleeing into exile.

Fearing the wrath of Charles and his supporters, Poullain fled Lille sometime in the early 1540s, becoming a refugee for the Reformation. His initial destination was the free city of Strasbourg, a popular destination for Protestant refugees. In Strasbourg, Poullain met many of the most prominent reformers in Europe. On 6 October 1543, Poullain penned a letter to the French reformer and refugee Guillaume Farel, ending with the valediction: "From the House of Bucer."[141] Bucer, a former Dominican, had also fled to Strasbourg looking for refuge after his patron, the German knight Franz von Sickingen, had been killed by imperial forces in 1523. Himself a reformer and refugee, Bucer became a father figure to Poullain, much as Bucer had been to Calvin. In a letter to Calvin in 1544, Poullain called Bucer, "my parent."[142]

Poullain encountered a large community of French refugees living in Strasbourg. In 1538, this refugee community had formed its own congregation—the first such refugee church in German lands—under the leadership of Calvin, who had served as its minister.[143] It is possible that Poullain had never heard the Lord's Supper celebrated in French until joining the French refugee congregation in Strasbourg, over which Pierre Brully, Calvin's successor, presided. Poullain became close friends with Brully. In 1543, Poullain wrote to Farel from Strasbourg in defense of Brully's fitness as a pastor. Poullain defended Brully in a confident and commanding tone, one that would get him into trouble with some of his fellow refugee reformers. Farel had accused Brully of absenteeism, and Poullain responded: "It pains me more than a little, that your contempt is so great and has opened a rift against our preacher Peter [Brully]."[144] Poullain then went further and accused Farel of absenteeism for leaving his own post in Geneva to travel to his native France: "Certainly there are many of you [in Geneva], as almost all men err, who not infrequently go for a few days according to their own business, to their homes."[145] Poullain then grouped himself with Farel, a man decades older than him, with the phrasing "we young men" and then reassures Farel that he understands Farel's natural inclination to envy.[146] It is likely that Farel shared Poullain's letter with Calvin, because the letter found its way into Calvin's collected correspondence.

Nineteen letters from Poullain to Calvin survive, and they reveal Poullain as a young man searching in vain for a permanent home and a stable job as minister. In May 1544, Poullain traveled north to the County of Nieder-Isenburg to serve as tutor for the two sons of Count Heinrich.[147] Poullain related to Calvin that "the boys [of the Count] are not curious for letters but in morals and piety are satisfactory."[148] Poullain hoped to bring the Isenburgs into the Protestant fold, but after a few months, he realized his efforts were futile.[149] His failure to convert the Isenburg boys would become even more glaring years later, when the younger son, Salentin, became the Catholic archbishop-elector of Cologne.[150]

Returning to Strasbourg in late 1544, Poullain assisted Brully as pastor of the French refugee church in Strasbourg. When Brully left Strasbourg a few months later to help establish Protestant churches in the Low Countries—a task for which he would be executed by the Habsburg authorities—Poullain stepped in as Brully's replacement.[151] We know of Poullain's position from a letter, written by Bucer in December 1544, in which he included in a list of Strasbourg ministers an entry for "Valerandus Pollanus, minister Eccl. Gallic."[152] Poullain was not a particularly popular minister, and he had vocal opponents within his congregation in Strasbourg. He wrote to Calvin complaining, "you would not believe all the troubles that Satan provoked here," and elaborated that much of the trouble was "on the part of our own people."[153] Although Poullain claimed that he "was able to calm down" his congregants, we know that he was not successful.[154] A significant portion of the French refugee church in Strasbourg disliked Poullain and supported Jean Garnier of Avignon for the post of pastor in Poullain's place, but the community's electoral system prevented many members from voting for pastor.[155] Bucer attempted to mediate and arranged for Poullain and Garnier to share the duties of minister, but this arrangement proved short-lived, and a new election became necessary.[156] The electoral process was supervised by the Strasbourg magistrates—as all clerical appointments had been since 1539—and involved multiple candidates, preaching demonstrations, and government examinations.[157] When the dust settled, Poullain had lost to Garnier, who was confirmed as minister to the French refugees in Strasbourg.[158] By then, Poullain had been exiled for nearly five years, and he had still not secured a permanent position.

Poullain left Strasbourg to search the Rhineland for another French refugee congregation in need of a minister. Tracing Poullain's travels through his letters to Calvin, we know that in 1545 he visited Frankfurt and Metz, the late Brully's hometown.[159] Unfortunately, Metz was a dangerous city, frequently besieged due to its position between the battle lines of Emperor Charles and King Francis of France. Charles had claimed the city in 1544, and in late 1545 Poullain reported to Calvin that he knew nothing more about the city.[160] Poullain moved north toward the cities of the Lower Rhine. He arrived in Wesel in the winter and wrote to Calvin, explaining that he had attempted to mediate the "disagreements with the Germans in the city" over "the ordinances of the Supper."[161] Poullain tried to win approval from Wesel's authorities for the refugees in the city to celebrate the Lord's Supper apart from the civic church.[162] He wrote to Calvin in the summer of 1546, describing his success in helping the Wesel refugees maintain the purity of their Eucharist, though a recent study of Wesel has shown that Poullain actually failed to win any concessions from the city regarding the practice of the Supper.[163] He moved on from Wesel to Aachen and Antwerp before ultimately returning to Strasbourg in late 1546.[164]

The next year proved disastrous for Protestants in Strasbourg, including Poullain. In April, Charles crushed the Schmalkaldic League at the Battle of Mühlberg. Poullain must have sensed that his days in Strasbourg, and indeed in the empire at large, were numbered. Earlier that year, another event of enormous consequence suggested to Poullain that he should resettle in England. On 28 January 1547, Henry VIII died. The throne went to his nine-year-old son, Edward VI, and control of the kingdom fell to Edward Seymour, Duke of Somerset, regent to the young Edward and a committed Protestant. England must have seemed even more inviting for Poullain as the situation in Strasbourg worsened. In 1549, the Strasbourg City Council acquiesced to the demands of the emperor and signed a religious treaty with the city's Catholic bishop, a treaty which returned Strasbourg's most important churches to Catholic control.[165] The Catholic Mass was reintroduced in the city. For Poullain, the despair of seeing Catholicism reenter his place of refuge was offset by a joyful event in his personal life. Sometime in 1548 or early

1549, Poullain married. We know about his marriage from a letter he wrote to Calvin from Strasbourg on 15 February 1549 that ends with the salutation, "My wife greets you many times."[166] Although we know almost nothing about his wife or the marriage, we do know that the couple spent their first year of marriage fleeing to England.

The Poullains fled Strasbourg with Bucer, leaving the free city in a small boat on 6 April 1549.[167] The party sailed for London. In London, the Poullains met one of the largest refugee communities in Europe, a community composed of displaced people from the Low Countries, both the southern French areas and the northern Dutch areas. Led by the Polish nobleman and reformer John a Lasco, this dual-language refugee congregation counted among its members some of the most prominent Protestant clergymen in Europe, including Lasco, Marten Micron, Jan Utenhove, and now Bucer. Poullain's services were not needed in London, so Utenhove, who grew up in Flanders not far from where Poullain had spent his own childhood, suggested he travel to Glastonbury in southwest England, where another refugee community sought a French preacher. Poullain followed Utenhove's advice and traveled to Glastonbury in 1550.[168]

In Glastonbury, Poullain joined the congregation he would eventually lead as minister and political representative. The Glastonbury congregation was a small community of only sixty-nine households, according to their application for English citizenship.[169] Like Poullain, they came from the southern Low Countries; at least two families of "silk-makers" were from Poullain's hometown.[170] The Duke of Somerset had permitted these refugees to settle on the property of a former monastery, which Henry had dissolved in 1539, hanging the monastery's abbot. Once settled, the refugees had written to the London refugee community and asked for their own minister. Poullain arrived with the recommendation of Utenhove, and the community in Glastonbury promptly elected him pastor. In Glastonbury, Poullain had finally found a fit: a congregation of his own and a stable place to live with his wife.

But the Glastonbury community enjoyed peace in England for only a few years. In the summer of 1553, King Edward died. One can only imagine the fear Poullain and his congregation felt when Edward's Catholic sister Mary took the throne. On 5 September, the Privy Council evicted Poullain and his followers from their Glastonbury homes.[171] On 17 September, Lasco, Utenhoven, Micron, and 175 members of the refugee community in London fled England.[172] Poullain's Glastonbury flock remained in London into December, and shortly before Christmas they sailed for the continent.[173] On 17 February 1554, Queen Mary officially ordered all remaining foreign Protestants to leave her realm within twenty-four days. Poullain's group had by then traveled via Antwerp to the city of Wesel and asked Wesel for protection and a church building of the sort they had had in England.[174] Poullain still insisted upon separate Eucharistic services as he had the last time he was in Wesel. After Wesel refused this plea, Poullain's group followed the Rhine farther upriver to Cologne, where Poullain met the wealthy Frankfurter Claus Bromm, who offered to help.[175]

## Religious Affinity and Frankfurt's Decision to Admit Refugees in 1554

Talking to each other about their communities' poor fortunes, Bromm and Poullain must have discussed religion. The Reformation and its aftershocks had led to their current predicaments. Bromm was a devoted follower of the great humanist reformer Philip Melanchthon, who decried the persecution taking place in the Low Countries and France, where "many pious families are expelled from their nests."[176] In Cologne, Bromm discovered just such a group of refugees, Poullain and his congregation of persecuted Christians from the Low Countries. This community offered Bromm the chance to demonstrate Frankfurt's charity toward fellow Christians and, at the same time, build a new industry and tax base in Frankfurt by bringing skilled weavers to the city on the Main. Poullain's description of his community's previous accommodation in Glastonbury, where they had settled on the property of a dissolved convent, may have triggered Bromm's memories of Frankfurt's convents, many of which had been reformed and turned over to the city's control. The two men agreed to resettle Poullain's community upriver in Bromm's native Frankfurt. The newcomers would receive housing and legal protection, and in exchange they would bring to Frankfurt their skills as weavers, even teaching the city's children their advanced techniques.[177] Bromm's plan demonstrates how religious, economic, and even political motives complemented each other. If Emperor Charles would not relax Frankfurt's debts, then Bromm could recoup the city's losses by taking in some of the emperor's fugitive subjects, a financially sound plan for Christian charity, profit, and redress.

At Bromm's suggestion, Poullain traveled to Frankfurt in early March 1554 and met with Adolf von Glauburg, a friend of Bromm's and an influential member of Frankfurt's inner circle. The Glauburg family was the second-oldest patrician clan in Frankfurt, and the Glauburgs dominated the ruling council throughout its long history. On fifty-two separate occasions a Glauburg assumed the role of mayor.[178] For his part, Adolf von Glauburg was less interested in politics than in his studies, his books, and his faith—although he did sit on the council from 1551 to 1555. Adolf pursued every manner of study he could, first enrolling at the University of Wittenberg, to study under Luther and Melanchthon (he developed a personal attachment only to the latter), before moving to Mainz to study philosophy and mathematics, while also cultivating interest in astrology.[179] He collected books and amassed an eclectic library of 959 titles.[180] We can gauge the extent of his eclecticism in the list of Reformation authors included in the "Theology" section of his library: Martin Bucer, Heinrich Bullinger, John Calvin, Johann Cochläus, Johann Eck, Desiderius Erasmus, Martin Luther, Philip Melanchthon, Johannes Oecolampadius, Peter Martyr Vermigli, and Huldrych Zwingli, among others.[181] Considering the breadth of Reformation perspectives represented on his bookshelf, it seems fair to call Glauburg a reform-minded Renaissance man, in the mold of the great civic humanist Willibald Pirckheimer of Nuremberg.

In one way, Glauburg's support meant much more for Poullain and his chances of swaying the city council than Bromm's. As junior mayor, Bromm had been an unmitigated failure. Before his unsuccessful mission to negotiate a reduction in the city's debts to the emperor, Bromm had involved the city in a disastrous copper mine venture meant to solve Frankfurt's postwar financial woes.[182] Bromm had convinced the council to borrow 150,000 gulden to invest in a copper mine three hundred kilometers to the northeast. Unfortunately, the mine proved worthless, and the city fell even deeper in debt.[183] And after Bromm suggested a negotiation with the emperor, which also failed, the prospect of a third experiment—the admission of refugees—would likely have met with serious reservations by his fellow councilmen. But whereas Bromm's ventures invited skepticism from the council at large, Glauburg's influence remained strong. His support of the refugee project proved invaluable for Poullain.

Glauburg introduced Poullain to a circle of the richest and most powerful councilmen in Frankfurt, patricians who had befriended Glauburg through the use of his extensive library and considered themselves reform-driven humanists: Johann Fichard (the city's attorney), Conrad von Humbracht (the senior mayor), Hans Bromm (Claus's brother, a councilman, and future mayor), Ludwig Martroff (another future mayor), and Johann Cnipius Andronicus, the head schoolteacher.[184] These were the most educated and affluent men in Frankfurt, and together with Claus Bromm and Glauburg, they formed the early core of council support for Poullain.[185] These seven men viewed Poullain as a kindred spirit, and they had the power to facilitate his community's admission.[186] Pastor Beyer summarized a year later how the patricians had helped Poullain: "He [Poullain] gained access to several council members, and became known through these men to other leading men—a number of these were related—as well; they helped him advance a supplication, in which he brought his desires to the entire council. He followed these men[,] presented a supplication and let it be translated into German."[187] Bromm and Glauburg provided the channel through which Poullain entered the city's political waters.

Glauburg also introduced Poullain to his family, notably his uncle Johann von Glauburg and cousin Karl von Glauburg, both council members.[188] Poullain came to trust Johann in particular, at least according to the English refugee William Whittingham. When Whittingham and several followers arrived in Frankfurt months after Poullain, Poullain quickly advised them to meet with Johann von Glauburg, which the Englishmen did: "Labor was made . . . to Maister John Glawberge one off the chiefest Senators[,] . . . who jentlie promised his furtherance, and that he also woulde move the whole Senate thereoff, the whiche he did accordingly."[189] A year later, in a letter to Calvin, Poullain continued to refer to "Dr. Glauburg, unique patron of our church."[190] Johann von Glauburg became an ardent supporter of refugees and helped admit them into Frankfurt. The Glauburg family remained patrons of the refugee community for generations.

Also supporting Poullain were the two eldest city ministers, Melchior Ambach and Johann Lullius, humanists and friends of Bucer.[191] Ambach and Lullius had served as ministers in Frankfurt since 1540.[192] They remembered the early Reformation in the city, before the death of Luther in 1546 and the subsequent backlash among Lutherans against Melanchthon's attempts at ecumenism.[193] The two old ministers still clung to the notion of a united Protestantism held dearly by their friend and mentor Bucer. Bucer had constructed the foundational reforming document of the city of Frankfurt, the *Concordia Buceriana*, as a subtle compromise between Luther and Zwingli.[194] His conciliatory influence could be felt in many other south German cities, like Augsburg.[195] Ambach and Lullius had acted as two of Frankfurt's signatories when Bucer's *Concordia* became the constitution of Frankfurt's church, in 1542.[196] In short, Poullain's earliest supporters were not only sympathetic humanists but also clergymen who adhered to the earliest and broadest reforming impulses in Frankfurt. Beyer would later appoint committed Lutheran partisans to replace Lullius and Ambach, but not before these men had supported the admission of Poullain and his group of refugees.[197]

Council minutes immortalized Frankfurt's decision to admit Poullain's community of refugees thusly: "Now that the petition from Dr. Valérand Poullain from Flanders has been read aloud again—the petition in which he asks for citizenship for himself and several silk-wool weavers from Flanders and in which he requests they be given their own church—these things should be granted to them and they should be welcomed in the name of God."[198] This brief and unassuming resolution from 18 March 1554 marks the official beginning of refugee accommodation in Frankfurt, when the council welcomed a community of refugees and granted its members rights, including the right to become citizens and the right to worship in a city church.[199] The council did not stipulate the terms of admission—beyond specifying which church would be granted—and instead accepted the terms proposed by Poullain in his petition.

In his petition, Poullain hinted at a major benefit his community would bring Frankfurt: economic growth through the introduction of an advanced weaving industry.[200] He proposed a reciprocal arrangement: "These people [my followers], want to be given city privileges and equipped with the necessary workspaces and houses, from which they will pay rents; they do not want to overburden either you caring and wise [councilmen] or the citizenry and instead want to feed themselves by their own work and trade and want additionally to teach the city children who are capable how to do silk-wool weaving."[201] Poullain's message was clear: provide for my followers and they will put their industry to work for you. His petition refers to the weavers' industry as "Bursat machen," a term best understood as a new type of textile manufacture in which wool was woven together with lighter materials—especially silk—to create a lightweight yet thermal cloth, well-suited for pants and jerkins.[202] Poullain's followers were the most technically advanced weavers in all of Europe, masters of light cloths that combined a warp made of wool with a weft made of lighter material—instead of wool for warp and weft—to produce light fabrics.[203] These lighter cloths were less cumbersome, more versatile, and truly sought-after. When the cities of the southern Low Countries began to produce lighter clothes, they revolutionized industry and became major centers of European manufacturing.[204] Poullain's weaver community from the Low Countries offered Frankfurt the chance to become a hub for this exciting and highly profitable new manufacturing sector. The refugees would even supply their own equipment, right down to the weights they used on their looms.[205]

Economics played a significant role in the admission of the refugees, which the wording of Poullain's petition suggests and an analysis of internal Frankfurt sources confirms. It is unlikely, though, that Poullain instinctively or serendipitously knew how to appeal to the city's industrial aspirations. Indeed, how could he have drafted the petition when he could not even write in German? His patrician supporters helped him construct his letter, beginning with the honorific used for almost every supplication to the council in the sixteenth century: "To the Honorable, Caring, Most Wise Mayors and Council of the Holy Imperial City Frankfurt."[206] Poullain later described to his Dutch colleague Pieter Datheen how he had first achieved accommodation in Frankfurt, and he made clear that he had first secured the support of several patricians. Datheen recorded Poullain's account: "Valerand Poullain remarked that . . . at the start of March 1554 he arrived in Frankfurt am Main. . . . And since he indicated his desire to several councilmen and the city ministers, upon their advice he submitted a supplication to the honorable council."[207] In short, Poullain had help from a number of influential council members who knew exactly what the council at large wanted to hear.[208] And while economics may have motivated the council at large, Poullain's earliest supporters—the Bromms, Glauburgs, and their inner circle—were motivated principally by their sympathy for fellow Protestants.

The clearest evidence that religion motivated the accommodation of the refugees appears in later writings from the city's official ministers, led by Beyer, who complained about the newcomers some months after their arrival. Letters of complaint written years later would seem unlikely sources for statements of Christian solidarity, but these invariably begin with an account of the initial reasons for welcoming the refugees. Frankfurt's ministers wrote how Christian charity had moved Frankfurt's most powerful patricians to support Poullain and admit his refugee congregation. In one letter, from 5 September 1555, Frankfurt's clergymen recalled that "the honorable council first admitted these foreigners out of charity [*Barmherzigkeit*]."[209] Eight weeks later, the ministers wrote a longer letter to the council, again explaining how the refugees had been "admitted in the beginning out of charity."[210] In 1563, Beyer and his colleagues authored a more detailed account of the initial admission of refugees into Frankfurt, one that described Poullain's appeals to patricians and to the city's ministers. According to this report, Poullain had "met a council member in Cologne," who subsequently "referred him to another council friend," (presumably Glauburg), who in turn suggested Poullain "now come to Mr. Beyer."[211] Upon entering the house of Beyer, Poullain "laid out his passport [*Pasport*] with which he together with twenty-four other households had safely sailed out of England and thereby further told what a great injustice and violence the papists once again practiced in the kingdom, and how miserably the foreigners were forced to depart [England] and scattered hither and thither."[212] Poullain's story moved Beyer. When the Frankfurt Council decided to admit the refugees in 1554, Beyer raised no objection, "because he [Poullain] complained about such great distress and appealed to Christian Love."[213]

Beyer and his colleagues narrated the admission of 1554 many years later as part of a campaign to suppress refugee religious services in Frankfurt. An obvious antipathy suffused their letters of complaint. They portrayed Poullain as a con man who won their support through disingenuous appeals to charity and references to revered Protestant figures: "He said he thought often about Dr. Martin Luther and Mr. Martin Bucer, God rest his soul, and emphatically said he had studied all of their theology and books."[214] The city ministers had come to resent Poullain's initial appeal to pan-Protestant sympathies, perhaps as the consequence of shame, because they knew it had worked on them. Beyer had to admit that he himself, along with his fellow clergymen, had approved of the council's admission of the refugees out of a sense of Christian charity. One letter from Poullain to Beyer survives, and in it Poullain expresses gratitude for the initial support offered to his congregation by minister Beyer: "You have always stood so bravely for the liberty of the church."[215] In 1554, Beyer had seen the newcomers as true Christians and supported their accommodation. Poullain's talk of a new weaving industry in Frankfurt may have swayed certain council members, but the most forceful supporters of Poullain and his flock, including the city's patricians and ministers, were swayed by the idea of Protestant solidarity.

## The Bonds Poullain Cultivated

In Geneva, Calvin received word of Poullain's congregation settling in Frankfurt. Calvin wrote to Poullain and congratulated him for having successfully secured "a place where you can keep busy grazing your little flock."[216] The twenty-four families entering Frankfurt in March 1554 must have been grateful for Poullain's leadership. His exchanges with Bromm, Glauburg, and other leading patricians had won the refugees a new home. While Poullain's official petition to the Frankfurt Council emphasized his congregation's industry, his earlier appeals to the patricians had stressed Protestant fraternity. The welcome Poullain secured resulted from the interplay of economic and religious motives.

To understand the vast numbers of refugees finding safety across Europe in the late sixteenth century, one must recognize the period as defined not only by the collapse of the political and religious order of the previous centuries—and the consequent persecution—but also by the development of new connections between religious communities meeting for the first time under such circumstances. The vicissitudes of the years 1517–54 had created a bond between displaced Protestants like Poullain and south German patricians, like those in Frankfurt. Both groups had rejected the Catholic Mass and provoked the anger of Charles V. In Frankfurt's case, the danger posed by Charles was mitigated by the city's privileged imperial context—the city enjoyed imperial immediacy and could thus claim jurisdiction over its own religious reforms. With no such institutional protection, Protestants in the southern Low Countries fled their homelands.[217] Poullain described his community's travails to Bromm, Glauburg, and Beyer. He reminded them of their shared goal of reform and their mutual enemy in Charles. Frankfurt's leaders acknowledged their bond with Poullain's group and welcomed the newcomers.

The decision of the Frankfurt Council to accommodate Poullain and his followers demonstrates how new religious sympathies were emerging alongside new religious hatreds. The plight of persecuted Christians assumed a new dimension in the middle decades of the sixteenth century as the despair of displacement was alleviated, somewhat, by the realistic hope for formal legal accommodation in sympathetic foreign communities. This hope inspired more refugees to follow Poullain's lead and travel to Frankfurt, where they were promptly "rescued by the most pious city council [*pientissimo Senatu*]," as one later arrival phrased it.[218]

Over the next few years, thousands more refugees arrived in Frankfurt and joined Poullain's congregation. Soon, though, their presence in Frankfurt began to destabilize the civic institutions that had made refugee accommodation possible in the first place. Native Frankfurters began to petition the council to end its generous terms of accommodation for refugees. How long could the city's rulers maintain their welcoming posture toward newcomers? And who, among Frankfurt's many citizens, would be the first to denounce the refugees within the city?

# 2

# Refugee Arrivals and the Advent of Confessionalism

⚜

They conduct their Eucharist to the great offense of many people
who see it or hear about it, because with them . . . the communicants take it into their hands themselves, eating it and drinking it in
this fashion, just as though it were a binge.
        —Frankfurt's ministers to the city council, March 1556

Frankfurt's patrician-dominated council may have admitted
the refugees, but it remained to be seen how the citizenry and other
residents would react. On the morning of Thursday, 19 April 1554, curious
Frankfurters decided to see for themselves who the newcomers were. They
walked to the southeast corner of the city and crowded around the Church
of the White Ladies (Weißfrauenkirche), where Poullain's congregation
had gathered to celebrate its first religious service in Frankfurt. Spectators
that morning witnessed a moving scene as Poullain baptized his own son,
born while the community had journeyed to the city.[1] Following this joyful
moment, Poullain asked his flock for a communal confession in French:

My brothers let every one of you appear before the face of the Lord,
with confession of his faults and sins, following his heart as follows:
Lord God, eternal-Father all powerful. We confess and recognize
without pretense, in front of thy holy Majesty, that we are sinners,
and we do recognize our iniquity and corruption, prone to do evil, incapable of any good, and in vice we continue and endlessly transgress
thy holy commandments.[2]

44

At the climax of the service Poullain broke bread and invited the congregants forward to eat it as a memorial to Jesus: "The bread which we break is a communion in the body of Christ."[3] Poullain had used this liturgy with his community in England, and they would have been familiar with the order of service, which called for them to receive the cup from a deacon.[4] The service ended quietly, not with the singing customary at the end of services in Frankfurt's churches but rather with a simple blessing: "The Lord bless you and keep you. The Lord smile upon you and be merciful to you. The Lord look upon you kindly and give you happiness."[5]

For Frankfurters, the novelty of the refugee service was clear. Poullain conducted the service in French, and his congregation began to call itself the Church of French Foreigners in Frankfurt or simply the French Church of Frankfurt. Notice of these foreigners spread quickly, and watching refugee services became a popular pastime for Frankfurters. Poullain and his followers began to complain. On 26 April 1554, council minutes discuss a grievance from the refugees about "sundry unsubtle behaviors" disrupting their services.[6] Poullain may have been especially sensitive to potential sources of distraction to his audience since his sermons were longer than those of other Protestant preachers—he believed a good sermon should last one hour.[7]

The Church of the White Ladies, where Frankfurters first witnessed the services of the refugees, had previously been empty. Originally built in the thirteenth century as part of a convent for penitential noblewomen, the Sisters of Mary Magdalene, the convent became contested property in the 1530s, when the prioress along with some (but not all) of the sisters embraced the Reformation.[8] In 1542, the Frankfurt Council declared the convent officially reformed and began appraising its property, which was still nominally controlled by the prioress until Johann von Glauburg assumed custodianship of the property after her death.[9] In March 1554, the council unlocked the church's doors and gave the building over to the refugees.[10]

The members of the French Church of Frankfurt delighted in their new temple, even with Frankfurters peering through the church windows, and they wrote letters to other exiled communities advertising their acquisition of a church building. Soon, Poullain's small congregation welcomed hundreds of other Protestant refugees from the Low Countries and other lands. The Church of the White Ladies became a place where ordinary Frankfurters saw the growth of the refugee community firsthand.

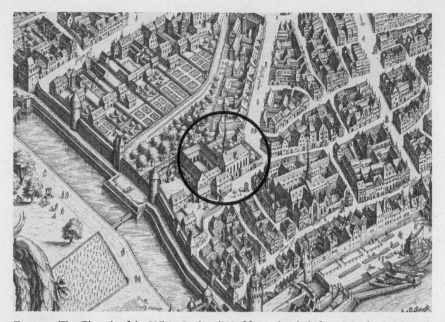

Figure 4. The Church of the White Ladies (Weißfrauenkirche), from Matthäus Merian's Großer Stadtplan, 1628. (Historisches Museum Frankfurt, photograph by Horst Ziegenfusz, adapted by author)

This chapter investigates the consequences of native Frankfurters witnessing refugee religious ceremonies, especially celebrations of the Eucharist. In the year following that April celebration, as hundreds more refugees arrived in the city (with the support of the council), as English- and Dutch-speaking refugee preachers joined Poullain in holding services in the Church of the White Ladies, and as the city's residents had ever more opportunity to view the ceremonies of the newcomers, the city's seven official ministers became alarmed. They had seen the rituals taking place in the Church of the White Ladies and were convinced that something was amiss about the religion of the refugees. Their initial alarm—evident in petitions they wrote to the council—morphed into distrust, and distrust inspired them to construct a new boundary between Frankfurt's civic church and the religion of the refugees. Two distinct religious confessions emerged: Lutheran and Reformed (though the native ministers usually referred to the latter as Calvinist or Zwinglian).

Documents authored by refugees—petitions to the council, letters to sister communities in exile, and printed accounts of the experience of exile—confirm the emergence of a new religious division from a second perspective. Refugees wrote accounts of their exile in order to make sense of their displacement and memorialize it for future generations.[11] Their words describe how Protestant fraternity dissolved once Frankfurt's ministers witnessed their liturgy. It was the witnessing of religious ceremonies, as opposed to the reading of religious tracts, that convinced the native ministers that the refugees fell outside the bounds of the civic church. Firsthand knowledge of refugee rituals fueled a process of religious differentiation in Frankfurt, with two different Protestant confessions emerging in contradistinction to each other.

Frankfurt's refugee community grew during the exact decade that Protestants across the Holy Roman Empire began to battle each other over the nature of Protestant reforms and rituals. One year after Poullain's arrival in Frankfurt, the imperial Peace of Augsburg based its protections of Protestant rulers and cities on the Augsburg Confession, to which Protestants were meant to adhere.[12] Thus the question of whether the refugees in Frankfurt adhered to the Augsburg Confession gained imperial implications. Frankfurt's ministers marshaled firsthand evidence to claim that refugees arriving in Frankfurt from the Low Countries, England, and France did not adhere to the Augsburg Confession and were therefore not protected by imperial law. Far from being spectators on the sidelines of these imperial controversies, or unlucky victims of their outcomes, refugees by their very presence instigated the process of confessional differentiation that would ultimately see them segregated from the city's official civic congregation.[13]

## Summer 1554–Summer 1555: A Year of Growth and Diversification within the Refugee Community

The refugee community grew in size and diversity over the next year. Poullain fostered this growth by writing to other refugee leaders and advertising the generous concessions his community enjoyed in Frankfurt. On 8 February 1555 he wrote to Calvin, "Our Senate [the Frankfurt Council], by God's grace, continues to be constant in its good-will towards the church."[14] Poullain's words had definite effect. His French-speaking refugee congregation expanded from the original 24 households in March 1554 to 165 households appearing on an internal list of members of the French Church of Frankfurt dated 25 November 1555.[15] And more than just French-speakers arrived in 1554 and 1555.

On the night of 27 June 1554, Poullain left his home and walked to a Frankfurt inn, where the leaders of a small group of English refugees, newly arrived in the city, had gathered to discuss their fate. The Catholic Queen Mary of England, who had expelled Protestant foreigners like Poullain in February, had now driven native English Protestants into exile.[16] One community of English refugees had traveled to Frankfurt. We know about these displaced English Protestants not only from their letters, which have been collected and printed several times, but also from a famous polemical account of their sojourn in Frankfurt written by one of their leaders, William Whittingham.[17] And while Whittingham's account, titled *A Brieff discours off the troubles begonne at Franckford* (1574), focuses mostly on a simmering conflict that would emerge within the English community in Frankfurt, it also describes the context of the English refugees' arrival in the city on the Main.[18] According to Whittingham, it was a small group which entered Frankfurt in the summer of 1554—just four men together "with their companies."[19] The four men were Whittingham, Edmund Sutton, William Williams, and Thomas Wood, and it was these four whom Poullain sought out that summer evening.

Poullain met the four Englishmen the night they arrived in Frankfurt and invited them to join his congregation. As Whittingham remembered it: "The same night came one Maister Valaren pullan Minister unto their lodginge and declared howe he had obtained a churche there in the name of all suche as shuld come owte off Englande for the Gospell."[20] English Protestants had been gracious hosts to Poullain during his time in Glastonbury under Edward VI, and now he could repay their generosity by welcoming one group of displaced Englishmen to Frankfurt and finding them a place within his congregation. Yet the English desired a congregation of their own, apart from Poullain's French-speaking refugees. They politely explained this to Poullain: "Answere was made him that as god was to be praised who had moved the Magistrats hartes to shewe the frenche suche favour: Evenso, for so muche as fewe off them [the English] understoode the frenche tonge, it woulde be small commoditie to them, or to suche as shulde come afterwarde to joyne themselves to that churche."[21] The English desired their own church with sermons and scripture readings in their own language. Poullain proved supportive, as did the other leaders of the French-speakers, including a recently arrived theologian and elder named Jean Morel, whom Whittingham referred to as "Maister Morellio, another Minister of the frenche churche."[22] Poullain, Morel, and three other men now constituted the consistory of the French Church of Frankfurt, a leadership structure the English arrivals planned to emulate. The English hoped to build a community in parallel to their French-speaking brethren in Frankfurt, and at the suggestion of Poullain, Morel, and other leaders of the French Church, they met with Johann von Glauburg, the custodian of the Church of the White Ladies, whom they asked for "a place or churche, wherin they and all their country men might have gods worde truly preached, and the Sacraments sincerely ministered in their naturall tonge."[23]

Poullain sounded a note of optimism about their chances of receiving support from Glauburg, and indeed Glauburg did not disappoint. He convinced the council to welcome the newly arrived English Protestants and grant them the right to join the citizenry. Mayoral records from that summer relate: "As it was again read aloud, what the Englishmen had discussed and what was heard, the petitioners—those amongst them who are otherwise common people—should be accepted into the citizenry."[24] Frankfurt did not accept nobles into its citizenry, and refugees—including Poullain himself—would have to argue that they were not nobles by German standards. "A report was made by Valérand," the council minutes from that week read, "that the nobles amongst them had a different form than in German lands."[25] Poullain gained a dispensation for foreign nobles, and Sutton, who seems to have been of some level of English nobility, took advantage of this and became a citizen in 1555.[26] The English refugees intended to "remaine and abide" in Frankfurt according to Whittingham.[27] The English must have believed that Catholicism would continue to reign in their homeland and that they should stay in Frankfurt permanently, an outlook that led the first historian of English refugees to call their stay in Frankfurt, "not a flight but a migration."[28]

In addition to Poullain, the English would have encountered at least one more familiar face in Frankfurt. Anne Hooper, the wife of the zealous reforming bishop of Gloucester, John Hooper, now lived in the city on the Main. Anne had fled England with her daughter Rachel soon after her husband was imprisoned by Queen Mary in late 1553 for, among other things, having married Anne. John remained steadfastly loyal to his wife, a loyalty that contributed to his condemnation. John Foxe's famous biography of Hooper in *Acts and Monuments* (1563) relates Hooper's loyalty:

At master Hopers commynge in, the lord Chancellour asked whether he was maryed?

Hoper: Yea my lord, and will not be unmaried tyll deathe unmarye me.... Wherupon they that were Scribes, were commaunded to wryte, that maister Hooper was maried, and said that he would not go frome his wyfe. And that he beleved not the corporall presence in the Sacrament, wherfore he was worthy to be deprived from his bishoprike.[29]

Around the same time that John was formally condemned by the English Catholic hierarchy, Anne and their daughter reached Frankfurt, a journey into exile she described in a letter to the Swiss reformer Heinrich Bullinger: "But since the Lord, by my husband's bidding and the advice of my friends, has at length driven me from England, and conducted me safe to Antwerp, I availed myself of an opportunity . . . and joined my female relative in Frankfort, where now, by the mercy of God, the senate has granted liberty to the foreign church for their whole ecclesiastical ministry both of the word and sacraments."[30] Her "female relative" was Poullain's wife; she called Poullain, "The husband of my relative and the chief pastor of the church."[31] Anne was a native of the southern Low Countries like Poullain himself. Foxe's *Acts and Monuments* describes her as "a Burgonso woman born, and of great parentage."[32] In a 1551 letter, Anne signed her name "Anne de Tserclas, now Hooper," and further research suggests that her birth name was Anne de Tilly.[33] In Frankfurt, Anne and her daughter lived with Poullain and his family. Indeed, we know about Poullain's first religious service in Frankfurt thanks to the letters Anne wrote to Bullinger.[34] She considered herself a member of Poullain's congregation and prayed, "May God grant to this church a due increase, and worthy of his name!"[35]

Together with Whittingham, Sutton, Williams, and Wood, Anne ensured that Frankfurt constituted a major nexus of the English Reformation. She was known and loved by reformers in England and beyond. As her correspondence with Bullinger in Zurich reveals, she provided a channel of communication with her husband, with whom she stayed in contact during his imprisonment: "by the goodness of God, he has always been allowed to write to me, and to receive my letters."[36] Anne cultivated her relationships with other leaders of the English Reformation; she needed connections to orchestrate the rescue of her son Daniel, who was still in England when she arrived in Frankfurt. Her network proved effective, and she reported to Bullinger in November 1554 that both her children lived with her in Frankfurt: "My Daniel and Rachel also salute you."[37] Anne had saved her children, though she could not save her husband, who was brutally executed in February 1555. When exactly Anne learned of her husband's death is unclear, though her regular correspondence with him and other English reformers suggests she would have learned soon after the fact. His death only increased her prominence, and her presence lent the refugee community in Frankfurt a symbolic importance in the wider English Protestant community. The city on the Main already housed one refugee flock that had previously lived in England under King Edward; now it also sheltered the family of the martyred reformer John Hooper, a bishop famous for his rejection of anything resembling the Catholic Mass.

By the end of the summer of 1554, there were two communities of refugees living in Frankfurt with the permission of the council, one comprised of French-speaking Protestants from the Low Countries and the other of native English Protestants. The council clearly considered the two groups as one, at least judging by the council minutes from 1554. The council ordered a French translation of the civic oath for the "English and Netherlanders," whom it also referred to as simply "foreign strangers."[38] The council ordered Poullain to help translate and administer the civic oath to all refugees, with those who were unable to recite in German doing so in translation "via Valérand."[39] The council expected the English to conform to the teachings and liturgy of the French Church of Frankfurt and, naturally, share the Church of the White Ladies with Poullain's rapidly growing French-speaking flock.[40] The English met some of the council's expectations, including the sharing of the Church of the White Ladies with the French-speakers, but they still separated themselves from Poullain's congregation by electing their own elders and deacons. Frankfurt's ministers raised no objection to the new English refugee congregation.[41] After all, the English newcomers barely increased the overall number of refugees living in Frankfurt. A census from late 1555 reveals that there were four hundred refugees from the southern Low Countries in Frankfurt, while a census from 1557—when the numbers from the Low Countries would have been even higher— lists only forty-five English-speaking households, many of which consisted of a single individual.[42]

Like Poullain before them, Whittingham and the English sought to expand their community. They did so by writing to their Protestant countrymen and encouraging them to travel to the city on the Main. On 2 August 1554, they authored a letter to the English communities in Emden, Strasbourg, Wesel, and Zurich: "We dowte not (dearely beloved) but yow have harde . . . off the excellent graces and mercy whiche oure good god and heavenly father hathe shewed unto our litle congregation in this citie off Franckford, for that he hathe not onely made the Magistrats and commons very favorable towards us and lovinge, but also, hathe geven them hartes, with muche compassion."[43] The authors of the letter—John Stanton, John Mackbray, William Williams, William Whittingham, William Hammond, Thomas Wood, and Michael Gill— explained how the city council "graunted that thinge, whiche amonge others and in other cities, we coulde not obtaine nor durste allmoste hope for."[44] They were referring to the Church of the White Ladies: "For what greater treasure or sweeter comforte can a Christian man desier, then to have a churche wherein he maie serve god in puritie off faithe, and integritie off lyfe."[45] Frankfurt had offered them a church building, in which to "preache, minister, and use Discipline, to the true settinge forthe of gods glorie."[46] Frankfurt's generosity was unlikely to be matched by other cities, according to the authors, and thus the city on the Main was "the citie moste forwarde to procure" those things essential for religious refugees—church space and the right to join the citizenry.[47] Whittingham and his companions invited the wider English Protestant diaspora to join them in Frankfurt: "Wherfore brethern, seinge your have indured the paine off persecution with us, we thought it likewise oure dewties to make your partakers off oure consolation."[48] In Frankfurt, the English explained, "everie man helpethe us, no man is againste us, muche love, no grudge, glad to please, lothe to annoie us, yea, and to declare this good will not to be off the meane sorte, nor so small as oure brethren have felte otherwere."[49] This letter and others like it attracted more English Protestants fleeing Queen Mary to Frankfurt over the next two years.

In 1555, a group of Dutch-speaking Protestant refugees numbering forty households entered the city on the Main. This group had traveled from London. Leading these newcomers was John a Lasco, the Polish nobleman and former head of the London congregation of refugees from the Low Countries. The journey from London had been long and arduous for Lasco and his followers. Jan Utenhove, an elder in London congregation and Lasco's close friend, recorded the story of their harrowing journey and published it as a testament to the refugees' perseverance. These people had actually fled England before Poullain's group, but their group of 175 had spent the winter of 1553–54 sailing around the North Sea unsuccessfully petitioning the Kingdom of Denmark and several German Hanseatic cities for admittance.[50] The rulers of Denmark and the Hanseatic cities refused to accommodate Lasco and his flock, and only the sick and very old were sheltered while the others were forced back onto their ship. As Utenhove described it, the Dutch-speaking flock faced a "grave storms of affliction" on their winter voyage similar to the suffering endured by Saint Stephen during his stoning or Jerusalem when the Romans destroyed the Temple.[51] Utenhove published his account in 1560, and his words became a legend within the Dutch refugee community (though recent research has revealed that the winter of 1553–54 was actually quite mild).[52] Eventually Lasco and his Dutch-speaking followers from London disembarked in Emden, a small city that belonged to the County of East Friesland.[53] Lasco knew Emden from a previous stay when he had helped reform the civic church there, and he knew the city's ruler, Countess Anna von Oldenburg, well. Still, he decided not to stay in Emden and traveled deeper into the empire to the imperial city of Frankfurt.

Lasco's biographers disagree about his motives for traveling to Frankfurt. Perhaps he was dissatisfied with his community's treatment by the Emden authorities and chose to settle in Frankfurt, or perhaps he was traveling through Frankfurt on his way back to his native Poland.[54] "I think of my homeland," Lasco explained to Calvin in a letter from 19 September 1555.[55] Frankfurt lay on the major north-south and east-west travel routes across Europe.[56] Yet in another letter to Bullinger, Lasco states that he was "invited to serve the community of Dutch" in Frankfurt, suggesting that he had intended to settle in the city on the Main.[57] Corroborating this latter possibility is the fact that Lasco did not travel alone and instead brought with him several families of Dutch refugees who sought the same independence from civic authorities that Poullain and the English had achieved in Frankfurt and which was not possible in Emden at that time.[58] The most likely scenario is that he intended to stay for a year or two because he ultimately did not apply for citizenship and instead registered as a denizen [Beisass], a category which would have permitted him to accumulate assets in the city and work, though not as an artisan.[59]

In May 1555, the Frankfurt Council "rescued" Lasco and his followers "most humanely," according to Utenhove's account.[60] Lasco found that the city already had a sizeable and rapidly growing community of refugees who spoke Dutch and had arrived directly from the Low Countries over the past few months.[61] He set about organizing Dutch-language services that summer, with the help of Marten Micron, a reformer from Ghent who had served as the Dutch preacher in Lasco's London refugee church.[62] The council treated the Dutch as it had the English before them—they were meant to join Poullain's refugee congregation and worship with them in the Church of the White Ladies.[63] Lasco and the Dutch did so. Moreover, unlike the English refugees, the Dutch joined with the French in both temple and church institutions, becoming a dual-language congregation under the same elders.[64] Lasco would serve as superintendent over the French-Dutch refugee congregation, as he had in London, meaning that he would be the community's political representative to the council, a position granted to him by the council itself. Utenhove described Lasco's promotion thusly: "From the most pious council . . . he obtained power not long after [his arrival] because the Belgic Church [Belgicae Ecclesiae] needed to be set up for the use of pious foreigners [peregrinorum], and it needed to be built according to the model of the divine word."[65]

Lasco was a reformer of international renown and a man whom Poullain admired. Poullain accepted Lasco's leadership of the entire congregation of refugees from the Low Countries and contented himself with his governance over the French-speaking services and community. He remained the preacher to the French-speakers.[66] A membership list of the Church of French Foreigners from late 1555 lists at its top "Dr. John a Lasco, Polish Baron."[67] Poullain's name appears directly under Lasco's and above the names of six elders.[68] For the Dutch-speakers, Lasco installed as preacher Pieter Datheen, a twenty-four-year-old reformer and former Carmelite monk from Flanders (though Lasco's first choice had been Gaspar van der Heyden, who refused to leave Antwerp).[69] Datheen offered his first Dutch sermon in Frankfurt in the Church of the White Ladies that September. Lasco remained the superintendent of the French-Dutch refugee community until he departed for his homeland of Poland in the fall of 1556. The French and Dutch remained united in their church hierarchy until 1570, when the Dutch withdrew and formed a separate congregation with separate elders.[70]

We know much about Lasco and the Dutch-speakers from the words of Datheen, the twenty-four-year-old whom Lasco trusted to preach in Frankfurt. Datheen published an account of his time in Frankfurt in 1563, an account that provides valuable information about Lasco, the refugee community, and the relationship between the refugee community and Frankfurt's native clergy.[71] Datheen recalled Lasco's efforts in Frankfurt: "As the persecution in the Low Countries grew ever-stronger, and ever-longer and ever-greater, so too were expelled Christians from the Low Countries in June of the year 1555, through the advertisement and intercession of Mr. John a Lasco, of blessed memory, mercifully permitted refuge and public church services [in Frankfurt]."[72] Datheen became an important reformer in his own right.[73] Despite his lack of formal theological training, he helped shape the Dutch refugee community in the city and beyond.[74] In later decades Datheen would translate the influential Heidelberg Catechism into Dutch and author the articles of the Convent of Wesel, which has been remembered as a founding conventicle of the Dutch Reformed Church.[75]

The presence of an influential reformer like Lasco lent Frankfurt's refugee community a new importance in the world of the Reformation. In Frankfurt, Lasco published his most influential text, a church order based upon the institutions and ceremonies he had organized for his congregation of refugees in London, a text which he advertised to many correspondents—including the Duke of Prussia.[76] (Poullain had already witnessed the workings of Lasco's London church and had modeled his own church order upon Lasco's.) In this church order, titled *Forma ac ratio tota ecclesiastici ministerii in peregrinorum*, Lasco outlined a robust system of discipline including public repentance, public confessions of faith, weekly catechesis on Sunday afternoons, and obligatory communion.[77] Governing these rituals would be a church hierarchy that would faithfully honor its secular ruler, "to whom we fully profess that all our faith in the Lord owes submission and obedience."[78] Below the secular ruler and directly governing the church would be "two excellent orders of extraordinary ministers," which Lasco divided between elders—who "sustain the needs of the whole church" and include the community's ministers in their number—and deacons, "who have management of the needs of the destitute."[79] Lasco went on to explain: "One man presides over this whole order of elders and is elected from their number, so that by his authority the consensus of all, as if of one mind, may be preserved in all affairs, and he is called superintendent."[80] In London, Lasco had assumed this position himself. He brought this church order with him to Frankfurt. There he published it in order to share what he viewed as the ideal church arrangement for refugees, people who had to be especially careful to remain free from the incorrect teachings of the world around them, from which their superintendent was meant to protect them. The publication of Lasco's *Forma ac ratio* confirmed that Frankfurt was not only a welcoming destination for refugees but also a center of refugee thinking and a source of refugee ecclesiology. Its publication must have made Frankfurt an even more attractive destination for persecuted Protestants.[81]

A new destination for Protestants was much needed. Mary's reign over England persisted, and the Habsburgs continued to violently suppress Protestantism in the Low Countries. Protestants in both places faced serious danger for openly practicing their faith, and dissimulation was absolutely unacceptable, at least according to a tract published by Lasco in 1553, *Whether Christian faith maye be kepte secret in the heart, without confession.* Lasco had coauthored the text with Anne Hooper's husband, John. The two authors reminded their readers that dissimulation entailed attendance at the Catholic Mass, which constituted participation in idolatry. They encouraged their readers: "Let us praye to him [God] that we pollute not our selves, with any rites, ceremonies or usages, not instituted by god. In this case, a faythful man to be at the Masse, is to be considered with what mind those thete he accompanieth himself withal."[82]

Lasco and John Hooper insisted that good Christians should abandon the Mass entirely and find a place in the world where they could openly confess their faith and take part in "the right use of the Lordes Supper."[83] Their insistence on avoiding the Mass put Lasco and Hooper in accord with Poullain, who five years earlier had translated Wolfgang Musculus's antidissimulation tract *Prosakairos* into French under the title *Le Temporiseur. Le Temporiseur* denounced as "cowardly" any Protestants who "do not refrain to assist and to be present at the execrable Mass and superstitious idolatries."[84] Poullain, Lasco, and Hooper all agreed with Calvin, who had denounced Protestant dissemblers in France and the Low Countries who justified their dissembling by insisting they were following the example of the Pharisee Nicodemus from the Gospel of John who visited Jesus at night.[85] Calvin had already begun using the term "Nicodemite" in a pejorative way in 1544 in a work titled *Excuse à Messieurs les Nicodémites*, a tract which he wrote in response to an inquiry by Poullain about how Protestants ought to respond to Catholic rule.[86] Calvin, Poullain, Lasco, and Hooper (along with numerous other reformers) all agreed that Protestants could not in good conscience attend Mass in order to avoid persecution.[87] Good Protestants must either die for their resistance—as Hooper soon would—or flee to a place where they could worship properly—as Calvin, Poullain, Lasco, and Hooper's family had. Frankfurt afforded the possibility for Protestants to rebuild their religious lives in exile. Indeed, it was developing into a bastion of international Protestantism.

Lasco's writing, like those of Whittingham, succeeded in attracting hundreds more Protestant foreigners to Frankfurt. A list of Dutch-speaking refugees from 12 April 1556 lists 43 households including Lasco's.[88] Combined with the 165 households of French-speakers, there were more than 200 households of refugees from the Low Countries in Frankfurt by the end of 1555. One historian who charted the growth of this congregation from the Low Countries calculated that the congregation comprised 400 individuals at the end of 1554; 700 by the end of 1555; and 1,000 by the end of 1556.[89] To this must be added the 45 households and 226 individuals of the English Church of Frankfurt cataloged on a list from January 1557.[90] Thus in 1556, the entire community of refugees in Frankfurt numbered more than 1,000 individuals divided into two congregations: a dual-language congregation from the Low Countries led by Lasco—with Poullain preaching in French and Datheen preaching in Dutch—and an English congregation. The two congregations shared the Church of the White Ladies.

Frankfurt's population grew from around 11,500 residents in 1548 to 13,000 residents at the end of 1555, and while the city also attracted German Protestant migrants from nearby territories, refugees represented the bulk of the growth, and their community grew at a pace much faster than the city as a whole.[91] From the twenty-four families that first had entered the city in March 1554, the refugee community grew to around one-tenth of Frankfurt's population in under two years. Many of the refugees applied for citizenship, including eighty-three French-speakers from Poullain's initial band and fourteen Dutch-speakers.[92] The community had welcomed new language groups and installed new preachers to support Poullain, and soon the Church of the White Ladies hosted so many religious services that scheduling events became a contested matter among the various refugee language groups. A new church building was needed.

## A FIGHT OVER CHURCH SPACES AND THE ADVENT OF CONFESSIONAL CONFLICT

In 1555, Lasco, Poullain, Datheen, and Whittingham realized that the ever-expanding community of refugees they supervised needed a second church building. As more refugees arrived, more church services were

necessary. It was the English who first approached the council and requested an additional church, and their attempt to secure one inadvertently provoked a fight over religious jurisdiction in Frankfurt. The city's
seven civic ministers clashed with the most prominent patrician families
over who exactly had the authority to grant churches to refugees. Who
controlled Frankfurt's Protestant churches? The presence of refugees
seeking their own religious services forced the city to confront this question. Soon, the frustration felt by the city's ministers about the growing
refugee community morphed into indignation that these newcomers
were granted church space despite being exempt from the city's religious
hierarchy.

Frankfurt maintained seven official ministers for the city's Protestant
congregation: Melchior Ambach, Hartmann Beyer, Christian Egenolph,
Peter Geltner, Johann Lullius, Matthias Ritter, and Marcus Sebander.
These men had initially welcomed Poullain and his congregation of
foreigners. The two oldest ministers, Ambach and Lullius, had been
especially supportive of Poullain since he was a disciple and friend of
Martin Bucer, who had worked with Ambach and Lullius to implement
the Reformation in Frankfurt. Yet even Ambach and Lullius had become
dissatisfied with the proliferation of refugee services in the city. These
two, along with their five colleagues, were dismayed that Frankfurters
were spectating at refugee services in the Church of the White Ladies.
The chief minister, Beyer, rebuked curious Frankfurters and told them
to stop "crowding about [the services of the refugees] as they would
only confuse the foreigners and not understand anything themselves."[93]
By 1555, Frankfurters could witness refugee services in Dutch, English,
or French. Still, all refugee services were confined to the Church of the
White Ladies in the extreme southwest of the city, and as long as the
services stayed there, Frankfurt's ministers remained content—or at least
unmotivated to protest to the council about the religion of the refugees.
In late 1555, though, the English sought to expand into a second church.

"It has come to our attention," Beyer and the city ministers wrote to the
council on 5 September 1555, "that there is a plan to grant St. Catherine's
Church to the foreigners."[94] The ministers must have been monitoring
the situation closely, as their letter reached the council before the refugee
petition formally requesting the use of St. Catherine's. Council minutes
relate the ministers' preemptive opposition to any such plan, real or imag-
ined: "The local ministers together write and ask that the English not be
granted what they desire, [namely] that they be granted St. Catherine's

Church."[95] As the ministers explained to the council, introducing refugee services in the already busy St. Catherine's would require "the appointed preacher, Herr Matthias [Ritter], to move his preaching to nine o'clock on Sunday, which is difficult for him and for all of us to understand."[96]

Frankfurt's ministers acted quickly as St. Catherine's was uniquely important to the city's Protestant tradition. It had been the site of the first Reformation preaching.[97] St. Catherine's had been built by the patricians for their daughters, and it stood under their patronage.[98] The patricians' control over the building had enabled Protestant preachers to access its pulpit in the 1520s. Now, ironically, the city's ministers feared that patrician control over the building would imperil their preaching and degrade clerical authority over the church. Beyer and his colleagues could not abide the idea. They believed they should govern all the churches in the city, or at the very least those churches which had been cleansed of the Catholic Mass. Frustrated by the English plan for a second church, the ministers protested that they should have jurisdiction over the city's churches "as the teachers in our Christian community and as Christ's evangelists."[99]

In the era before the Reformation, Frankfurt's churches had been the only institutions in the city that had remained beyond the control of the council and its patricians.[100] The city's twenty-seven churches and religious houses maintained some independence from the council and answered principally to a collegiate chapter, monastic house, military order, or the archbishop of Mainz. The Reformation had changed this. In 1533 the Frankfurt Council assumed control over the city churches. And although a modicum of Catholic authority reentered the city after the Schmalkaldic War—when the council relinquished control over the three collegiate churches, which reintroduced the Catholic Mass—anyone seeking access to the city's non-Catholic churches had to go through the council. The council ruled Frankfurt's twenty-four Protestant church buildings, and the patricians dominated the council, ensuring that Frankfurt's civic congregation, like its government, was oligarchical in nature.[101] Empowered by the Reformation, the patricians had opened the Church of the White Ladies for Poullain in early 1554, though with the approval of the city's ministers.

The patricians and the ministers of Frankfurt had previously worked in concert to implement and defend the Reformation in the city, and while the arrival of more refugees seeking religious services now divided Frankfurt's religious and secular leaders, both sides still sought to work in harmony. After reading the ministers' letter from 1555 aloud, the council accepted their demand that St. Catherine's be refused to the refugees: "It is resolved that the English should be remain at this time in their Church of the White Ladies."[102]

In their letter denouncing the expansion of refugee services, Beyer and his six colleagues went further than merely opposing the opening St. Catherine's to the refugees. They also denounced, in detail, the existing refugee services in the Church of the White Ladies. The detailed nature of their attack makes it clear that the city's ministers had joined their curious congregants in peering through the windows of the Church of the White Ladies at the services of the refugees. They described what they witnessed thusly: "Among these people, all manners of pestilence reign; they even bring their young children with them into the church and hold them, even though they are unclean, so that there are many bad smells."[103] Repulsed by the smells emanating from the refugee gatherings, Beyer and his colleagues also recoiled at the site of the refugees taking the communion bread in their own hands. Something was amiss about the religion of the refugees. As the city ministers explained to the council, "they use unusual ceremonies so that it seems that they do not believe in the presence of the body and blood of Christ."[104] The continuation of these services in Frankfurt's churches would "be a great detriment to us, the clergy, as it would seem that we agree with them, and that we adhere to their obscure and erroneous opinions."[105]

Beyer and his colleagues insisted that they were at the very least responsible for assessing whether the refugees were in conformity with the civic church. And a proper examination of the displaced Christians had not yet been conducted. Throughout Poullain's earliest negotiations for a church in the city, Beyer and his colleagues had only "heard" that the newcomers would "conform with us in our doctrines and our church."[106] Now the ministers insisted that conformity to civic religion meant conformity to the Augsburg Confession of 1530, and they explained that it was "unknown to us" whether the refugees had ever truly held to the Confession.[107] Witnessing the refugee services had made the ministers skeptical.

The council took the concern of the ministers seriously, especially in late 1555 as the emperor (now Charles's brother Ferdinand) and the imperial estates gathered in Augsburg to settle the matter of religious governance in post-Reformation Germany.[108] Frankfurt's patricians and ministers alike sought to preserve Protestant reforms in the city, and they watched the imperial meeting in Augsburg closely. Ultimately, the patricians and ministers shared the same basic goal with respect to

Frankfurt's religion. They sought to maintain a harmonious civic church based around biblically focused preaching and the right administration of the sacraments, although the specific details of the latter remained a contentious issue between the patricians and the ministers. When the emperor and imperial estates agreed in September that Protestantism as defined by the Augsburg Confession was the only permissible alternative to Catholicism, the Frankfurt Council recognized the danger inherent in accusations by the city ministers that the refugees did not conform to the Augsburg Confession.[109] Alarmed about possible nonconformity, the council agreed that "it should be learned from the ministers—and they should specifically report—in what points and instances the Walloon [Welsche] and English ministers do not match and agree with the Augsburg Confession."[110] The council demanded a thorough account of any religious difference, and the ministers spent extraordinary energy crafting one.

Several weeks later, on 29 October 1555, the council finally received the petition from the English for a new church. Interestingly though, the petition does not mention St. Catherine's. It begins with a glowing statement of admiration for the "most distinguished and most celebrated senate of Frankfurt" and continues with a lengthy expression of gratitude for the many generous concessions afforded to refugees by the city.[111] The English must have feared that the city's ministers had begun to poison the council against the refugee community. The petition goes on to entreat the councilmen "most ardently that these kindnesses of yours never be suspended."[112] After further expressions of gratitude and an assurance to the patricians that all refugee services included a prayer for "your safety and that of your state," the English finally made their request for a new church: "we ask you most resolutely, and beseeching with the most ardent vows, that it also be permitted through your agreement for us to use that chapel [sacello] of yours, and since we are outsiders [extra urbem vestram] the chapel should be in the outermost corner [of the city]."[113] The English were not asking for St. Catherine's in the center of the city but rather the All Saints Chapel outside of the old city and against the city wall in an area called Neustadt.[114]

The All Saints Chapel stood in the extreme northeast corner of the city and thus very far from the Church of the White Ladies, which lay in the extreme southwest. Perhaps the English sought to separate themselves from the rapidly expanding community from the Low Countries. The choice of the All Saints Chapel makes one thing very clear: the

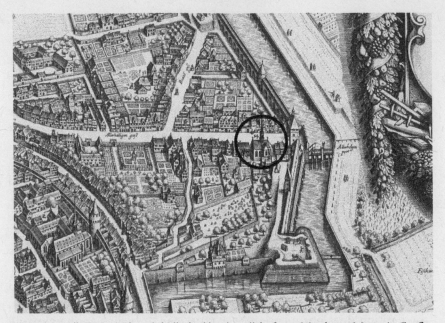

Figure 5. All Saints Chapel (Allerheiligenkapelle), from Matthäus Merian's Großer Stadtplan, 1628. (Historisches Museum Frankfurt, photograph by Horst Ziegenfusz, adapted by author)

English realized that St. Catherine's in the city center was out of their reach now that the city's ministers had mobilized preemptively to prevent the council from permitting refugee services there.

Whittingham and his countrymen presented good reason for needing a second church. Put simply, the Church of the White Ladies had become too crowded. While the English congregation could physically fit in the building, they had trouble scheduling a time to do so because of the many Dutch and French services also taking place there. As leader of the congregation from the Low Countries, Lasco called for two Sunday services—a morning service consisting of a Bible reading and hour-long sermon plus an afternoon service consisting of a shorter sermon and catechesis.[115] And since both the French-speakers, led by Poullain, and the Dutch-speakers, led by Datheen, sought to follow Lasco's standards, there were at least four Sunday services for the people from the Low Countries. Thus, the English had trouble scheduling their own services. Ultimately, the English had to use the building in the very early mornings, when it was bitterly cold. They explained this to the councilmen:

We have already been assembled for a long time in one temple with the French church but we have been confined in that temple on the Lord's day beyond measure, and also shut out at times. Moreover, everyone, indeed, is intolerably distressed by gloomy winter, which is already falling upon them, but especially those among us who are weaker, such as old men and women. For we gather at six o'clock, the top of the morning darkening more and more, to approach the temple; we also gather at the last part of the day, near six o'clock, and return home in the darkness.[116]

Fortunately for the cold English congregation, the All Saints Chapel belonged to a single patrician family, the Neuhaus family, and they welcomed Whittingham and his community. The council certified this decision on 29 October 1555, the same day the English petition first arrived.

The acquisition of a new church by the English proved a pyrrhic victory. That same day, Beyer and his colleagues submitted their long-awaited report regarding religious difference. The initial desire by the English for a new church had impelled Beyer to start crafting his report seven weeks earlier, and his account proved scathing. Indeed, its uncompromising denunciation of the religion of the refugees divided Beyer from the council and even sowed discord among the city ministers themselves. Beyer insisted that the refugees had, upon their initial arrival in March 1554, pledged to abide by the Augsburg Confession of 1530, which he called the foundation of the city's Protestant church. Poullain, the council, and two of Beyer's colleagues disagreed, and a new boundary began to divide Protestants in Frankfurt. The Reformation in Frankfurt entered a new stage.

## LITURGICAL DIFFERENCES AND THE END
## OF UNITED PROTESTANTISM IN FRANKFURT

Beyer crafted his report to the council with the help of five colleagues, four of whom had signed the earlier letter insisting the English be denied St. Catherine's—Egenolph, Geltner, Ritter, and Sebander—plus one new colleague named Andreas Saxo recently arrived from rural Saxony.[117] These six men submitted their report on 29 October, and began by reminding the city's rulers of their purpose: "Since your honorable council requested from us ministers a more specific analysis and clarification regarding our recently submitted supplication, which regarded the foreigners, in which we asserted that they are not one with us in their teachings, we are therefore letting it be known to you, that such disunion primarily concerns the Holy Sacrament of the body and blood of our Lord Jesus Christ."[118] The Eucharist was the source of controversy. And now, after another seven weeks of refugee services in Frankfurt, the ministers of the city had collected firsthand evidence of the refugees' religious wrongdoings.

The first and clearest piece of evidence cited by the ministers was an item they had already mentioned in their first letter to the council: a booklet containing Poullain's liturgy, which he had had printed in Frankfurt and which the ministers found in the Church of the White Ladies and labeled a collection of "opinions."[119] The booklet contained a plethora of troublesome passages, according to the ministers, but they would "leave these in peace" and focus solely on the issue of the Lord's Supper.[120] The booklet stated the following: "Thus, we say with constancy, that these words (namely, 'this is my body, this is my blood') are no reason or source from which corporeal presence may flow or be understood."[121] Frankfurt's ministers explained to the council that the beliefs of the refugees contradicted the Augsburg Confession of 1530, which established the real presence of Christ in the bread and wine of the Supper. Furthermore, the ministers claimed that the Augsburg Confession of 1530, along with the supplemental Apologia written by Melanchthon in 1530, comprised the articles of faith "which we [in Frankfurt] confess."[122] The city's patricians disagreed. The much more accommodating *Concordia Buceriana* of 1542, with its broader understanding of Jesus's presence in the Eucharist, was the true foundation of the city's civic church, according to the patricians.

Poullain's printed booklet was not the only evidence of refugee heterodoxy submitted by Frankfurt's ministers. Beyer's report continued by describing one troubling omission in the refugee services that was witnessed by the city clergy: "[The refugees] pass the bread with these words: 'the bread which we break, is the community of the body of Christ, take this and eat, remembering that the body of Christ was broken for us, for the forgiveness of your sins' and in the same way they pass the chalice with these words, 'the chalice which we bless is the community of the blood of Christ,' and they [the refugees] completely leave out these words of the Lord Christ, namely 'this is my body, this is my blood.'"[123] Beyer and his colleagues argued that this omission represented heterodox thinking regarding the presence of Christ. The refugees treated the

Supper as a "mere memorial" rather than an actual encounter with the physical body of Jesus.[124]

For the six Frankfurt clergymen who signed the new report, it was scandalous that the refugees understood the Lord's Supper differently. It betrayed the city's hard-fought Reformation by introducing a new, incorrect form of the Supper into the city. As Beyer reminded the council, he and his elderly colleagues Ambach and Lullius (whether or not they now agreed with Beyer) had fought together to rid Frankfurt of the Catholic Mass precisely because the Mass distorted, in their minds, the central ritual of Christian faith, the Eucharist. Additionally, incorrect worship represented incorrect belief, and incorrect beliefs within Frankfurt would only further fracture the city's religious unity, which had already been jeopardized by the reintroduction of the Catholic Mass following the emperor's victory in the Schmalkaldic War. Two forms of Christianity could not be permitted "under one roof, even temporarily, in good conscience," as Beyer himself had argued in 1549.[125] All Frankfurters should celebrate the Eucharist in the same fashion, and though the emperor had violently reintroduced the Mass into certain of the city's churches, the city's Protestants could still be united in their manner of Eucharistic celebration.

The Eucharist was the focal point of the religious changes taking place in Frankfurt, and for Frankfurt's clergy, the Eucharist as celebrated by the refugees contradicted an understanding of the ritual accepted by all right-minded Protestants: "Such a mistake about this item [the Eucharist] is opposed to the Augsburg [Confession] and also opposed to the Saxon and Wittenberg Confession, submitted a few years ago to the Council of Trent, and likewise opposed to the Concordia established by the blessed Dr. Bucer and other distinguished teachers ... with the blessed Dr. Luther, and in sum it is opposed to all our doctrine."[126] Here, the ministers acknowledged the *Concordia Buceriana* as a foundational religious text for the city's church, but not the only one. Moreover, they suggested that it supported their understanding of the real presence of Jesus in the Eucharist. Jesus's presence was essential for Frankfurt's ministers, and they were not alone in emphasizing it. Recent scholarship has demonstrated how diverging understandings of Christ's presence in the Eucharist account for confessional distinctions emerging across Europe.[127] Such distinctions emerged very sharply in areas of Germany hosting refugees.

Frankfurt's ministers based their diagnosis of theological error on first-hand evidence of the refugee ceremonies. Put simply, Poullain's services looked different from the ones of Frankfurt and other German cities. The council needed to take the foreignness of the newcomers seriously and enforce religious uniformity based on Frankfurt's native church. And while the ministers did not want Frankfurt to be quite as "merciless" toward the refugees as the city of Emden—which had "refused them a place to sleep"—the ministers did recommend the council "follow the example of the city of Strasbourg," which had enforced liturgical uniformity.[128] The city council of Strasbourg had acted "immediately" when the city's ministers brought forth evidence of refugee heteropraxy and ordered an inspection of church services to ensure they conformed to the Augsburg Confession "through a fee or corporal punishment."[129] The presence of refugees and refugee religious services provoked a regime of religious policing in Strasbourg, which Frankfurt's ministers sought to emulate.

At the very least, the city ministers wrote, the Frankfurt Council should prevent the refugees from printing their books and liturgical texts. Printed texts had helped establish the Reformation in Frankfurt (in many ways, print was the essence of the Reformation in Frankfurt), and Frankfurt's clergy worried that Poullain and his followers would use the city's printing presses to spread erroneous teachings and thereby "give great offense to the people and cause listlessness and discord."[130] The council did not share the clergy's concerns about listlessness, though it would eventually agree that publications caused discord, as we will see in the next chapter.

Not all of Frankfurt's clergy signed the October letter protesting refugee services and publications. Ambach and Lullius, the two oldest ministers, refused to sign even though they had signed the earlier protest about jurisdiction over church spaces. The absence of their signatures did not go unnoticed by the council. Minutes from 29 October recorded the official reading of the letter of protest as well as the council's response: "It was decreed, that this text should be submitted to Lullius and Ambach, and it should be heard from them, why they did not sign it and whether they are of the same opinion as the others."[131] The two old ministers replied immediately. It was their advanced age that kept them from signing the letter, they insisted.[132] Ambach explained that they were too exhausted to quarrel about the Lord's Supper, a fatigue not shared by his younger colleagues. Two generations of ministers split over the treatment of the refugees.[133] On 31 October, the council expressed its sympathy with Ambach and Lullius and decided to reject the "sharp" treatment recommended by Beyer and the other, younger ministers.[134]

In earlier decades, Ambach and Lullius had crusaded against the Catholic Mass in Frankfurt. They had signed and promoted the text of Bucer's *Concordia* before the council eventually approved it. For them the Reformation in Frankfurt continued to center around a rejection of the Catholic Mass and its replacement by a Supper in which the body and blood of Christ were truly present (thus agreeing with Luther's theology) yet not spatially circumscribed (thus appeasing possible detractors from Zwingli's camp). Ambach and Lullius clung to a broad understanding of Christian reform, an understanding that could accommodate Protestants like Beyer and Poullain. Unfortunately, the next generation of ministers in Frankfurt—dismayed by the unfamiliarity of the refugee liturgy and encouraged by imperial political developments stressing the Augsburg Confession—insisted on conformity with the unaltered Augsburg Confession of 1530. Led by Beyer, these younger ministers claimed that the Augsburg Confession was the real foundation of the city's Protestant Eucharist. They denounced the refugees for nonconformity with the Augsburg Confession and demanded the council close the Church of the White Ladies.

Throughout the winter of 1555–56, Beyer and his colleagues penned additional letters to the council. Ambach and Lullius signed none of these. In the letters, the city ministers protested the council's lack of decisiveness and maintained that the refugees did not perform proper Christian services. Notably, the ministers began to refer to specific geographic areas where the Lord's Supper was properly understood and practiced: "Saxony, Denmark, Meissen, Thuringia, Hesse, Württemberg, and the cities of the empire."[135] These places were meant to serve as points of reference with their Eucharistic ceremonies serving as measuring sticks by which to assess the religion of the refugees. No location in the Low Country or France appeared on the ministers' list. Still, Beyer and the other Frankfurt ministers continued to begrudgingly concede the refugees were "belonging to our church."[136] But over the next two years, as more and more refugees arrived, the tone of the ministers' letters to the council changed dramatically. Furious that Frankfurt's rulers refused to curtail refugee services, Beyer began to lash out at the refugees' political supporters.

Beyer began to view the Glauburgs as the chief obstacle to religious unity in Frankfurt. The Glauburgs continued to support the refugees and frustrate Beyer's efforts to change their Eucharistic practices. Worse still, Johann von Glauburg maintained a regular correspondence with Calvin, whom he called a "pastor most faithful to the Lord and a friend."[137]

In his letters to Calvin, Johann expressed loyalty to Calvin's vision of a reformed Christianity. And Johann seems to have passed his religious inclinations on to his bibliophile nephew Adolf, unsurprising considering that Johann raised Adolf from infancy. Adolf also became an ardent supporter of the refugee community. Following an acrimonious council meeting about the refugees and Beyer, Adolf supposedly murmured to Beyer's supporters on the council, "Your preachers are desperate criminals."[138] Adolf stood with the refugees against Beyer, who, upon hearing of Adolf's utterance, became convinced of the Glauburgs' wrongheadedness. The presence of the refugee congregation allowed Beyer to identify heretical Frankfurters—namely those who proved loyal to the newcomers including the Glauburgs and ministers Ambach and Lullius.[139] Beyer worked to marginalize his older colleagues and by 1556 had succeeded in ousting both men from the ministry and replacing them with a zealous new preacher from Saxony.[140]

Soon after the fraught council meeting, Adolf von Glauburg died on 26 September 1555.[141] At Adolf's burial, Beyer launched a vicious verbal assault on the displaced Christians and their patrician supporters on the council. Beyer offered a eulogy in which he denounced the now dead Glauburg for his support of the refugees, an attack subsequently described to Calvin in a letter from Adolf's uncle Johann.[142] Beyer announced that the refugees and their supporters were in disunion with the Frankfurt church.[143] Glauburg had propagated this disunion when he first supported the admission of Poullain and his followers. Beyer went on to claim that the city ministers had not even been consulted at the time of Poullain's admission: "After the honorable council first admitted these foreigners out of charity, they were at the same time given a church in which to hold their sermons and baptisms and ceremonies. Albeit we, the teachers in our Christian community and evangelists for Christ, were not consulted about the decision."[144] In response to Beyer's claim, the council summoned the city ministers and reminded them that they had not been bystanders in the admission of Poullain's followers but rather had "in the beginning" certified to the council "that the foreigners were in unity with the teachings of the church in Frankfurt."[145] In subsequent letters to the council, the ministers admitted that they had supported the admission of the refugees and had done so out of "Christian love."[146]

A new letter from Beyer and his colleagues reached the council in March 1556. The letter accused the refugees of "errors and fanaticism" and included the following facts about Poullain's services: "They have other odd opinions about ceremonies and material things, because they can suffer no crucifix or image, even for true historical reasons. They conduct their Eucharist to the great offense of many people who see it or hear about it, because with them several sit around the table upon which are several large glasses with wine and wafers of bread, they distribute such in their manner, and the communicants take it into their hands themselves, eating it and drinking it in this fashion, just as though it were a binge [Zech]."[147] Clearly, this was the account of someone who had witnessed a refugee Supper and, upon seeing the foreigners take the bread and wine in their own hands, concluded that this was a grossly improper expression of Christianity.

Poullain may have noticed Beyer or other clergymen observering his services in the Church of the White Ladies. He arranged to meet with the city ministers to defend the ceremonies of his congregation. But a series of meetings with Poullain did little to assure Beyer and his colleagues. On the contrary, Poullain's statements only convinced Frankfurt's clergy that he concealed "other opinions in secret."[148] Poullain's duplicity was obvious, the ministers felt, for they had witnessed the troubling ceremonies he conducted in the Church of the White Ladies themselves.

Yet Poullain had not deceived the ministers of Frankfurt in March 1554, when he guaranteed his community's conformity with the city's Protestant church. The document they have given him to read and accept—the document they had considered the standard of orthodoxy—was the Concordia Buceriana of 1542, the city's foundational religious text which had been crafted by Bucer as a compromise between Luther's and Zwingli's views of the Eucharist. In short, they had presented Poullain with a document deliberately seeking Protestant solidarity, and Poullain had agreed to abide by it.[149] The refugees and their descendants remembered these circumstances and continued to cling to the Concordia Buceriana. In the eighteenth century, the descendants of the refugees still living in Frankfurt sued the city for worship rights, and the Concordia Buceriana became compelling evidence that their ancestors had not deceived Frankfurt's ministers in 1554.[150] The city ministers had restricted and redefined their understanding of the Eucharist after the arrival of the refugees. Only then did Beyer insist on conformity to the unaltered Augsburg Confession, which was not the text laid before Poullain in 1554.

Judging from his letters to the council, Beyer hated Poullain and feared the refugee minister's writings would poison Frankfurt permanently. Inadvertently, though, Beyer preserved for future generations one of the few texts written by Poullain. Beyer saved an undated Latin letter Poullain sent to him sometime between 1556 and 1558 among his papers. That letter now sits alongside some of Beyer's fieriest sermons against the refugees within his literary remains at the archives of the University of Frankfurt. It represents a last attempt, by Poullain, to repair Protestant unity in Frankfurt.

"I ask you in the name of Christ, most dear and venerable brother, to take pains so that in no way can this little church complain that it has been now betrayed by some false expectation," Poullain began.[151] The "little church" was his own refugee congregation, which he maintained had come under unfair scrutiny for failing to abide by rules that had first been implemented well after the refugees had arrived. According to Poullain, his community had never agreed to the set of standards Beyer now sought to impose. The Augsburg Confession, not the refugee community, was the real newcomer in Frankfurt, and it had the potential to fracture the fraternal bond established between the displaced people and their Frankfurt hosts. Beyer had previously guaranteed that the refugees "would always be free," and his new campaign to end refugee services marked a departure from the city's previous religious course.[152]

Poullain recognized that the Eucharist was the central point of dispute, and he referred in his letter to previous efforts to settle the matter with Beyer quietly: "You know how carefully I have conducted my business with you before calling the council about the bread of the Supper."[153] Beyer disapproved of the refugee congregants breaking the bread with their hands while standing, and Poullain had therefore offered to end this practice within his congregation—"there will be no business of the breaking of the bread with the acceptance in the hands while standing."[154] Yet this concession did not appease Beyer. Beyer and his allies continued to complain about the refugees, prompting Poullain to write to the council and eventually print his liturgy to quell suspicions of religious error: "Then finally I conducted this case before the magistrate and in printed books as you know."[155]

Poullain insisted he had never deceived anyone about his congregation's liturgy, "nor have I lied about these ceremonies of ours, and good men have supported my words and faith."[156] He hoped his letter would placate Beyer, and he ended by praising Beyer and begging him to end his campaign against the refugees: "And so I beg you and our piety through Christ, most clement and venerable brother, as much as you have always stood so bravely for the liberty of the church, take care so that no yoke be placed upon you and let it be permitted to us to speak to one another face-to-face.... I do not doubt that you equally will love this little church from which deservedly the highest is demanded."[157] Poullain reminded Beyer of their fraternal bond as Christian ministers: "V. Pollanus sends this to you, your most beloved brother and minister in Christ."[158] Yet this expression of love could not repair Protestant unity in Frankfurt. Beyer soon intensified his campaign against the refugee congregation.

By 1561, Beyer had begun using the term "Calvinism" to refer to the religion of the refugees. He insisted that the city's rulers should extirpate Calvinist doctrine and liturgy from within the city walls. He faced stiff resistance from the councilmen, who supported the refugees. The Glauburgs noted that the reformer Melanchthon in Wittenberg continued to support the admission and protection of refugees from the Low Countries (though by 1561, Melanchthon was himself facing accusations of being a crypto-Calvinist).[159] The council held firm in defense of the refugees. Beyer's counterpart in Hamburg, the fiery preacher and chief minister Joachim Westphal, wrote to Beyer in disgust that Frankfurt's rulers continued to believe the "monstrous alteration before the council," by which he meant Poullain's claim that the refugees were in conformity with the city's religion.[160]

The Frankfurt Council ordered the refugees to respond to the accusations of "errors and fanaticism" leveled against them by the city ministers.[161] Were the newcomers indeed Calvinists, as Beyer and his colleagues insisted? Distraught by this slur against them, the refugee congregation responded with a letter to the council that insisted, "we are not fanatics, not Sacramentarians, indeed we are also not Calvinists or Zwinglians, because we are devoted to no man but instead to the Truth, as it is composed in the Biblical text."[162] The refugees continued to view themselves as Christians in the same reformed mold as Frankfurt's civic congregation. Unfortunately, the leaders of that civic congregation now drew a boundary between Frankfurt's Protestants and the refugee flock. In the span of seven years, the refugees had transformed in the eyes of Frankfurters, from Christians, to fanatics, to Calvinists. This change in perception epitomized the sixteenth-century phenomenon of confessionalism—the effort by reformers to define, regulate, and separate their beliefs and rituals from those of other Christian traditions—and it occurred after the city ministers, led by Beyer, witnessed the refugee Eucharist firsthand.

## REFUGEES AND CONFESSIONAL EXCLUSION

The city of Wesel, 260 kilometers to the northwest, confronted similar confessional controversies when it admitted refugees in the 1550s. Wesel had previously rejected Poullain's community due to Poullain's insistence on ecclesiastical independence from the civic congregation. But Wesel later admitted a different group of displaced people who did not make this demand. Wesel's rulers worked to mitigate religious conflict by obscuring confessional differences between the newcomers and the native residents, deliberately ignoring what one historian called "the manifest confessional divide" within the city.[163]

Frankfurt's story was a bit different. The Frankfurt Council formally admitted Poullain's community; permitted the newcomers to maintain their own independent congregation based in one of the city's churches; and defended the refugees' conformity with the civic church against the complaints of the city ministers. In taking these three steps, Frankfurt's councilmen were not obfuscating a confessional discrepancy dividing the civic congregation from the refugees but rather demonstrating that no such discrepancy existed, at least according to the *Concordia Buceriana*, which contained Frankfurt's officially adopted understanding of the Eucharist. Frankfurt's rulers genuinely held that Poullain's flock conformed to civic Christianity in Frankfurt.

In 1554, when Poullain had stressed his congregation's dedication to the "true religion," he had not done so duplicitously, as Beyer and the city ministers would later claim.[164] Poullain had read the *Concordia Buceriana* and believed that his community was in accord with Frankfurt's Eucharistic practices. For at the time of the refugees' arrival, the divisions between (Lutheran) hosts and (Reformed) guests were still unclear. Frankfurt refugees did not bring a discrete Reformed confession with them into the Holy Roman Empire, as historians sometimes describe.[165] On the contrary, Poullain and his flock had deliberately sought out a city with a shared vision of religious reform.

Only after repeated personal encounters between refugees and natives did a religious division develop between them and harden. Over the course of 1554–55, Frankfurt's clergy and the refugee community began to view each other as distinct and misguided, especially regarding the Lord's Supper. Should one break the bread at the Lord's Supper? Beyer and Poullain answered this question differently, and both men became adamant in their resolve. As the case of Frankfurt demonstrates, refugees fueled confessional differentiation over the issue of the real presence of Jesus simply by celebrating their Eucharist where their hosts could see.[166] Encounter led to exclusion. (In France, too, the encounter between German-speaking Protestants and French-speaking Protestants resulted in a crystallized distinction between Lutheran Christians and Reformed Christians, with the former insisting on holding to the Augsburg Confession of 1530's understanding of the real presence.)[167] The experience of exile also determined Lasco's view of German Protestants. The rejection he and his followers faced in Hamburg and Lübeck over the winter of 1553–54 convinced Lasco of the wrongheadedness of the Germans who insisted on belief in the real presence. And as we will see in chapter 3, Lasco published a highly influential church order in Frankfurt in which he deliberately differentiated his community from the uncaring and misbelieving Protestants of north German cities.[168]

Two confessions began to emerge and diverge in Frankfurt, divided over the issue of the Eucharist. This divergence not only separated refugees from citizens but also Frankfurters from each other. Frankfurters disagreed about whether the city should accommodate the religion of the newcomers. Two of the city's leaders, Minister Beyer and Councilman Glauburg, came to see each other as heretical. Refugees did not simply arrive in a city experiencing confessional conflict, as historians have traditionally described.[169] The very presence of refugees, the accessibility of their religious services, and the challenges of their communities' growth caused a rift to form in Frankfurt as the city's religious leaders redefined and zealously guarded the borders of what they deemed to be Frankfurt's civic church. By 1555, Protestants in Frankfurt could be categorized as either Lutheran (part of the civic church) or Reformed (part of the refugee community). Clear evidence of the new divide between Reformed and Lutheran residents of Frankfurt emerged in the 1580s, when a different group of refugees from the Low Countries accepted the authority of Frankfurt's clergy and accepted the real presence of Jesus in the Eucharist. This group became known as the Low Country Congregation of the Augsburg Confession (Niederländische Gemeinde Augsburger Confession). And while these newcomers shared much in common with their Reformed countrymen—their minister, Casiodoro de Reina, would live in the house of Augustin Le Grand, one of the richest members of the Reformed community—their treatment by the city clergy differed markedly.[170] Frankfurt's clergy celebrated the Lutheran refugees, approved of their use of French, and considered this group from the Low Countries to be an integral part of the city, unlike their fellow refugees, whom the ministers deemed outside the bounds of the true confession.[171]

Still, whatever the posture of Beyer and the city ministers, in the 1550s and early 1560s the patricians who supported Poullain and his refugee flock continued to control the Frankfurt Council. The council refused Beyer's demands that the Church of the White Ladies be shut, and that the refugees be compelled to attend Frankfurt's civic church services. Soon though, events within the English congregation and the congregation from the Low Countries would force the council to abandon its support for the refugees and agree to implement the restrictions on refugee religious services demanded by Frankfurt's ministers.

# 3

# Refugee Controversies and the End of Accommodation

❧

For it standethe your wisedomes in hande to consider, that howe muche commoditie the goodnesse off the Senate dothe deserve, so muche envie shall yow be giltie off, or charged withall, yf yow have abused their lenitie or gentlenesse, whiche were so well affected towardes your nation.

—Calvin's warning to the English refugees in Frankfurt, May 1555

STARTING IN 1555, Frankfurt's Lutheran clergy, led by Minister Hartmann Beyer, wrote frequent letters to the city council demanding a ban on the religious services of the Reformed refugees living in the city. The city clergy explained, "If they [the refugees] do not want to join our views nor hold identical ceremonies with our church (which, after all, the foreigners in Strasbourg did), then an honorable city council has sufficient reason to refuse them a church."[1] The point of contention remained the Lord's Supper. Beyer insisted that the Reformed should practice the Supper in a manner consistent with a physical understanding of the bread as Christ's body, and if they refused, the council should ban refugee services and admit only displaced people who accepted the Lutheran understanding of the Eucharist. The Frankfurt Council refused these demands. To the horror of the city's ministers, Reformed services continued in the Church of the White Ladies as hundreds more refugees joined the English refugee congregation and the congregation from the Low Countries over the years 1555–58. Reformed

75

newcomers continued to enjoy the protection of the council's most powerful patricians.

Gradually though, the council at large and even some of the patricians who had supported the refugees became suspicious of the newcomers and listened more attentively to the complaints of the city ministers. By 1561, seven years after the arrival of the first refugees, a political realignment was complete—the council decided to shut the Church of the White Ladies to the services of the refugees, a surprising step considering the council's previous steadfast support for the Reformed.

Historians have ascribed Frankfurt's turn against the refugees in 1561 to socioeconomic motives, blaming jealousy toward the wealth and "commercial aptitude" of the newcomers.[2] The city's guilds are the central antagonists in this story line; they agitated against refugees because they resented the refugees' "modern economic and social forms, all of which contravened the spirit of guilds [Zunftgeist]."[3] Yet a broader study of Rhineland refugees has shown how the arrival of refugees actually benefited the guilds.[4] More importantly, whatever the guilds felt about the refugees and their industry, the guilds had negligible influence on the council. Indeed, the guilds maintained a long tradition of petitioning the council in vain.[5] The guild representatives who sat on the council constituted the third and lowest bench and could not hope to wrest control from the patricians on the upper benches. After all, the patricians determined which guilds were "council-eligible" in addition to choosing which men would represent these specific guilds.[6]

The patricians dominated the council, and a discussion of the council's motives in the mid-sixteenth century is, ultimately, a discussion of the patricians and their thinking. Why did these oligarchs begin to heed the complaints of the city's clergy about the refugees? While petitions to the council from the city ministers and from the refugees allow for an indirect examination of the councilmen's thinking, council minutes and mayoral records provide a direct view. Together, these sources provide a clear picture of the context and events that led the patricians to slowly abandon their protection of the refugees' religious independence.

The council slowly came see the refugees as troublemakers due to a series of religious controversies emanating from within the growing refugee community, controversies that spilled into print, embarrassed the council's patricians, and imperiled Frankfurt's position within the Holy Roman Empire. Permitted to govern their own religious affairs, the refugees struggled to agree among themselves about the shape of their religious institutions and the nature of their ceremonies. The arrival of new groups with different ideas about church governance and liturgy led to new intramural controversies. Controversies led to factionalism, and factionalism led to loud, publicized fights that caught the attention of not only Frankfurt's leaders but also reformers and rulers across western Europe. Frankfurt's patricians realized they would need to rescind the independence they had previously granted the displaced Christians they had welcomed and sheltered.

The earliest controversy involved accusations that the refugees were harboring Anabaptists, individuals who believed Christians should be baptized as adults. Such accusations of Anabaptism had swirled around the refugee community since its arrival. Then, a fierce and public feud over liturgical practice emerged within the English refugee community, a fight that resulted in the publication of a tract critical of the emperor. Additional tracts published by Reformed refugees—even several tracts aimed at lessening controversy—raised further alarm. Finally, a long-simmering conflict in the French-speaking community over leadership boiled over, costing Valérand Poullain his position as minister. Thus, the man who had won the refugees a place in Frankfurt, a man trusted by the city's patricians, departed Frankfurt in controversy. Alarmed by these escalating conflicts, and frustrated by the refugees' ongoing internal discord, the council closed their church after Easter 1561.

## ACCUSATIONS OF ANABAPTISM
## AND BREWING CONFLICT

The vulnerability of the bond between the refugees and their political patrons became clear as early as August 1554, only a few months after the admission of Poullain's group. Frankfurt's rulers received reports (we do not know from whom) that the city had been infiltrated by Anabaptists, radical Protestants who rejected oaths and infant baptism, two of Frankfurt's most fundamental civic rituals. On 23 August, the minutes of the council read: "Reported: there are two Anabaptists arrested because they would not make the oath to the mayor."[7] Frankfurt's two mayors enjoyed executive, judicial, and legislative authority over the city and constituted the purest representation of the city's political independence. By refusing to swear an oath to the mayoral office, the two suspected Anabaptists offended the city's political authority most profoundly. Were these two men members of either Poullain's congregation or Whittingham's newly arrived group of English people? The timing suggests so, as this mention of Anabaptist effrontery appeared at a time of major growth within the displaced community in Frankfurt. The refugees were quick to defend themselves and dispel the rumor that their number included Anabaptists. On 13 September, the council minutes recorded: "About Valérand [Poullain] and the other English it is reported; they are denounced as Anabaptists; they have therefore printed their confession [of faith]."[8] An account of their religion was needed, Poullain believed, or else the refugees would be branded as Anabaptists, a dangerous mark ever since a group of Anabaptists overthrew the government of the city of Münster in 1535. After this uprising, German rulers treated Anabaptists as dangerous rebels.

Anabaptists blurred the line between religious dissent and political insurgency, according to their opponents. Frankfurt's patricians and clergy shared the view that Anabaptists were not only lurking rebels but also spiritually dangerous heretics because they rejected the baptizing of infants. The city ministers insisted the council act quickly to ferret out radical elements within the city by compelling foreigners to be interrogated about their beliefs by the city ministers.[9] Beyer and his colleagues sensed something amiss about the displaced population in the city, and even if Poullain and the majority of the newcomers conformed to the city's idea of Christianity, some portion of the refugees may still have been Anabaptists. The first written complaint by Frankfurt's ministers to the council—which was cosigned by Ministers Ambach and Lullius, the two ministers most supportive of the refugees—reminded the councilmen that "various opinions exist among them [the refugees], indeed they do not (as we hear) agree together, rather there are numerous antagonisms among them, such that it is fair to assume that they want to separate themselves from each other going forward."[10] The harboring of Anabaptists, factionalism, and general disorderliness were the initial complaints lodged against the refugees by Frankfurt's ministers.[11]

Refugee ministers like Poullain cooperated with civic efforts to ferret out Anabaptists. They cooperated out of a desire to prove their civic loyalty and out of a genuine disdain for Anabaptists. When the French refugee minister Richard Vauville arrived in Frankfurt in 1555, he wrote a letter to Calvin describing the refugee community's favorable position in the city, and how the refugees were turning over troublemakers to the civic authorities:

Truly in this do their [the councilmen's] goodness and zeal in respect to Christianity exhibit themselves, since they wish for no foreigner [*peregrinum*] in this city to remain, whose faith is not known to the ministers of the foreign churches. But if, for instance, some broken man were wanting to make a disturbance, then we are ordered to take him down to the magistracy, so that it may exile him after he has paid the penalties for his impudence, and thus not only our church but also the entire state is cleansed of secular and wicked men who are used to disrupting churches.[12]

In spite of this cooperation on the part of the refugees and their ministers, accusations that the newcomers harbored Anabaptists and troublemakers persisted. On 19 March 1556, for example, Beyer and his colleagues asserted that the refugees had been chased out of England "not for the pure Gospel but for errors and fanaticism."[13] The ministers insisted the council should "publicly post an edict threatening a great punishment for [those refugees] housing or harboring Anabaptists and Sacramentarians and those from suspicious towns."[14] Anabaptists and other fanatics gravitated to the refugee congregation, Beyer believed, because of the ecclesiastical independence the city granted to the newcomers.[15] They were not subject to oversight by the city ministers.

In at least one important respect, Beyer was right. The refugees were having serious trouble controlling their own congregants, especially as newcomers continued to pour into the city. As new voices joined the refugee community, disharmony emerged and became ever-louder. Eventually, refugee conflicts reached a level that began to disturb the city's rulers. The council began to reconsider its initial decision to permit the refugees to govern their own religious community. Rather than promoting communal harmony, the refugees' ecclesiastical independence resulted in discord and even the expulsion, by the Reformed, of some of their own members.

## English Refugee Discord

The case of the English demonstrates how challenging it was for refugees to maintain communal accord as new groups arrived. After the foundation of the English congregation in Frankfurt under Whittingham in the summer of 1554, the English enjoyed only a brief period of intramural harmony before the effort to attract additional groups of English Protestants resulted in unexpected and fractious outcomes. Letters of invitation resulted in the arrival of new members and new problems. Yet the first conflict confronting the English community originated from the outside, from correspondence with a sister congregation in exile in Strasbourg, two hundred kilometers to the south.

Upon their arrival in Frankfurt, Whittingham and his colleagues had written a letter of invitation to the English Protestants refugees living in Emden, Strasbourg, Wesel, and Zurich. The invitation seems to have been heartfelt. The Frankfurt Englishmen began by describing their remarkable situation in the city on the Main: "[Here in Frankfurt] it is graunted in so ample wise, that beinge subjecte to no blemishe, no, nor so muche as the evell off suspition (from the whiche fewe churches are free) we maie preache, minister, and use Discipline, to the true settinge forthe off gods glorie, and good ensample to others."[16] The response from Strasbourg's English leaders dismayed Whittingham and his group. Evidently, the Strasbourg leaders had misunderstood the letter of invitation; they responded not by addressing the invitation but instead by suggesting that one of the Strasbourg members should travel to Frankfurt and supervise the nascent community's formation. Whittingham recalled his group's reaction to the Strasbourg letter: "Nowe, when the answere that came from Strausbrough was read, and compared withe the letter written unto them, it did not in anie pointe answere it. For the congregation [in Frankfurt] wrote not particulerly for anie certaine nomber [of desired ministers], but generally wishinge all [English] mens presence, nether did they require to have anye superintendent to take the chieff charge and governement, for the choise and election theroff (yff suche a one had bene necessary) ought to have byn reserved to the congregation."[17] Whittingham and his fellow Englishmen in Frankfurt did not appreciate Strasbourg's attempt to govern their choice of minister, a matter they considered their own affair. Moreover, the Strasbourg refugee community structured its religious institutions slightly differently, in a manner common among some English exile congregations but distinctly different from the English church in Frankfurt.

Whittingham's community had, upon their arrival in Frankfurt, agreed to abide by Poullain's church order, which had been based on the one Calvin had developed for the French refugees in Strasbourg, but modeled its electoral system more on the order John a Lasco had created for his refugee congregation in London. In Poullain's order, as in Lasco's, all the men of the congregation, not just their elders, would elect the minister and other church officers.[18] Put simply, the English refugees in Frankfurt maintained a more democratic church order than Englishmen elsewhere. Lasco's order describes all the men of a community participating in the election of ministers: "When the church has need for one or more ministers, a public fast is proclaimed to the whole church, and a fixed day is set by the elders for this public fast and public prayers in the church, and it is announced from the pulpit to all the people, so that . . . the entire church may convene on that very appointed day . . . on which all of the most capable men are discussed."[19] The leaders of Frankfurt's English refugees, the elders and the ministers who comprised the consistory, answered to the congregation's entire male membership. Among the English refugees in Strasbourg, only the elders were eligible to vote for the minister.[20] Strasbourg's less-democratic system may have resulted from the fact that Strasbourg's Englishmen had previously held high positions within the English church. The leader of the Strasbourg refugees was John Ponet, the former bishop of Winchester. In 1554, he was the highest-ranking member of the English Protestant church in exile.[21] Frankfurt's English community did not include former bishops, and its members embraced a more egalitarian structure. The two communities of English refugees, displaced in two different German cities, disagreed about the optimal structure of English Protestantism. (This disagreement is not surprising when one considers the character of Ponet in Strasbourg, whom the classic history of Marian exiles calls "quarrelsome, avaricious, unscrupulous and a coward.")[22]

Whittingham and his community in Frankfurt ultimately rejected the minister suggested by Strasbourg and instead invited a man of their own choosing to lead their religious community, John Knox, a Scotsman living in Geneva. Knox joined them in Frankfurt in October 1554. His preaching proved popular with Whittingham and the other founders of the English congregation in Frankfurt. Knox also conformed to the rituals of Poullain's French-speakers. Yet his appointment caused the Strasbourg Englishmen serious consternation.

Beyond questions of hierarchy, the English communities in Frankfurt and Strasbourg stood at odds regarding liturgy.[23] A prayer book divided them. The displaced Englishmen in Frankfurt refused to use the 1552 Book of Common Prayer, which had been constructed by the Archbishop of Canterbury Thomas Cranmer during the reign of King Edward. After Edward's death, Queen Mary rejected Cranmer's religious reforms and had the archbishop arrested. But despite Mary's considerable efforts, she could not abrogate the reverence Cranmer enjoyed among English Protestants, both those in England and those in exile. Cranmer's prayer book remained especially influential among the English Protestants who had taken refuge in Strasbourg. The Englishmen in Strasbourg insisted—and would continue to insist throughout their exile—that all English Protestants should respect the authority of the bishops who had governed Christianity in England under King Edward, the ministers and bishops led by Archbishop Cranmer. Strasbourg's community endeavored to police other English refugees' adherence to Cranmer's prayer book, especially the 1552 version. In late November, Strasbourg's Englishmen sent two representatives to Frankfurt with a letter declaring that the delegation had been sent "to helpe to set in order and stabilishe" the community in Frankfurt.[24] According to Whittingham, the theologian leading the delegation, Edmund Grindall, told Frankfurt's Englishmen that stability demanded use of the prayer book: "Grindall declared the occasion of thier comminge whiche (amonge other things) was chieflie for the stablishinge of the booke off England not that they mente, (as he saied) to have it so strictly observed but that suche ceremonies, and thinges whiche the countrie coulde not beare, might well be omitted."[25] According to the Strasbourg delegation, several features of the liturgy that were prescribed by Cranmer's Book of Common Prayer were being omitted from the English ceremonies in Frankfurt, and the English church as a whole "could not beare" such omissions.[26] Chief among these features were candles, vestments, and versicles with refrains.

Whittingham and his flock in Frankfurt did not believe the Book of Common Prayer to be the measure of good English Christianity, and they chose to honor the agreement made with Poullain and the Frankfurt Council, which insisted that the English conform to Poullain's simpler liturgy, which did not include candles, vestments, or the recitation of the versicles.[27] As Whittingham saw it, he and his founding colleagues had accepted Poullain's liturgy as the bedrock for their refugee congregation. What right did other refugee communities have to insist that the English of Frankfurt change course and use the 1552 Book of Common Prayer? The English community in Frankfurt dismissed the Strasbourg delegation's demand that they use the prayer book. Soon, though, their own community would swell with newcomers who agreed with the

Strasbourg community that the Book of Common Prayer was an essential element of English Protestant life.

Throughout 1555, more English Protestants responded to Whittingham's invitation and moved to Frankfurt. Most of these newcomers agreed with Strasbourg's English refugees that the Book of Common Prayer should govern the ceremonies of English Christians. The disagreement between two sister exile communities morphed into an internal division among the English of Frankfurt. The city on the Main quickly became the site of a major clash over liturgy, a clash that would determine the trajectory of English Protestantism for centuries. One influential nineteenth-century historian of Anglicanism put it succinctly, "During the reign of Mary the history of the Prayer Book is traced at Frankfurt."[28] Another historian, writing more recently, described how "The *Book of Common Prayer* went into exile, following its users, to Frankfurt and to Geneva, where local religious licensing required interesting alternative versions."[29] The newcomers to the English refugee congregation in Frankfurt demanded the prayer book and rejected Poullain's liturgy. Crucially, the male newcomers had their own votes within the community as part of the democratic system established by Poullain and Lasco and agreed upon by the first English arrivals in Frankfurt. Thus, newly arrived Englishmen could implement the religious changes they preferred via the ballot box. They could elect new ministers, elders, and deacons who respected the authority of Cranmer and his prayer book. Whittingham and the founders of the community quickly found themselves outnumbered.

Whittingham captured the brewing conflict within his refugee congregation in a letter to England in which he reveals the intrinsic connection between community growth and dissension: "After certeine monethes that we had here lived in great consolation and quietnes it chaunced that as oure nomber did increase, some entred in, whiche busilie undermined oure libertie and labored to overthrowe oure discipline, whiche troubles grewe at lenght in so great quantitie, that by the greatest parte it was concluded, that no man shulde neede here after to subscribe to anie discipline."[30] The newcomers were not only malcontents but also troublemakers, according to Whittingham: "they altered oure orders in praiers and others thinges, thinkinge to bringe in place the full use off the great Englishe booke, whiche notwithstandinge, by reason off divers imperfections we coulde not admit."[31] He went on to describe efforts by the new arrivals to seize the pulpit from Knox: "A stranger [was] craftely brought in to preache, who had bothe byn at masse and also subscribed to blasphemous Articles. Many tauntinge bitter sermons were made (as they thought) to oure defacinge."[32] It was omissions from the Eucharistic liturgy, not additions, that angered the new arrivals, in particular the missing versicles, their accompanying refrains, and the litany—all of which were prescribed by Cranmer's prayer book but omitted by Knox.[33] Whittingham and the rest of the original English community agreed with Knox that the 1552 Book of Common Prayer was full of medieval accretions. As Whittingham proudly put it, Knox refused to "minister the communion by the booke off Englande, for that there were thinges in it placed (as he saied) onely by warrant of mans authoritie and no grownde in godds worde for the same."[34] Some Englishmen like Thomas Lever sought compromise, but Knox refused any element of the Eucharist which he deemed unbiblical.[35] Knox's steadfast omission of these elements stands to reason considering his admiration for the purified service instituted by Calvin in Geneva. For his part, Calvin was a staunch supporter of Knox, and he wrote to the Frankfurt Council advocating for Knox and Whittingham's position: "Verely no man well instructed or off a sounde Judgement, will deny (as I think) that lights and crossings or suche like trifles, sprange or issued owte off superstition, wherupon I am perswaded that they whiche reteine theis ceremonies in a free choise, or when they maie otherwise doo, they are over greedy and desyrous to drink off the dregges nether do I se to what purpose it is to burthen the churche with tryfflinge and unprofitable ceremonies."[36] Calvin's words may have found a receptive audience among the Glauburgs and their faction of the council, which supported the refugee community, but the letter inadvertently revealed to Frankfurt's rulers that the refugee community was in discord, and that this discord had become known in other parts of Europe. Soon, the English feud over rituals would boil over.

A clash of personalities escalated the disagreement. Richard Cox, the former dean of Westminster, chancellor of Oxford, and tutor to King Edward, arrived in Frankfurt on 13 March 1555, via Duisburg and Strasbourg.[37] Cox had helped Archbishop Cranmer draft the Book of Common Prayer.[38] Arriving in Frankfurt, Cox must have expected his fellow English Protestants to honor Cranmer's authority (and his own) and embrace the prayer book.[39] Yet Whittingham and his company did not. A quarrel developed between, on the one hand, Cox and the newest English arrivals in Frankfurt and, on the other hand, Minister Knox and founders of the community who had elected him.[40] Cox and Knox took this conflict to the pulpit, where neither man lacked ability or volume. The outrage of the intramural conflict reached the ears of Johann von Glauburg and the council. According to Whittingham's recollection: "The 22, off Marche master Glauburge came to the Englishe Churche and shewed the congregation, that it was commaunded them, by the magistrate (when by his procurement the church was graunted) that they shulde agree withe the frenche churche bothe in Doctrine and ceremonies, and that they understood howe the fallinge from that order had bred muche dissention amonge them."[41] As Whittingham remembered it, Glauburg had warned the entire English congregation to conform to the liturgy of Poullain's French-speakers. But Cox would not be defeated by a stern warning from Glauburg.

Cox found support from Glauburg's nephew, the bibliophile Adolf von Glauburg, thus dividing the patrician clan most supportive of the refugees. Whittingham related Adolf's role: "The verie same daie beinge the 26. off marche one Adulphus Glauburge (A Doctor off lawe and nephew to Maister John Glauburge the Senator) whom D. Cox and the rest had wonne unto them, sent for wittingham, and tolde him that there were presented to the Magistrates thre Docters, 13. batchelers off devinitie besides others, and that the magistrates at their suites had graunted them the full use off the Englishe booke comaunding and charginge him therfore not to medle any more to the contrary."[42] Cox had rallied the most distinguished of the English community—the newest arrivals included theologians who had been part of Cranmer's Protestant hierarchy—and impressed upon Adolf the soundness of Cranmer's prayer book. Furious, Uncle Johann insisted his nephew had overstepped the bounds of his assignment. Johann had only deputized Adolf to confirm that the English refugees were conforming to the liturgy of the French church not debate the merits of the Book of Common Prayer. Moreover, as Johann remembered it, Cox and his followers had left the earlier meeting with the magistrates on 22 March having agreed to conform to the French liturgy.[43] Beyond the internal Glauburg feud, the council as a whole insisted that the English at least agree among themselves regarding the rituals they would use. But agreement eluded the English in Frankfurt, and the two factions became ever more entrenched in their positions over the next two years.

Over the course of 1555, events in England would inflame the argument over Cranmer's prayer book. On 9 February, Queen Mary executed

John Hooper, the Protestant bishop of Gloucester and noted opponent of the Book of Common Prayer. Hooper's wife, Anne, was a prominent member of the English refugee community in Frankfurt. Already in April 1554 she had started referring to herself as a widow—"this burden of widowhood is very painful," she wrote to the Swiss reformer Bullinger.[44] By November 1554, with her husband, John, presumably in prison but possibly dead, Anne confessed to Bullinger: "I very often feel to be all but dead through grief. And I now require the aid of all godly persons, although I am never entirely forsaken of the Lord, who sometimes refreshes me with the anticipation of a better life."[45] Three months after Anne wrote these words, John Hooper became the first martyred Protestant bishop and the first bishop ever burnt to death in English history, lamentable distinctions which Mary deliberately reserved for Hooper due to the radical nature of his reforms.[46] Hooper had been a staunch opponent of all elements of Catholic worship that he deemed extrabiblical innovations, including vestments, exorcisms, and kneeling during the Eucharist. Many such elements remained in the first edition of Cranmer's Book of Common Prayer, which Hooper called "manifestly impious" in a letter to Bullinger.[47] Agreeing with Hooper were Knox and Lasco, now both in Frankfurt.[48] The execution of this advocate for simplified worship, whose family and friends now lived in Frankfurt, must have inspired steadfastness on the part of those English refugees rejecting the prayer book. Whittingham and Knox's refusal to adopt Cranmer's book now bore personal and emotional meaning.

Yet it was not only Hooper, the radical opponent of the Book of Common Prayer, whose mistreatment by Queen Mary inspired steadfastness within Frankfurt's English refugee community. Archbishop Cranmer himself spent months withering in prison for heresy. Foxe's *Acts and Monuments* (1563) describes Cranmer "offering hymselfe to peryl for hys true religion, wher otherwise he might haue quietly liued, but also that all cruelty extended afterward against him, was not for the enforced matter of supposed treason, but for hys voluntarye professing of hys true Christian fayth."[49] Cranmer, the chief author of the Book of Common Prayer and famed champion of Protestantism in England, faced almost certain execution. Thus, support for compliance with the full English service, by refugees like Cox and the majority of English community in Frankfurt, became an act of solidarity with the soon-to-be martyred Cranmer.

Out of loyalty to Cranmer and his prayer book, Cox decided it was necessary to remove Knox as leader of the English refugees in Frankfurt.

Cox decided on a bold tactic aimed at making Knox look dangerous in the eyes of Frankfurt's rulers. Cox submitted Knox's printed text, *A Faithful Admonition to the Professors of God's Truth in England*, to the council.[50] In this tract, Knox—never one to mince words about tyrants—referred to the emperor as "no lesse enemy unto Christe then ever was Nero."[51] These were, of course, incendiary words in an imperial city like Frankfurt, which depended on the emperor for its independence. Much like the refugee population in Frankfurt, the city itself tried to remain inconspicuous to the emperor during this period. A printed denunciation of the emperor by the chief minister of a refugee congregation harbored in Frankfurt posed great danger for the city. The Frankfurt Council certainly thought so. It ordered Knox to leave the city in late March 1555. Disgusted by the situation in Frankfurt, Knox moved south to Calvin's Geneva, which he embraced as "the maist perfyt schoole of Chryst that ever was in the erth since the dayis of the Apostillis," according to a letter he sent a friend the following year.[52] Knox went on to compare Geneva to Frankfurt and other places where, despite true preaching, the ceremonies of the church remained lamentably unreformed. Frankfurt's English clung to nonbiblical worship accoutrements, items like the candles and vestments that Cox now brought into the Church of the White Ladies during the English services.

The English conflict forced the Frankfurt Council to face the same question that confronts all governments seeking to accommodate a minority community: to what extent should the community be permitted to govern its own affairs? Judging from the council's negotiations with Poullain in 1554 and the subsequent admission of English- and Dutch-speakers, Frankfurt's rulers expected the refugees to manage their own religious institutions and rituals. Poullain had proposed this system at the end of his initial petition requesting a church: "Moreover, so that nothing disorderly or harmful should arise from such a church and gathering, may you . . . [councilmen] order an earnest church discipline [*Kirchenzucht*] be established among [us]."[53] The English had, upon their admission, delighted in the fact that Frankfurt allowed them to "use Discipline, to the true settinge forthe of gods glorie."[54] The council's plan to allow the newcomers to oversee their own religious community makes sense considering language barriers. In many ways, the council's strategy for governing these foreigners matches systems of group accommodation still advocated for today, with the same possibilities for the maltreatment of members of the accommodated group by its leaders.[55] This possibility became reality in Frankfurt. Once Cox and his followers had achieved a sizeable majority, they forced Knox and his supporters to flee and seek new homes abroad.

Whittingham decried Cox's tactic of "accusinge him [Knox] before the Magistrates off treason againste the Emperour."[56] Whittingham and most of the original group of English refugees to arrive in Frankfurt followed Knox to Geneva in the fall of 1555. From Geneva, Calvin wrote to Cox, "Maister Knox was in my judgemen nether godly nor brotherly dealt withall."[57] Calvin not only lamented the departure of Knox, he appreciated the danger of the new attention centered on refugees in Frankfurt.[58] He admonished Cox: "It standethe your wisedomes in hande to consider, that howe muche commoditie the goodnesse off the Senate dothe deserve, so muche envie shall yow be giltie off, or charged withall, yf yow have abused their lenitie or gentlenesse, whiche were so well affected towardes your nation."[59] Cox had won. But by plucking Knox from his position and expelling Knox's supporters, Cox and the new arrivals had inadvertently precipitated the unraveling of the privileges enjoyed by the refugees in Frankfurt. They did so by alerting Frankfurt's leaders to the strong discord among the refugees. Clearly, granting the newcomers independence had not resulted in a well ordered, controversy-free Reformed community.

## Refugee Publications and the Escalation of Conflict

In their first few years in Frankfurt, as intramural conflicts began to divide them, the refugees published religious tracts. Poullain started the practice himself as part of a broader effort to clarify his followers' religious ceremonies and reconcile them with the city's. He was acutely aware of the council's disdain for controversy. Unfortunately, his efforts only exacerbated tensions between the Reformed and the city. Soon, refugee publications became a major headache for the council and provoked concern among the city patricians who had secured a place for the newcomers in Frankfurt.

Poullain had been meeting privately with the city's seven official ministers to mollify their concerns about religious innovations and divisions since the summer of 1554.[60] He knew that the ministers could influence the council, and he attempted to dissuade them from raising concerns about the ceremonies of the refugees. In response to the early accusations

of Anabaptism leveled at his community, Poullain wrote a brief letter to
the local ministers, whom he greets with the salutation "Most High Men,"
before rejecting the recent language used by Frankfurters that referred to
his flock "as if we were Anabaptists."[61] Poullain spoke for all his fellow
refugees when he wrote, "We owe all obedience to the most holy and
most noble Senate," before insisting to the native ministers, "We offer to
you all friendship and all obedience [obsequium] in Christ."[62] To prove his
refugee community's good standing and rejection of Anabaptism, he ap-
pended to his letter a printed copy of his liturgy, Liturgia sacra, which he
had designed in Glastonbury and brought to Frankfurt as the standard
for refugee services in the Church of the White Ladies. He published the
text in late 1554 and submitted it as proof of his community's rejection
of any fanaticism.[63]

Poullain's Liturgia was meant to quell the suspicions about the refugees
prompted by the arrival of Anabaptists and the onset of English infighting. Ironically, Poullain's text convinced Beyer and the other Frankfurt
ministers of the heterodoxy of the refugees. When Poullain reprinted
the text in 1555, he further inflamed tensions. Beyer and his colleagues
wrote to the council demanding a ban on further refugee publications
about the Supper. Beyer's fellow minister Peter Geltner drafted the letter
to Frankfurt's rulers, and he quoted Poullain's Liturgia directly—both
in its original Latin and in his own German—to prove that the refugees
failed to subscribe to the proper understanding of the real presence in
the Eucharist: "Their dictums repeatedly say, that there is no corporeal
presence, neither the body nor the blood of Christ."[64] Beyer, Geltner, and
their colleagues now had printed evidence that the refugees were "turning the Supper into a mere commemoration [blosse Gedachtnüs]."[65] Thus
Poullain's effort to defend the refugees from accusations of factionalism
and Anabaptism had backfired and led the city's ministers to call more
loudly for a ban on refugee publications and an imposition of conformity
upon refugee services.

Following Poullain's lead, Lasco published his own church order in
Frankfurt in 1555. And while Poullain's Liturgia failed to achieve much
notoriety outside the city, Lasco's Forma ac ratio proved an international success. It was the most influential publication emerging from
the Frankfurt refugee community. According to a recent survey of Reformed Protestantism, Lasco's Forma ac ratio was "one of the era's fullest
published blueprints for properly reformed church practice."[66] In particular, the text became a model "for the organization of underground

[Reformed] churches."[67] Reformers across Europe read the *Forma ac ratio*, which brought distinction to Lasco, his community, and their position in Frankfurt.[68]

Beyer and his Lutheran colleagues were deeply displeased by the growing fame of the Reformed community living in their midst. In the same letter to the council from 29 October 1555, the Lutheran ministers described the embarrassment they had felt at the autumn trade fair when dozens of visitors approached them to ask about the refugee community in the city: "We had to hear all kinds of things about the foreigners from many honest people who were astonished that the honorable council would accept such a crowd of strange foreign people from three different lands and languages into such a stable city, situated in the middle of Germany."[69] Frankfurt's Lutheran clergy, proud of their stable city, resented the fame that Lasco's publication had brought to the Reformed community in Frankfurt.

Beyond any frustration felt by Minister Beyer at the blossoming of a rival Protestant tradition within Frankfurt's walls, he must have especially recoiled upon reading the contents of Lasco's *Forma ac ratio*.[70] The text begins on a polemical note. In the prefatory letter of dedication to the king of Poland, Lasco deliberately positions his refugee church in contradistinction to the Lutherans of north German cities like Hamburg and Lübeck—cities which had rejected Lasco's beleaguered community during its winter voyage out of England in 1553–54. These north-German Lutherans were not only cruel, according to Lasco, but also wrongheaded in their understanding of the real presence in the Eucharist. Via this eroneous doctrine, he explained, they had "dragged the tyranny of the pope to themselves, indeed under the praiseworthy title of Evangelism."[71] When speaking about the Lutheran clergy who had so detested his community, Lasco's tone was not only polemical but also sardonic: "It would not be astonishing if they should be called Luthero-Papists [Lutheropapistae]."[72] People who rejected his community's services understood neither the Marburg Colloquy of 1529 (an agreement on most issues of reform drafted by Luther, Zwingli, Bucer, and others) nor Luther himself, claimed Lasco.[73] Beyer must have been shocked by such statements. He maintained a regular correspondence with the chief ministers of Hamburg and other north German cities, and he undoubtedly resented a Polish foreigner expounding on the correct understanding of Luther's thinking. Lasco's tract helped crystallize the new confessional boundary dividing Frankfurt's Protestants. It also reveals how the experience of exile—especially the failed effort to gain refuge in Hamburg, Lübeck, and other Baltic cities—had resulted in Lasco defining and emphasizing a theological and liturgical chasm between his congregation and the callous north German cities. Lasco seems to have embraced the role of refugee superintendent, whose chief task, according to the *Forma ac ratio*, was "defending it [the church] against all the endeavors of all adversaries and holding fast in doctrinal controversies."[74] Lasco recognized a religious distance separating his flock from German Protestants, and he believed it his task to protect his flock from wrongheaded theologies that threatened to lead vulnerable Christians astray.

Dismayed by Poullain's *Liturgia* and shocked by Lasco's *Forma ac ratio*, Frankfurt's ministers proposed an official ban on the printing and dissemination of all Reformed tracts.[75] They suggested that the refugees had only settled in Frankfurt in order to disseminate religious texts: "They [the refugees] think they have gained a convenient location here from which to spread their error about the Holy Supper ... via the printing press."[76] Frankfurt was the nexus of the European book trade. Its fairs facilitated distribution of printed texts across the continent. Undeniably, the refugees were aware of the importance of Frankfurt's fairs, which Poullain had extolled. His initial petition for entry into Frankfurt mentions the "wide praise of the city [for] its business and two fairs."[77] Now the city ministers feared the refugee community was taking advantage of Frankfurt's position and demanded the council stop the spread of Reformed ideas by banning refugee publications.

Yet as we saw in the previous chapter, not all the city's ministers agreed that the refugees were pursuing a dangerous religious project separate from the city's Reformation. When the councilmen gathered to discuss the ministers' petition the next month, the battle lines became clear. Ministers Beyer and Geltner were joined in their attack on the refugees by Ministers Christian Egenolph, Matthias Ritter, and Marcus Sebander. But Ministers Ambach and Lullius dissented and submitted their own position paper to the council. To the dismay of Beyer's group, the council read both texts aloud. Worse still, the council agreed with Ambach and Lullius that only the *Concordia Buceriana* and the Wittenberg Concord—another document of compromise between Wittenberg and Swiss conceptions of the Eucharist—should be accepted as evidence in the dispute over refugee religious nonconformity. Leading the council's prorefugee faction was Johann von Glauburg, who agreed with Ambach and Lullius that conformity to Frankfurt's church meant conformity to the *Concordia Buceriana*, a document which Glauburg knew Poullain had approved of in 1554. Council minutes state that "Glauburg [said] the *Concordia* of 1542 should be shown to the foreigners as a point of reference."[78] Conrad von Humbracht—a patrician from the highest bench who had been Frankfurt's senior mayor when Poullain had been admitted—agreed with Glauburg that the "foreigners be shown the *Concordia*, and they should hold to it."[79] Mayor Carl Kuhorn agreed with Glauburg and Humbracht. Council minutes record Kuhorn responding "similarly" on the issue of refugee ceremonies.[80] In short, Frankfurt's most powerful rulers rejected Beyer's idea that the refugees refused to conform to Frankfurt's civic rituals.

Beyer's faction did succeed in one respect. The Frankfurt councilmen agreed that publications about the Supper were instigating conflict, and they banned further refugee publications on the matter. But the ban did not target the refugees alone. To the dismay of Beyer, Geltner, and their supporters, the council banned all publications on the Supper, including those by Frankfurt's clergy. Now Beyer and the native ministers could not legally respond to Lasco's and Poullain's pieces in print.[81] When it came to religious publications, keeping the peace, not promoting orthodoxy, was the chief concern of Frankfurt's rulers.

Beyer resented the prominence of the Reformed refugee ministers in Frankfurt. His efforts to silence these men had backfired, and it seemed the council esteemed the refugee and native clergy equally. Beyer reserved a special hatred for Poullain, the first refugee minister in the city, if not the most prominent. Poullain had orchestrated the advent of refugee accommodation in Frankfurt, and he had done so duplicitously, according to Beyer. Poullain's days as refugee minister in Frankfurt were numbered. Ultimately, though, it was not Beyer who orchestrated Poullain's downfall but rather Poullain's own refugee congregation.

## POULLAIN'S LEADERSHIP QUESTIONED

Poullain had had detractors in his community since late 1554, when new groups of refugees traveled to Frankfurt to join his initial flock from Glastonbury, although open calls for his resignation only emerged in 1555. The French Reformed refugees experienced growing pains like those that had afflicted the English—the admission of new members led to ruptures. French refugees arrived at an astonishing rate so that by the end of 1555, seven hundred refugees from the French-speaking southern Low Countries were living in Frankfurt.[82] Among the new arrivals was Jean de Poix, Lord of Séchelles, who wrote to his friend Guillaume Farel to report on "the state of our [Frankfurt] church, which is increasing daily, at this time we are (as I believe) about three hundred and fifty souls."[83] De Poix was a prominent Reformation figure in his own right, a nobleman from the borderland between the Habsburg Low Countries and France's Picardy region and a friend of Calvin's. Poullain's refugee congregation had added prominent religious reformers, individuals who challenged Poullain's dominance over the community.

Conflict erupted between Poullain and his growing flock over the issue of elections for the French-speaking elders on the consistory governing the congregation from the Low Countries. As new groups of displaced people arrived in Frankfurt and made the confession of faith required to join Poullain's community and attend its services, it became clear that the community needed more elders to supervise the services and monitor the community's behavior. A substantial number of community members had arrived directly from the Low Countries, and these people desired elders who had not come from Glastonbury with the first core group under Poullain. Leading the charge against Poullain was Augustin Le Grand, a wealthy merchant from Bruges and the richest man in the community from 1554 to 1578.[84] Le Grand had arrived from Bruges with twenty-five other households several months after Poullain's initial flock.[85] This merchant had the resources to buy his own house in the city—a house that would assume central importance in the refugee communities as a gathering place.[86] Le Grand had the wealth and the confidence to challenge Poullain, and an anti-Poullain group quickly coalesced around him.[87] Poullain wrote to Calvin in February 1555 describing "vain whispers" against him.[88] In his apologia to Calvin, Poullain inadvertently revealed something of his imperious tendencies: "I do not know what they have said against me on this occasion, and because of that I am not easily admitting any of them into the communion of the church (which however is not my private rule but the public rule of the entire church)."[89] Poullain's personal control over the church infuriated those who did not agree with him.

Recognizing the French refugees' frustration with Poullain, Superintendent Lasco and Councilman Glauburg suggested that another minister be appointed to serve as a counterweight to Poullain—someone more prominent than Juan Morillo, who was currently serving as a second preacher.[90] Lasco nominated Richard Vauville, a reformer from Bourges who had fled France for London after the Affair of the Placards in 1534. Vauville had worked with Lasco in London, serving as one of two French preachers in the London congregation of refugees from the Low Countries.[91] In 1553, Vauville and Lasco escaped England together on the same unfortunate ship of refugees who could not find a harbor over the winter of 1553–54.[92] Now Vauville traveled to Frankfurt to assume the same position he had held in London—French preacher in a dual-language congregation of refugees from the Low Countries. Vauville arrived in Frankfurt in March 1555.[93]

Everybody liked Vauville. Lasco referred to him lovingly as "our Richard," in a letter to Calvin, a letter that reported the sad news that Vauville's wife died soon after the couple arrived in Frankfurt.[94] Calvin heartily approved of the choice of Vauville. Poullain may have resented the appointment of Vauville as a check on his own influence, but his personal affection for Vauville seems to have alleviated matters. Poullain also liked Vauville. He described him as a "man of truly perfect Christian piety."[95] Poullain's supporters agreed, even if they too were dismayed that Le Grand's faction had succeeded in installing a new preacher. Le Grand's supporters were pleased with the choice of Vauville.[96] In short, Vauville seems to have been the ideal compromise and was elected by the entire congregation in late March 1555.[97]

Vauville wanted to help Poullain, not supplant him. Writing to Calvin, Vauville referred to Poullain as his "dearest brother in Christ" and explained that the appointment of a second French preacher in Frankfurt involved "no other consideration . . . than to alleviate the labor of Valérand."[98] Vauville described how he and Poullain worked together: "As soon as I was confirmed in the ministry, my colleague [Poullain] and I began to take turns leading the catechesis."[99] Still, Vauville's appointment did not resolve the simmering animosity toward Poullain within the congregation of refugees from the Low Countries. Parishioners continued to complain about the man, as Lasco related to Calvin in late 1555. The congregation suffered from a "health so broken into pieces," as Lasco put it.[100] Worse discord was still to come. That winter, the newly elected and widely popular Vauville succumbed to the plague like his wife before him.[101] Calvin wrote to the "the French Church of Frankfurt" on 26 December 1555 lamenting the death of "your good brother, master Richard Vauville."[102]

Vauville's tenure provided only a brief respite from the intramural fight over Poullain's leadership. At the next election for a new elder, Poullain nominated only one person, and resentment over his authority grew more furious. Johann von Glauburg wrote to Calvin to describe "grave divisions" among the refugees from the Low Countries.[103] Glauburg worried that refugee discord would attract attention from the council and imperil the refugee community's independence. Vauville's replacement—a man named Guillaume Houbraque whom Lasco nominated and the community elected in April 1556—could not quell the anger aimed at Poullain.[104] Lasco, Glauburg, and Poullain himself asked Calvin to mediate the conflict personally. Calvin traveled to Frankfurt to adjudicate the dispute and enlisted the help of Lasco and the English minister Robert Horne in examining the complaints lodged against Poullain.[105] Calvin and his team interviewed Poullain's chief opponent, Le Grand, and quickly learned how fractious matters had become. Calvin recorded the answers that Le Grand gave to him:

11. Augustin [Le Grand] replies that he does not know if anyone has used outrageous [words] toward Master Valérand and he does not believe so. But he knows well that . . . their zeal was good and right.

16. Augustin replies that Master Valérand said this was a fact and he puts such a charge in his own sermons, wherein he has done only himself injury.

17. Augustin replies that he agrees to leave all other quarrels to Master Glauburg.[106]

It is easy to imagine the questions Calvin must have asked to elicit such replies from Poullain's chief antagonist. Outrageous accusations against Poullain clearly swirled within the community. Le Grand was likely the source, though he insisted that Poullain was merely paranoid in bringing up such claims against himself from the pulpit.

Calvin and his team, along with the councilman Glauburg, determined that Poullain was innocent of any impropriety in his governance of the church. But they also realized he was simply too unpopular to remain in his position.[107] By the start of 1556, Poullain suspected that Calvin could not (or would not) save him. He wrote to Calvin expressing his hope "to be allowed to choose another in my place."[108]

## Poullain's Resignation and Refutation

In the autumn of 1556, both Poullain and Lasco gave up their leadership positions within the refugee congregation in Frankfurt, though under different circumstances. Following Calvin's summer intervention, Poullain reluctantly surrendered his position as preacher to Frankfurt's French-speaking refugees in September. The next month, Lasco voluntarily gave up his post as superintendent to return to his native Poland, "from which he had for twenty years been exiled by his own choice in the name of religion," as his friend Utenhove described it.[109] Lasco's renown as a reformer had grown during his time in Frankfurt and inspired the king of Poland to invite him with "at least forty letters."[110] Utenhove and Lasco traveled to Poland, a trip Utenhove records in language evoking the gospels: "after we left Frankfurt on 21 October (with divine favor), we arrived in Poland[,] . . . where the harvest is plentiful, but the laborers are few."[111]

Poullain's whereabouts after his resignation remain unclear. Frankfurt's mayoral records include the following entry from 20 October 1556: "Mr Valérand Poullain, the French preacher, if he moves away from here, should be granted an exit [letter] in the customary fashion."[112] Yet Poullain did not leave Frankfurt immediately. He witnessed his replacement as French preacher assume the pulpit in January 1557.[113] Later that year, Poullain published a controversial new text in Frankfurt. Titled *Antidote*, the text defended the refugee community's understanding of the Eucharist and refuted the claims of Lutheran detractors.[114]

The full title of Poullain's text was *The Antidote of Valérand Poullain: That Is to Say a Thorough Refutation of the Unchristian and Poisonous Counsel Recently Written under the Name of Joachim Westphal to the Council of Frankfurt*.[115] Poullain now attacked not only Beyer but also Beyer's more famous associate, Hamburg's Superintendent Joachim Westphal, a chief antagonist of refugees in Frankfurt and the empire at large.[116] Poullain maintained that both Beyer in Frankfurt and Westphal in Hamburg had broken from the true spirit of the Reformation.

Poullain began his thirty-seven-page treatise with a history of the initial admission of his flock into Frankfurt. In the beginning, Poullain explained, Beyer had been fully informed of the refugees' beliefs. More than that, Beyer had assented to their admission into the city. Poullain described "our church's agenda [*Agenda*], which was already printed in England, and also the confession of our faith and the complete content of our teachings, which we conveyed to both the honorable council and Hartmann Beyer."[117] Beyer had not even been the most senior minister at the time of the refugee arrival, in 1554; Ambach and Lullius were his senior colleagues, and they had supported Poullain's congregation wholeheartedly, though they were too infirm to help the refugees for long. Poullain called them "the two oldest of the ministers of the city of Frankfurt, who were already known to me before, whose sickness prevented them from helping me in this current business."[118] Poullain also claimed that Beyer and his allies in Frankfurt were responsible for first disturbing the accord between Poullain's congregation and the city at large.

After setting the historical record straight, Poullain continued his *Antidote* by defending his congregation's liturgical practices and attacking those prescribed by Beyer and Westphal. He insisted that the two men maintained an erroneous understanding of the Supper, which resulted in a bizarre form of idolatry. As he phrased it: "It necessarily follows from the monstrous theology of Westphal, that where Christ's body is—namely in the bread, under the bread, and with the bread—should also be worshipped. . . . This we consider unchristian, this false opinion of Westphal's, about the corporeal presence."[119] From his community's admission into Frankfurt in 1554 until now, Poullain's strategy in dealing with Beyer and his Frankfurt allies had been to defend the refugees' conformity with the prescribed civic liturgy. After three years of exile in the city, he attacked the ceremonies of Frankfurters as idolatrous and resultant from a flawed Christology. Poullain now buttressed the same boundary between refugees and citizens that Beyer had worked hard to construct.

As he continued in the *Antidote*, Poullain attacked Westphal's character. The Hamburg superintendent's "bitter and tyrannical" attacks against the vulnerable displaced Christians living in Frankfurt and other cities of the empire reminded Poullain of "the accusations of the Jews against the Lord Christ in front of Pilate, that Christ was an enemy of the emperor."[120] Westphal spread salacious rumors, saying that refugees in Frankfurt were arsonists and robbers.[121] Poullain also accused Westphal's allies in Frankfurt, chief among them Beyer, of having informed the council about Knox's attacks on the emperor in order to force Knox out of the city. This claim actually contradicted Whittingham, who had blamed Cox for informing on Knox, but whether Whittingham or Poullain had identified the correct informant, both reveal how the refugee presence in Frankfurt had provoked a conflict with imperial implications.

The charitable accommodation of refugees had morphed into a scandal dividing Protestants across the empire, raising the specter of conflict with the empire's Catholic authorities.

The *Antidote* remains the last extant text by Poullain. He died in the fall of 1557, probably still in Frankfurt.[122] Yet the conflicts between Poullain's faction, the original group from Glastonbury, and his detractors, the more recent arrivals, persisted in Frankfurt beyond his departure, much to the dismay of Calvin, Glauburg, and the Frankfurt Council.[123] Frankfurt's rulers had previously trusted Poullain's goodwill. He was the one who had negotiated the refugees' admission into the city. His ouster by newcomers alarmed the council, which now scrutinized more carefully the entire refugee community.

Poullain's replacement was a man named François Perucel. Before coming to Frankfurt, Perucel had served alongside the late Vauville as a French preacher to the refugees in London.[124] Since then, Perucel had been serving the same role in the refugee congregation in Wesel, where he had fought for his parishioners' independence from the civic church.[125] Le Grand and much of the anti-Poullain faction had previously lived in Wesel, and they liked and supported Minister Perucel immensely.[126] Indeed they had advocated for Perucel to replace Vauville instead of Houbraque.[127] Invited to Frankfurt by Le Grand's group, Perucel traveled up the Rhine from Wesel and arrived in Frankfurt in the spring of 1557. Almost immediately, he and Houbraque came into conflict as Houbraque felt Perucel had not been fairly elected by the entire community.[128]

Two letters to the council, one from Houbraque's supporters and one from Perucel's, reveal the points of contention between the two camps. Houbraque's supporters defended him against accusations of "heavy-handedness," while Perucel's camp insisted that Houbraque exercised too much control over the election of elders.[129] The Houbraque-Perucel fissure that emerged in the years after Poullain's forced resignation centered on the same point of contention, namely authority over elections. Concerned, the Frankfurt Council stepped in. A letter written by Houbraque's supporters to the council, in early 1559, makes it clear that the Le Grand–Perucel faction had succeeded in convincing Frankfurt's leaders of Houbraque's autocratic tendencies. The letter mentions the council's recent ban on Houbraque's preaching: "On the 23rd of January, an order appeared in the French Church from the senior mayor that the well-learned Master Guillaume Houbraque should neither preach nor proceed in his office of preacher."[130] The mayor's records from the same day reveal that the letter from Houbraque's supporters was read aloud in the council chamber:

> As it was read aloud, what Master Guillaume Houbraque, one of the French preachers, together with his supporters complained and wrote against Master François Perucel and his like-minded followers, and also what Perucel with his supporters on the contrary complained and wrote against Houbraque; both sides should be ordered by the council on account of peace, to necessarily cease their errors and afflictions and so much as possible to settle; and it was thereafter ordered that Mr. Johann von Glauburg, Mr. Daniel zum Jungen, and Doctor Conrad Humbracht should determine for themselves the state of the matter.[131]

Although the three councilmen commissioned to investigate the conflict were decidedly sympathetic to the refugees—Glauburg and Humbracht had been two of Poullain's earliest patrons—they nonetheless prioritized civic order. Glauburg, upon interviewing Houbraque, found him "unruly" and prone to the company of "several private people ... who make disquiet and aversion to service."[132] The commission ultimately ruled in favor of Perucel in the dispute between the two French ministers, but something much more serious resulted from the commission's investigation. The refugee congregation lost the support of the Glauburg family, and when Johann von Glauburg reported the results of the fact-finding mission to his fellow councilmen, political support for the refugees collapsed. The refugees had alienated their closest patrons and consequently lost the support of the council at large.[133]

On 1 September 1560, after the three-man commission had finished its work, the council voted to ban public Reformed worship in the city.[134] This meant closing the city churches to refugee services, as the city ministers had originally demanded. On 18 March 1561, the council ordered the Church of the White Ladies to be closed: "As Mr. Johann von Glauburg, Mr. Daniell zum Jungen, and Dr. Conrad Humbracht—all jurors and commissioners assigned to the strife between Wilhelm Houlbraque ... and Francisco Riverio [Perucel] these ordained commissioners having delivered their advice to be heard, the church of the foreigners, which they have had here for some time, should be shut, though the execution of this act will remain until Easter."[135] With the closure of the Church of the White Ladies, the Reformed in Frankfurt could no longer worship in one of the city's churches as their own, independent congregation. This was the beginning of the end of religious accommodation in Frankfurt. The city's ruling councilmen would soon grant the city's clergy governance over the refugees' baptisms and marriages—as will be explored in the next chapter—but these impositions mattered much less to the Reformed than the closure of their church, which forced their celebrations of the Lord's Supper underground.

It is no coincidence that the council's decision to close the church came during the same meeting that the commissioners reported on intrarefugee conflicts. Intramural conflict worried Frankfurt's rulers. That April, a special advisory committee of the council explained that the decision to close city churches to the services of the refugees resulted from "the errors and division, which for a time have existed among the ministers of the French and Dutch churches here."[136] The English refugees eluded criticism in this instance because they had already returned to England, but not before their own intramural conflicts had added to the city's perception of Reformed Christianity as prone to factionalism and strife. A series of petitions from the Reformed over the summer of 1561 achieved nothing. The council would not permit the Reformed access to any city church.

## Intrarefugee Disputes and the End of Accommodation

In their first seven years in Frankfurt, the refugees experienced major upheavals within their community. Knox was banished in March 1555. Whittingham and the founders of the English congregation left in late 1555, mostly for Geneva. Poullain lost his position in September 1556, and Lasco left Frankfurt to return to Poland later that year.[137] The conflict between Houbraque and Perucel persisted until late 1560, and, by 1561, the minutes of the Frankfurt Council were filled with references to refugee conflicts, especially the one between Houbraque and Perucel since both sides petitioned the city for redress in their personal dispute. Moreover, Perucel and his supporters remained adamant, as they had been in Wesel, that the refugee parishioners avoid the civic religious rituals.[138] By 1561, the Glauburgs became unable (or perhaps unwilling) to defend the refugees further.

In 1563, Beyer compiled an exhaustive list of all the religious transgressions committed by the newcomers since their earliest arrival, titling the work a "Counter-Report and Answer of the Ministers of Frankfurt am Main to a Number of Unfounded Complaints by the Foreigners, Namely the French and Flemish Ministers and Their Congregations." In his report, Beyer focused on the various episodes of confusion, conflict, and infighting arising within the refugee community. He began with the story of an Anabaptist, alledgedly a member of Poullain's flock, sowing discord—"a Flemish man, a craftsman, let all kinds of rude errors be heard."[139] Beyer's list of rude errors appears to be a laundry list of Reformation-era accusations, and he specifically begins with a charge that the man denounced his fellow refugees. According to Beyer, the Flemish heretic claimed:

1. Firstly that neither the strangers here in Frankfurt nor those in Geneva preach the Word of God or are a church of God, because they are not without sin.

2. The Anabaptists in many lands, have all possessions in common, and are the most pious. . . .

3. Sebastian Franck has the best teachings and belief, he [the Flemish man] holds him in highest esteem. This opinion is held by others amongst them [the refugees] and seduces our people.

4. Jews, Turks, Anabaptists, and Libertines are all holy. . . .

5. The servants of the Word preach nothing by naked letters because if they did preach the Gospel their preaching would not be so unfruitful.[140]

Beyer continued with a litany of other scandalous opinions held by the refugees, and he insisted that the troubles emerging from the refugee congregation resulted, quite naturally, from the fact that the community of newcomers enjoyed independence from the civic church.

Ultimately, it was not the repeated claims of heterodoxy or heteropraxy hurled by the city ministers against the Reformed refugees that convinced the city's patricians and the council at large to restrict the religious privileges of the newcomers but rather fears about factionalism and conflict. Intramural fights among the Reformed in Frankfurt prompted the city authorities to investigate the entire refugee community and conclude its ecclesiastical autonomy led to factionalism, disruption, and—in the case of Knox—attacks on the emperor, who had troops garrisoned within the city. Even the Glauburg family and other patricians previously supportive of Poullain began to worry that controversies emanating from within the Reformed community might threaten civic harmony. Intramural conflicts cost the Reformed refugees the support of their earliest patrons. Eventually, the privileges won by Poullain disappeared.

From the very beginning of their stay in Frankfurt, the refugees had trouble assimilating newcomers. The foundational communities—the groups led by Poullain, Whittingham, and Lasco—may have called themselves "churches" [*Ecclesiae* or *Kirchen*] or sometimes "congregations" [*Gemeinden*], but they were, in the first instance, a handful of families who agreed to travel and work together. The first group to settle in Frankfurt consisted of Poullain's Glastonbury congregation, only two dozen families. The arrival in quick succession of new families, sometimes as many as forty-five families at once, tested the sinews of the established English and French-Dutch congregations. Moreover, the refugees arriving in Frankfurt came from immensely diverse backgrounds, often sharing very little in common. Newcomers and established refugees did not see eye to eye, yet they coexisted within a religious community that elected its own leaders. As the number of refugees in Frankfurt swelled, the newcomers elected new elders and new pastors. New leaders emerged. With new leaders, the refugee communities assumed different identities, and in the case of the English refugees, different rituals.

The displaced individuals in Frankfurt were not necessarily predisposed to factionalism, dissent, or error. Yet the democratic nature of their central institution, a consistory comprised of the elders and ministers elected by male members, ensured that leadership remained an endless point of contention. As new groups of refugees arrived, they wanted one of their number to serve on the consistory. With each new group of arrivals, it became increasingly difficult for Poullain and other ministers to imprint their vision upon the leadership structures of the community. When Poullain, Whittingham, and Lasco advertised their communities to other displaced people and thereby attracted newcomers to Frankfurt, they unintentionally sowed the seeds of discord within the entire Reformed community in Frankfurt. Newcomers had very different ideas about how religious services (in the case of the English) or elections (in the case of the French-speakers) should proceed. By the start of 1555, it was already clear that the refugee communities, not the city at large, had trouble integrating new arrivals in Frankfurt.

Historians trying to account for Frankfurt's eventual hostility toward the refugees have ascribed blame to Lutheran extremists in Frankfurt and other parts of the empire—men like Beyer and Westphal—who denounced the refugees to the council.[141] The Lutheran clergy did indeed advocate for the council to close the Church of the White Ladies to refugee services. Pieter Datheen, the Dutch preacher explicitly blamed Beyer and the other Lutheran ministers for the worsening fortunes of the refugee community in Frankfurt: "The [Frankfurt] preachers boast almost always of their godliness and Christian love etc., virtues which they give fine example of as they do not let themselves be content by slandering the expelled Christians in their pamphlets but rather also blaspheme and vilify them to the finest and most felicitous councilmen of the city of Frankfurt."[142] Yet if we consider the years it took the council to finally resolve to close the Church of the White Ladies, it seems clear that the Lutheran ministers' denunciations proved insufficient to prompt governmental action. When the council finally acted against the refugee community, it did so in response to the troubling number of leadership contests and conflicts emerging within the displaced population. Datheen's account fails to mention the intense discord among the competing factions within the Reformed community of Frankfurt. When the council did restrict the privileges of the refugees, it did so in response to conflicts arising from within the refugee community.

The Frankfurt Council concluded that refugees' religious services and religious independence led to dissension and controversy and should therefore be outlawed. Put simply, the refugees could not get along with each other, and they lost their religious privileges as a consequence. The refugees from the Low Countries who had come to Frankfurt, and their children who had known no other city, realized that their status had been greatly diminished in Frankfurt. They began to conceive of new ways to repurpose their consistory in order to mitigate future conflict and arbitrate disputes in Frankfurt. First, though, they had to decide whether or not to stay in Frankfurt after the closure of their church in 1561. Perhaps better destinations lay farther afield, with rulers more sympathetic to Reformed religious services. Many of the Reformed residents of Frankfurt left the city, but many also stayed behind and continued to build a religious community in exile.

# 4

# The Quest for Legal Protection
# outside of Frankfurt

❧

It is truly a deplorable thing, that the expelled Christians are not
permitted to preach the true doctrine of the Word of God and the
Augsburg Confession publicly and in their own language, considering that the idolatrous papists and the horrid Jews—who daily
blaspheme the Son of God, deride and trample on him as much
as they can—are permitted to publicly carry on and preach their
damned frightful heresy and blasphemy.

—Pieter Datheen's account of his departure
from Frankfurt, 1563

THE DAY AFTER EASTER 1561, the Frankfurt Council locked the
Church of the White Ladies and banned the refugees from the Low
Countries—who in that year numbered around two thousand Dutch- and
French-speakers and collectively called themselves Reformed—from wor-
shiping in the city churches or public spaces.[1] The Dutch-speaking refugee
elders wrote to the council on 7 August 1561 insisting that they had always
been faithful subjects. The claims being levied against them by the Lutheran ministers were fallacious innovations, they wrote, "because we are
certainly not fanatics, or sacramentarians, or Calvinists, or Zwinglians."[2]
The letter achieved nothing. In a 25 to 9 vote, Frankfurt's rulers reaffirmed
their decision to close the church on 28 August, insisting the refugees "become united and settled with the native ministers" or else depart the city.[3]

Locked out of their church and banned from using public spaces, the
Reformed from the Low Countries gathered to worship in a private barn

belonging to a man named Peter Gaul.[4] He apparently consented to let the Reformed use it for free, even though his name did not appear on the original membership list of the Reformed refugees.[5] No record of payment to Gaul exists. The Reformed did pay to rent private space for their poor from the city's Hospital of the Holy Spirit, and this poorhouse soon became a second site for religious services, though they continued to worship in the barn until at least 1570.[6] The Reformed recognized the unsuitability of a barn for the Lord's Supper, and their descendants recalled this embarrassment for centuries. In 1732, when the Reformed community in Frankfurt sued the city before the Imperial Aulic Council (Reichshofrat) for the public exercise of their religion, the unsuitability of Gaul's barn became evidence of Frankfurt's malice toward the Reformed faith.[7]

By the time the Dutch and French refugees were ejected from their church and other public spaces in 1561, the English refugees in Frankfurt had already departed the city. Whittingham and his allies had left for Calvin's Geneva "in some heate" in 1555, and the rest of the English community had departed for their homeland in the winter of 1558–59, after the death of the Catholic Queen Mary and the ascension of her Protestant half sister Elizabeth.[8] Thus the English had left before Frankfurt banned refugee services, and they remained grateful for Frankfurt's kindness. The last group of English to leave commissioned the construction of a small gilded column to be given to the council, along with a letter expressing "gratitude to the honorable council."[9] Yet the English refugees' celebration of Frankfurt should not obscure the fact that a much larger French–Dutch refugee community remained in the city, subject to the council's increasing restrictions.

The Reformed from the Low Countries missed the Church of the White Ladies dearly. In November 1561, the French members drafted a letter to the council, focusing specific attention on the issue of language. They insisted that entire congregation of refugees from the Low Countries, French and Dutch, shared an "inexperience of the German language," and they should therefore be given ecclesiastical independence and a church building in which they could organize both French and Dutch services.[10] The German-language barrier meant they could not effectively "make use of the public ministry."[11] They sought the return of public services in the refugees' native languages. (The French petition was signed by its elders but not its preacher, possibly because the elders realized the councilmen had grown tired of hearing from or about

Minister Perucel.) This petition, like the earlier one authored by the Dutch, achieved nothing.

The French refugees did not give up. In December 1561, they beseeched the council to at least open the Church of the White Ladies for Christmas. In this instance, the council relented. On 23 December 1561, the council minutes recorded: "As reported, that several Walloons appeared in the city hall [Römer] yesterday and requested that they be given the privilege to preach in their church on the Christmas holiday. It is resolved that early tomorrow the entire Council should be requested to gather and talk about the matter further."[12] The city's rulers agreed to allow the Reformed admission to the Church of the White Ladies for Christmas, but the following day, the church would be locked once more.

On 6 February 1562, the council went a step further and forbade the two thousand Reformed residents of the city (French and Dutch alike) from using any of the city churches, "until that time when the foreign ministers become unified and matching in all things with the local [ministers]."[13] In doing so, the city council acquiesced to the demands of the city ministers, led by Superintendent Hartmann Beyer, that they be the ones to arbitrate all future questions of appropriate worship.[14] Thereafter, services in the city's two dozen Protestant churches were controlled by the official Lutheran ministry in Frankfurt, led by Beyer.[15] (The three collegiate churches, which were Frankfurt's oldest and largest churches, had been reclaimed for Catholic services by Charles V in the Schmalkaldic War.) By forbidding the Reformed refugees from the Low Countries access to any religious space, the Frankfurt Council tried to force them to join the civic church.

The council further decreed that the refugees should "have their children baptized by the Evangelical [Lutheran] ministers and allow their would-be married couples to be consecrated."[16] The Reformed community complied with this order and ceded authority over its congregants' baptisms and marriages. Reformed men and women who sought to marry did so before a Lutheran minister, and children of Reformed couples were baptized by the city's Lutheran clergy, the same men who were actively fighting to suppress all Reformed religiosity. This compliance mirrored concessions by religious minorities in other parts of the empire, where marriage and baptism were often deemed civic rites.[17] Still, the Reformed in Frankfurt remained wary of Lutheran baptism and marriage ceremonies, and they repeatedly discussed the matter of their compliance with sister communities of Reformed refugees in nearby cities.[18]

While the Reformed refugees in Frankfurt mostly accepted the council's demand that their baptisms and marriages be officiated by the Lutheran city clergy, they refused to accept Lutheran control over the Lord's Supper. They insisted on conducting their own Eucharistic services in their own space. This determination left the Reformed with two choices: worship in private or leave Frankfurt. Those Reformed individuals who wanted to stay in Frankfurt—such as Jean de Bary, a bachelor from Tournai who had arrived in late 1555 and would stay in the city and build a large family there—spent the next decades hunting for private worship space while continuing to petition the council to reclaim the free exercise of religion.[19] Those who could not abide the new situation in Frankfurt abandoned the city for places more accommodating of their faith. But Frankfurt did not make it easy to leave. The city charged emigrants an exit fee of 10 percent of all removed property, and those Reformed residents who had become citizens—and many of the first arrivals had taken this step—were required to now take an oath upon leaving that they accepted their perpetual disqualification from citizenship in Frankfurt, along with all their descendants.[20] Even if the Glauburg family were to sway the council to again permit Reformed worship in the city—which it never managed—those Reformed citizens who had already departed could not reapply for citizenship. These restrictions on emigration suggest that Frankfurt's authorities wanted the Reformed to stay in the city and join the civic congregation. The refugees' departure was not the rulers' first choice for a solution to the problem of Reformed religious ceremonies in the city. Yet the authorities could not stop hundreds of Reformed individuals from abandoning the city on the Main.

This chapter follows two groups of refugees departing Frankfurt: those who left after the restrictions of 1561–62 and those who left after Frankfurt's authorities became even more restrictive in 1594. Although historians of Frankfurt have often paid more attention to the fact that the Reformed community in Frankfurt continued to exist, hundreds of Reformed refugees departed the city in the late sixteenth century.[21] By comparing these departing individuals' perceptions of Frankfurt, recorded in memoirs and letters, with the terms of accommodation they received in their lands of resettlement, codified in refugee treaties, it is possible to see what privileges and conditions really mattered to sixteenth-century refugees and how they thought they deserved to be treated. Why exactly had Frankfurt become intolerable? And what did these people seek in a new home-away-from-home?

## Resettlement to the Palatinate and
## the Emergence of the Refugee Treaty

The first group of refugees from the Low Countries who quit Frankfurt resolved to do so in the days after the Reformed service held in Gaul's barn. Leading this group was the Dutch preacher Pieter Datheen. Furious about the council's restrictions, Datheen renounced his citizenship and made plans to depart as soon as possible.[22] Other members of the dual-language Reformed community shared Datheen's determination to leave the city.

There were many nearby destinations from which to choose. While Frankfurt controlled a hinterland of fields, forests, and rural communities (Landgemeinden), its total acreage was relatively small, especially compared to the massive hinterlands controlled by other imperial cities like Nuremberg. Frankfurt's neighbors were only a few kilometers beyond the city wall. On a map, Frankfurt's territory looked like an inkblot, with twisting borders and isolated enclaves touching upon the lands of several nearby rulers. (Over the next four centuries, the entire area would come to be dominated by the modern metropolis of Frankfurt.)

The city bordered the lands of the archbishop-elector of Mainz (a staunch opponent of the Reformation), the Lutheran Landgrave of Hesse (who in 1536 had strong-armed the city into joining the Schmalkaldic League), the Count of Solms (who in the late sixteenth century remained a loyal partisan of the emperor's despite embracing the Reformation), the Count of Isenburg (who in the 1550s began to implement Reformation reforms and construct a grand palace slightly upriver), and the Count of Hanau-Münzenberg (who had begun to implement the Reformation through the gradual replacement of retiring priests with Lutheran ministers).[23] Frankfurt's neighbors understood the Reformation in different ways, and the city's borders marked religious as well as political boundaries. In 1562, no neighboring land beckoned to the Reformed refugees seeking a new home.

Datheen and the first group seeking to leave Frankfurt looked beyond Frankfurt's immediate vicinity to more distant parts of the empire. The northern city of Emden on the border with the Habsburg Low Countries beckoned. Unfortunately, Emden's Lutheran ministers thwarted any plan to welcome Frankfurt's Reformed, and the Reformed already in Emden suggested to their Frankfurt brethren that they look to England, Hesse, or the Palatinate.[24] The Palatinate was situated on both sides of the Rhine, about eighty kilometers to the south, with its capital in Heidelberg. The Palatinate's ruler was one of the empire's seven designated electors. And, luckily for the Reformed in Frankfurt, a dynastic shift had recently occurred in the Palatinate. In 1559, the Lutheran Elector Ottheinrich suffered a heart attack and died in his bed.[25] He died without an heir, and the electorate of the Palatinate passed to his distant cousin Friedrich, who became Elector Friedrich III. An intensely spiritual man, Friedrich had personal connections to Catholicism, Lutheranism, and the Reformed tradition. During the first years of his reign, Friedrich set out to define his own beliefs and resolve the confessional animosities dividing the empire's Christians.[26] Studying the Bible and consulting with the faculty of theology at Heidelberg—including several refugee theologians from France and the Low Countries—Friedrich became enamored of the Reformed tradition and convinced that the Reformed understanding of the Eucharist was correct.[27]

In the years following his ascension, Friedrich's sympathy for the Reformed faith developed into an ardent devotion, and he transformed the Palatinate into a center of Reformed learning.[28] He wrote to the imperial city of Worms, interceding on behalf of a Reformed community hoping to move there.[29] The empire's Lutheran princes worried that the elector's Reformed faith might be viewed by Catholics as a breach of the Peace of Augsburg and thereby result in a Catholic backlash against all Protestants.[30] Friedrich defended the legality of his faith and worked to make the Palatinate a political and military bastion for Reformed worship throughout the empire and beyond.[31] His ascension gave hope to Reformed refugees like those in Frankfurt. Perhaps Friedrich's interventions could sway the Frankfurt Council.

Friedrich wrote to the Frankfurt Council on 15 August 1561 on behalf of "the foreign expelled Christians from abroad," whom he insisted were "happy to sign and accept the Augsburg Confession."[32] Friedrich denounced the "bitterness" of the Lutheran city preachers in Frankfurt and called for the council to "order your preachers to be held to fairness."[33] But the elector's enthusiastic support for the Reformed of Frankfurt did not sway the council. The council demurred and instructed the city's attorneys to draft a reply explaining to Friedrich that the Reformed in the city were "not troubled [nor] caused hardship."[34] Still, the Reformed would not be granted a church in Frankfurt until they assented to the Augsburg Confession as interpreted by a recent gathering of Protestant princes (including Friedrich) in the town of Naumburg, a meeting which reaffirmed the Augsburg Confession of 1530 as the standard of true Christianity.[35] In short, Friedrich's intervention for the Reformed in Frankfurt failed, though it did earn the appreciation of the Reformed themselves. The Reformed began to consider whether Friedrich's own lands could serve as a new, permanent place of refuge.

Minister Datheen wrote to Friedrich in order to explore the possibility of resettling in the elector's lands, and in early 1562, Datheen journeyed to the Palatinate to inspect its potential as a home for those refugees who, like him, found Frankfurt's increasing religious restrictions intolerable.[36] Arriving in Friedrich's lands, Datheen met with Vice-Count Christoff Hund von Lauterbach, who governed an area on the left bank of the Rhine just south of the imperial city of Worms that included two largely abandoned convents in a place called Frankenthal.[37] Lauterbach and Datheen—much like Poullain and Glauburg before them—agreed that Datheen's Frankfurt followers would resettle on the lands of one of the convents in Frankenthal.[38] (Several friars who had embraced the Reformation still lived on these lands, but the elector removed them to another location.)[39] As had been the case in Glastonbury under the Duke of Somerset in 1550, and again in Frankfurt in 1554, the Reformed refugees entering the Palatinate in 1562 were granted property once consecrated to the Catholic Church. Moreover, in the case of Frankfurt and the Palatinate, it had been a head minister who had traveled to meet with a ruling authority and negotiate a place for his flock. What refugees sought in both Frankfurt and the Palatinate proved the same: legal protection for themselves and their spiritual lives. In these three respects, urban and territorial refugee accommodation looked similar.

The major difference between the negotiations taking place in Heidelberg in the spring of 1562, and those between Poullain and the Frankfurt Council eight years earlier, was a matter of specificity. Datheen and Lauterbach hammered out the terms of refugee accommodation in great detail, constructing seventeen articles in a "capitulation"—that is, a formal, written agreement—which covered a variety of topics from religious practices to fishing rights.[40] The agreement, known as the Frankenthal Capitulation, essentially established the refugee settlement in Frankenthal as a new town, with residents owing obligations to the elector just like other subjects of the Palatinate.[41] For example, the Frankenthal Capitulation guaranteed the newcomers ample access to "meadows and firewood ... for household usage [and] if these commodities are not needed in Frankenthal, these commodities should be offered for purchase to the [native] subjects at a good and appropriate price."[42] The articles in the capitulation lent the refugee project in the Palatinate a level of formality, a degree of legality, and a sense of negotiated accord that distinguished it from the initial settlement within Frankfurt. In 1554, the Frankfurt Council had not authored terms of accommodation but had simply accepted Poullain's petition.[43] Influenced by his experiences in Frankfurt, Datheen now sought a formal treaty.

The Frankenthal Capitulation began with a brief history. Datheen and his followers had sent "most subservient solicitations and pleas" to the "most serene, highborn prince and lord, Lord Friedrich, Count of the Palatinate of the Rhine, Arch-steward and Elector of the Holy Roman Empire, Duke of Bavaria, etc.," who then granted the Dutch permission to settle in Frankenthal.[44] The capitulation mentioned Frankfurt's hostility to the "expelled Christians," who could no longer remain in the city due to "emerging affairs."[45] A confessional chasm had opened between Lutherans and Reformed Christians in the empire, and Frankfurt's authorities now joined Charles V and Mary Tudor in the line of rulers who persecuted true Christian worship. Elector Friedrich accepted this narrative and recognized the refugees as his own Christian subjects.[46]

The capitulation went on to list the seventeen articles negotiated by Datheen and Lauterbach that would govern refugee accommodation in the Palatinate. The first article required the newcomers to make "a bodily oath, sworn to God, to be true, faithful, and obedient to his merciful elector and his appointed heirs."[47] Bodily oaths, as opposed to spoken oaths, derived their legitimacy from contact with a holy item: in this case, a Bible. The capitulation's second article promised that, in return for this bodily oath, the newcomers would receive "their own church" in the lands of the former Augustinian monastery, where they could preach and administer the sacraments without restriction.[48] They would be permitted to do so in their native language, though the capitulation noted that this allowance was "out of necessity."[49] The newcomers would organize their own church services and religious education, although the elector could resolve religious disputes that were brought to him.[50] The third article of the capitulation specified that the refugees would also be subjects of the elector's designated head official (*Schultheiß*) in Oggersheim or, if they moved to another part of the Palatinate, the designated *Schultheiß* of that area.[51]

The capitulation permitted Datheen's congregation "the administration of the holy sacrament" and further specified that they would have complete control over the Supper, including both the liturgy and admission to the ceremony, "so that in the future there will be no misunderstanding among them."[52] Datheen must have appreciated his congregation's control over their own celebrations of the Supper since Eucharistic practices had been the source of conflict in Frankfurt—both internal conflict among refugees and external conflict with the city's authorities. Lauterbach and the elector had obviously heard of the refugees' many conflicts in Frankfurt and cited communal accord as the reason for allowing the newcomers to govern their religious ceremonies.

Datheen and his followers would still have to conform to the ecclesiastical ordinances of the Palatinate, and such conformity entailed submitting to the religious supervision of the elector's ecclesiastical advisers.[53] In this important respect, the situation for the Dutch refugees would be no different than it had been in Frankfurt, where the right to public worship required compliance with the standards of the native ministers. The major difference between the two settings, for the refugees, was that the Palatinate's spiritual leaders were men like Kaspar Olevianus, who shared the refugees' Reformed understanding of the Lord's Supper.[54] Relocating to the Palatinate would gain for Datheen and his followers the public worship rights they desired; this was not because the elector believed in allowing his subjects to worship as they wished but because his religious inclinations matched the those of the refugees. The refugees who chose the bucolic setting in the Palatinate over the metropolis on the Main were enticed by the prospect of religious life under the protection of a like-minded prince.

The capitulation with Friedrich also delineated the structure of religious discipline for the community settling in his territory.[55] Datheen's flock would have a consistory of elders who would elect their own minister, appoint their own deacons to provide for the community's poor, and examine all other refugees seeking to join the community's services. This arrangement matched the communal structures developed by the refugees in Frankfurt, but here in Frankenthal, this ecclesiastical autonomy would be more than a communal norm; it would be a legal prescription.

Sixty families from Frankfurt's Reformed community embraced the capitulation Datheen had negotiated.[56] These families, mostly native Dutch-speakers, totaled approximately 250 individuals and constituted more than 10 percent of the population from the Low Countries living in Frankfurt.[57] Presumably, many were bilingual as they came from cities on the linguistic frontier between the Dutch and French Low Countries and had been members of a dual-language religious community in Frankfurt. They departed Frankfurt that spring, sailing down the Main River to the point where it joined the Rhine and continuing downstream on the Rhine for another thirty kilometers. Their ships then took a left turn up the Nahe River, which led into the Palatinate. They arrived in Elector Friedrich's lands on 3 June 1562.[58] They disembarked near the village of Roxheim and finished their journey overland.[59] The group walked sixty kilometers to their new home in the abandoned Augustinian monastery in Frankenthal. Upon their arrival on 13 June, fifty-eight men signed the treaty negotiated by Datheen. Five men signed at the top as the representatives of the "entire community": Pieter Datheen, Jacob Libert, Christian Gillis, Peter von Bentheim, and Franz von Köcken.[60] The refugees elected four of them (Datheen, Gillis, Bentheim, and Köken) as the first councilmen for their new town.[61]

By signing the Frankenthal Capitulation, the Reformed refugees from Frankfurt became subjects of Elector Friedrich. They agreed to honor the prince and his deputies in return for religious freedom. They were under no illusion that the 1562 capitulation would be the final word on their situation or their relationship to the elector. More negotiations and mandates would come. The capitulation described the process through which the refugees would be able to "receive a decision [about] their misunderstandings of a mandate [of the Count's]."[62] They could petition the elector for redress via a letter of grievance, and the same negotiations that had taken place between Datheen and Lauterbach could be reopened. Indeed, upon arriving in Frankenthal, the Reformed realized that the monastery's lands were insufficient for all the refugees, and a French-speaking contingent traveled an additional forty kilometers to Schönau, a village near the elector's capital of Heidelberg, where the elector granted them a confiscated Cistercian monastery.[63] The Schönau community then signed its own treaty with Friedrich on 25 June.

In the Palatinate as in other early modern territories accommodating refugees, the terms of settlement underwent regular revision. Community growth necessitated new terms, and despite a devastating plague year in 1564, the population of Frankenthal doubled in the decade following the capitulation.[64] By 1573, a new treaty had become necessary. The new Frankenthal Capitulation of 1573 included fewer articles than its predecessor, but its articles were longer and contained more detail about the relationship between the Reformed refugees and Elector Friedrich.[65] The Reformed community would now assume control over additional lands in Frankenthal, lands which had formerly been part of a female Augustinian convent.[66] Entry fees paid to the elector by new arrivals were reduced by half, and the community now gained its own *Schultheiß*, its own court, plus a new system for electing *Rottenmeister*, men who represented groups of ten individuals and reported to the councilmen. The 1573 capitulation was, for the most part, a political supplement to the previous treaty; the religious situation evidently had been settled in 1562. The 1562 accord had already granted the refugees the essential religious privileges that had been denied them in Frankfurt—control over their own church building and the right to govern their own religious life, including baptisms, marriages, and celebrations of the Eucharist.

Thus, in the decades following the closing of the Church of the White Ladies, it was Elector Friedrich, not Frankfurt's councilmen, who offered the Reformed the protections they sought. Frankfurt had abandoned the legal guarantees it had granted to Poullain in 1554, guarantees of religious independence and church space that Datheen and others deemed essential for life in exile. The Reformed community as a whole considered private worship in Frankfurt to be an odious restriction, and some like Datheen considered it sufficient reason to leave the city. Datheen and his followers refused to worship surreptitiously in a barn or a home. They sought explicit legal sanction for their religious services—what some historians have called "freedom of worship"—and they received this from Elector Friedrich in the capitulation of 1562.[67] Over the next two decades the Reformed refugees in Frankenthal sought additional legal language to protect their position in exile. Laws mattered to the refugees, and legal protection was evaporating in Frankfurt. Datheen recognized this fact. And as we will see next chapter, Datheen's brethren who stayed behind in Frankfurt likewise recognized and lamented the narrowing of Frankfurt's religious protections.

To gain a political sponsor, Datheen had taken steps that became common features of refugee accommodation across the empire in the late sixteenth and early seventeenth centuries. First, he had written a letter of supplication to a nearby lord. (In later decades, the consistory of the Reformed who stayed in Frankfurt would sometimes draft such letters in the name of all congregants, suggesting that those who wanted to remain in Frankfurt still supported their brethren's attempt to relocate.) Then, Datheen had traveled to the elector's territory, met with his deputies, and negotiated articles that would govern accommodation. After bringing the treaty back to Frankfurt and receiving the approval of his followers and the Reformed community as a whole, Datheen began the process of physically relocating. Upon arriving in the Palatinate, the newcomers—at least, the men of the group—finally signed the treaty negotiated by Datheen.[68]

The refugee treaty became a common legal institution in late sixteenth- and early seventeenth-century Europe (at precisely the same time that the term refugee itself came into usage). One recent survey identified nearly 250 refugee treaties from the late seventeenth century dealing solely with Waldensian refugees from the Cottian Alps resettling in German-speaking lands.[69] In Germany, these treaties were sometimes stylized as edicts but were more frequently called privileges [Privilegien] or capitulations [Kapitulationen], the latter term normally used within the empire to denote an agreement between a new emperor and the imperial estates under him.[70] As thousands of displaced people crossed the continent in search of refuge—a mass movement sometimes called "confessional migration"—negotiated treaties became an essential feature of resettlement.[71] Many of them were printed and advertised, either by newly resettled refugees seeking to enlarge their community or by a magnanimous ruler hoping to attract further settlers. Treaties were preserved and treasured by the refugees who accepted them and resettled outside of Frankfurt. These documents were expressions of communal identity and testimonies to the legacy of those individuals who chose to leave the city and form new communities elsewhere.[72] In the decades after 1562, hundreds of Reformed individuals in Frankfurt chose this path, following Datheen out of the city.

## Spanish Persecution and Institutional Longevity

The departures of Reformed residents from Frankfurt after 1562 are hard to detect because of a widening stream of new refugees entering the city over the next four decades. From 1556 (when the Dutch, French, and English communities listed their membership) until 1573 (when the city commissioned a census of all the "Netherlanders"), the number of refugees actually increased, despite the departure of both English refugees in 1558 and Datheen's group in 1562.[73] Even as refugees fled Frankfurt, many more arrived.

The person most responsible for the growth of the Frankfurt refugee community was the Spanish general Fernando Álvarez de Toledo, the Duke of Alba, whom King Philip II of Spain sent to Brussels in

1567 to eradicate Protestantism in the Low Countries. Viewing Protestant reform as heresy, Alba established a court called the Council of Troubles that tried and condemned to death five thousand Protestants, though many had already fled and were sentenced in absentia.[74] Alba was the greatest Spanish general of the age, and the Protestants of the Low Countries—indeed Protestants across Europe—could not expect to defeat him militarily.[75] He successfully secured control over the major cities of Flanders and Brabant, the hometowns of many of the Reformed refugees who fled to German lands. Alba ordered the construction of a state-of-the-art citadel in Antwerp to secure the city and the area.[76] A statue of the duke erected in the citadel symbolized his power in the southern Low Countries and captured the miserable condition of Protestants under his rule. The statue showed the victorious Alba standing on top of the bodies of Protestants, represented as iconoclasts with chisels.

As a result of Alba's rule, many new groups of refugees fled the Low Countries after 1567 and entered Frankfurt and other German Rhineland cities.[77] Persecution in the Low Countries sustained the refugee community in Frankfurt as well as the budding communities in the Palatinate. German destinations proved far more enticing than ones in the Low Countries that were either directly controlled by Alba and his "Council of Blood"—as the generalissimo's Council of Troubles was called by Protestants—or situated near enough to Alba to be vulnerable to invasion.[78]

The case of one woman who appears on the 1573 census of refugees in Frankfurt highlights the situation Protestants faced in the Low Countries. Gorgette de Marle, a widow, lived alone in Frankfurt after being forced out of her native Tournai, "on account of the faith," as the census lists it.[79] Gorgette's two brothers stayed behind and fell victim to Spanish persecution. One of her brothers was "burnt," while the second was sentenced to beheading if he did not "recant."[80] Luckily, and "according to God's will," the second brother escaped and made it to Frankfurt, where he reconnected with his sister. Neither he nor Gorgette (nor Gorgette's late husband Jacob) received citizenship, and her brother seems to have departed soon after arriving. Gorgette, on the other hand, chose to stay.[81] The entire family must have remembered the elder brother burnt at the stake by Catholic authorities. Frankfurt, however unaccommodating it had become toward the religion of the refugees, still held appeal, for dangerously vulnerable Protestants in the Low Countries who sought safety and sometimes family members in exile.

Figure 6. Statue of Fernando Álvarez de Toledo, Duke of Alba, in Antwerp, from Pieter Christiaanszoon Bor's *Oorsprongk, begin, en vervolgh der Nederlandsche oorlogen* (1621).

Life on the Main River among fellow Reformed refugees, even if such a life involved clandestine worship in houses and barns, appealed to many Reformed individuals who faced death under Alba. Robert de Neuville was one such man, a merchant bachelor who had fled Antwerp and arrived in Frankfurt after 1561 with his brother and as many as ten other household members.[82] For these refugees, anything was better than life under Alba, and by this low standard Frankfurt can be seen as demonstrating some form of early modern toleration, in the sense of begrudgingly permitting private worship.[83] But the reality of religious life in Frankfurt did not satisfy all the Reformed newcomers, and after learning that their petitions to the council for public worship and the right to apply for citizenship achieved nothing, many left the city once they could afford the city's exit fee.[84] Thus while the refugees' religious institutions displayed remarkable endurance, many individual congregants did not endure Frankfurt for long. A turnover occurred as some Reformed refugees, after experiencing life in Frankfurt's large refugee community, opted to join the smaller communities in Frankenthal or elsewhere where Reformed services were permitted. Large imperial cities and small villages offered different possibilities for accommodation, and both beckoned to Protestants from the Low Countries threatened by Alba.

The Reformed already in Frankfurt welcomed the newcomers, but they also sensed that the city around them was growing increasingly hostile to their community. They remembered the restrictions of 1561 as unjust encroachments on their religious tradition, and they passed on this sense of being wronged to their descendants. (The eighteenth-century lawsuit against Frankfurt by the Reformed marked the year 1561 as the beginning of Frankfurt's religious repression.) The initial refugees and their descendants detected a nefarious, downward trajectory of toleration in late sixteenth-century Frankfurt. To worship "publicly"—or as they further elaborated, "practice their religion openly"—was forbidden to the Reformed residents of Frankfurt, whether newly arrived refugees or the children of refugees born in the city. Marriages and baptism could only be performed by the city's Lutheran clergy—a matter some Reformed accepted and some did not. Reformed sermons and the Reformed celebration of the Supper were forbidden in any of Frankfurt's churches.[85] The Reformed rented a house for their poor, a house owned by Frankfurt's Hospital of the Holy Spirit, and they began conducting the Supper there.[86] The congregant with the largest house was Augustin Le Grand—the wealthy merchant from Bruges who had challenged the community's first minister, Poullain—and services became a regular occurrence in Le Grand's house until 1578, when he sold his house and moved to Hanau-Münzenberg with his brother Johann.[87]

Frankfurt assumed an odd position in the world of Reformed refugees, a position which the historian Michelle Magdelaine captured with the term *Drehscheibe*, that is, a turntable onto which refugees stepped before being redirected to various other destinations.[88] Magdelaine's incisive description was aimed at seventeenth-century Frankfurt, when Huguenots entered the city from France and subsequently departed for other German territories (notably Baden and Brandenburg).[89] Yet Frankfurt's role as *Drehscheibe* emerged in the late sixteenth century, with the Palatinate and the nearby territory of Hanau-Münzenberg attracting the largest number of departing refugees. Frankfurt still attracted refugees from the Low Countries, but escalating restrictions on the Reformed minority in the city impelled many to look for greener pastures elsewhere in the empire.

## FRANKFURT TO HANAU: REFORMED SURVIVAL ON THE MAIN RIVER

Near the end of the century, County Hanau-Münzenberg, bordering Frankfurt to the immediate west, became a second major destination for the Reformed refugees leaving Frankfurt. The county's capital, a town called Hanau, lay just nineteen kilometers up the Main at the mouth of a small tributary river, the Kinzig. In the final decades of the sixteenth century, hundreds of refugees from the Low Countries made the journey from Frankfurt to Hanau. Frankfurt remained an important point of debarkation for displaced people fleeing the Low Countries, and thousands did so after 1585. But during these same years, the city's rulers became increasingly restrictive toward the Reformed faith, prompting many of the new arrivals to press on to other destinations in the empire like nearby Hanau.

Local hostility toward the Reformed in Frankfurt often resulted from wider imperial developments, and the Reformed of the city recognized that fact. In the winter of 1571–72, the French Reformed wrote to the council claiming that a recent religious colloquium in Dresden, which had been called by Augustus, Elector of Saxony, to mollify tensions within Lutheranism over its relationship to the Reformed faith, had been deliberately misinterpreted by the Lutheran clergy in Frankfurt, resulting in "a great envy and hatred being kindled with many men, as if that Dresden Colloquium so opposed us."[90] Hard-line Lutheran ministers continued to denounce the Reformed presence in the empire. In short, as the Lutherans of the empire further defined the bounds of their church, they strove to exclude the Reformed. In 1577, the *Formula of Concord*, which unified Lutheranism, explicitly rejected any symbolic or spiritual understanding of Jesus's presence in the Eucharist. Frankfurt's ministers seized on this *Formula* and insisted that the Reformed be expelled from the city.

Despite the city's suppression of public Reformed worship, thousands more Reformed refugees entered Frankfurt, especially after Spanish forces conquered Antwerp and expelled all Protestants in 1585. Spanish forces did not differentiate between those who accepted the Reformed understanding of the Supper and those who accepted the Lutheran understanding; both groups found themselves forced out of Antwerp. Reformed and Lutheran refugees from Antwerp entered Frankfurt together—and even lived together once in Frankfurt—but the city only provided church space and poor relief for the Lutherans. They formed a semi-independent part of the city congregation called the Low Country Congregation of the Augsburg Confession.[91] Convinced that all newcomers should act like the Lutheran refugees, the city implemented even more restrictions on Reformed worship in the decade after 1585.

Local scandals often provided the impetus for new restrictions on Reformed worship. In late 1593 the Dutch Reformed preacher Franciscus Gomarus ran afoul of the city authorities. Gomarus had left the city in order to get married, flouting the native ministers' jurisdiction over the Reformed community's marriages, which the council had recently reasserted via a published edict.[92] Gomarus impugned the authority of the city's political and religious leaders, and the council responded by expelling Gomarus from Frankfurt.[93] Additionally, the council forbid the Dutch refugees from replacing Gomarus, thus leaving the community without a preacher.[94] By this time, the French and Dutch Reformed had split into two separate congregations, a divorce we will examine in chapter 5.

Stunned that the council would refuse to permit them to appoint a new Dutch preacher, many of the Dutch refugees who were citizens made plans to leave the city. On 24 January 1594, the council heard a report from the city's *Rechenherren*, officials with responsibilities for some the city's bills, that "several Dutch citizens here have left their homes and sold their household effects, and also—with wife and children—moved away from here."[95] Those who remained regularly petitioned the council to permit them to appoint a new minister, but to no avail.

Life for the Dutch and French Reformed in Frankfurt continued to deteriorate. In the summer of 1596, the council took steps to completely ban Reformed religious services in the city. On 27 July, the council terminated the lease on the house "wherein they [the Reformed] held their sermons, until now."[96] The Reformed rented this house from the Hospital of the Holy Spirit, which was itself owned by the city and administered by the mayor.[97] The Reformed demanded "an answer from the honorable council" regarding the termination of the lease, but the council remained silent.[98] In early August, 263 French Reformed congregants petitioned the council for the return of their right to worship (*Exercitium religionis*), which the council promptly refused.[99] On 12 August, the council explicitly banned even private Reformed celebrations of the Eucharist.[100] And on 26 August, the council formally rejected the French Reformed Congregation's request to "carry on the practice of their religion unhindered as before."[101] By rejecting this last formal petition, Frankfurt's rulers effectively banned all practice of the Reformed religion in Frankfurt.[102]

Distraught by the city's ban on their religious services, the Reformed had two options: they could either walk outside the city on Sundays to worship—a practice called *Auslauf*—or they could abandon Frankfurt altogether for a more welcoming German site.[103] Both options inspired letters to the nearby Count of Hanau-Münzenberg. Two days after the ban on private services, the French minister Jacques Caron contacted Count Philipp Ludwig II von Hanau-Münzenberg and learned that he was amenable to allowing the French Reformed to resettle upriver in Hanau.[104] The community in Frankfurt continued to correspond with the count, and on 24 January 1597, they began negotiations of a treaty that would allow them to leave Frankfurt and settle close by on the lands of Hanau-Münzenberg.[105]

In May, the Reformed—who referred to themselves as "obedient, dutiful citizens" of Frankfurt—sent another, more urgent letter to the count describing how the council had "arrested and imprisoned in St. Catherine's tower" a Reformed petitioner.[106] Clearly, the city had turned against them, they wrote, and they felt surrounded by "hate and envy" on the part of the councilmen and citizenry.[107] In May 1597, the council issued a decree denouncing the Reformed community's refusal to join the civic church. The Reformed called the decree "fierce" and rejected its use of the terms "rebellion and sedition" to describe Reformed independence.[108] Worse still, the Reformed found "in many common places of the city" a flyer accusing them of "rebellions and seditions."[109] According to the Reformed writing to Hanau, the flyers posted around Frankfurt claimed that the French and Dutch Reformed of Frankfurt "opposed the Holy Roman Empire and most highly ordered constitutions and decisions and also the oaths and duties [of the city]."[110] The city had become a dangerous environment for the members of the Reformed community. The inflammatory language found in the publicly posted bill frightened them. Their community collectively remembered the Saint Bartholomew's Day Massacre of 1572, during which ordinary Parisians killed their Reformed neighbors. By 1597, the massacre had come to represent a serious warning to the Reformed of Europe.[111]

On 1 June, the correspondence between the Reformed refugees in Frankfurt and Count Philipp Ludwig finally bore fruit in the form of a formal treaty inviting the refugees to resettle upriver in County Hanau.[112] This document, called the Hanau Capitulation, offered the refugees the count's "protection and shield."[113] It sheds light on the aspirations of early modern refugees and the protections they valued. Even though Poullain had died forty years before this treaty with Hanau, his influence on the document is clear (as it was on the Frankenthal Capitulation of 1562 as well). Poullain's original demands in 1554 for citizenship, workspace, and religious space still formed the pillars of refugee accommodation decades later, even though it was not a minister who negotiated the Hanau Capitulation but rather eleven wealthy French Reformed men, including a jeweler, two goldsmiths, one confectioner, one weaver of passementerie, one stocking weaver, four men who either wove or sold silk products, and another unspecified type of weaver.[114] The Frankfurt Council became aware of the negotiations between these prominent residents of the city and the nearby count, and a portion of the council found it distressing to hear of such wealthy and industrious men seeking to leave the city.

The Hanau Capitulation negotiated by the Reformed of Frankfurt and Count Philipp Ludwig in 1597 began by explaining that a treaty was necessary "on account of the Reformed religion" and guaranteed that it would be lawful for the Reformed religion to be "openly taught and exercised in the County."[115] It went on to grant the newcomers "the administration of the holy sacraments and blessing of their married couples in their hereditary mother tongue."[116] Here they would be able to institute what Calvin deemed the true marks of the church: the preaching of the Word and the right administration of the sacraments.[117] They would govern their community's broader religious life, including marriage. The right to practice the essential features of Reformed religious practice— the denial of which had driven the Reformed from Frankfurt—was formally codified.

The count welcomed the refugees to settle in the capital of Hanau, and he granted them the right to become citizens of the town and even serve in its government, but he thought it would be prudent for the refugees to build their settlement some distance from the town itself to reduce friction with the native population.[118] The newcomers instead built their settlement, called Neuhanau, directly adjacent to the old city's eastern wall, on land claimed by the archbishop of Mainz.[119] Before long, it dwarfed the old city of Hanau, prompting Count Philipp Ludwig to establish Neuhanau as its own city.[120]

The terms of the Hanau Capitulation of 1597 were remarkably similar to those in Datheen's 1562 capitulation, and in substance they reflected the terms Poullain had secured in 1554. And while the geographic dissimilarity between a small town like Hanau and a large city like Frankfurt probably mattered to a silk merchant like Nicolas Heldevier, the first signatory of the Hanau treaty, the terms offered by rulers like Count Philipp Ludwig and Elector Friedrich before him broadly matched the reality of accommodation in Frankfurt before 1561—refugees had the right to worship publicly and pratice customary trades in exchange for obedience. Ultimately, the political distinction between a territorial ruler and oligarchical council probably mattered little to Heldevier.

The Hanau Capitulation specified the terms of accommodation more precisely than previous refugee treaties. It included more details than Datheen's Frankenthal treaty of 1562—which in turn had included more details than the Poullain's petition of 1554. Familiar with those documents and their impact, Heldevier and his fellow Reformed realized that specific legal provisions were much more valuable than broad statements of sympathy. The experience of the Reformed in Frankfurt had proven that such statements were open to later reinterpretation. Thus, they made sure that the treaty with the Count of Hanau did not merely allow "true worship" but specified that the count would protect the "Christian liturgy, discipline, and church order" of those who conformed to the religion "commonly practiced at that time in the Reformed Churches of France and the Low Countries and also in Electoral Palatinate and in

Geneva."[121] The Hanau Capitulation listed countries which practiced Christianity correctly and specified that these would be the standard by which arriving refugees seeking protection would be judged. Gone were the days when Poullain could establish his Protestant bona fides by telling Frankfurt's ministers that he "thought often about Dr. Martin Luther and Mr. Martin Bucer."[122]

The desire for precision is evident throughout the Hanau Capitulation, and this desire was likely shared by guest and host alike. The count was probably concerned that the refugees might harbor Anabaptists as the French Reformed had previously been accused of doing. The Hanau Capitulation further stipulated that the refugee congregation should establish a system for vetting future members and preventing the accommodation of "sectarians."[123] A newcomer needed to "procure and submit good testimony [*Zeugnus*], reports [*Kundschaften*] and documents [*Urkunden*] from another Reformed Church or other honest and believable people pertaining to his religion, life, actions, and dealings."[124] The goal was to prevent troublemakers and schismatics from joining the congregation and fomenting trouble from within. The capitulation reiterated that the count would not tolerate "mobs or sectarians."[125] Philipp Ludwig insisted the newcomers agree to a clear system of examination. Ambiguity was the bête noire which both the Reformed and their future lord sought to avoid.

The Hanau Capitulation went on to define the political and economic conditions of refugee accommodation. The refugees were permitted to apply for citizenship in the city of Hanau, but they had to swear an oath to Count Philipp Ludwig (and his descendants) as their lord and respect the authority of the count and all his representatives.[126] For his part, the count would "guarantee the safety of the foreigners and their servants along with all of their goods and belongings," and he promised not to "unfairly or illegally arrest them," according to Article 5.[127] Yet the refugees were not free to hunt in the forests or fish and catch crabs in the streams of Hanau, which belonged to the count, according to Article 6.[128] The Hanau Capitulation reads as though the representatives of the refugees and the count's representatives sat across from each other, taking turns in suggesting articles for their respective parties. An obvious sense of reciprocity pervades the document and reveals its negotiated orgin.

Articles 8, 9, and 10 treat the refugees' livelihoods: "The denizens [i.e., refugees] as well as the citizens, merchants, traders, and craftsmen shall be free and prepared to pursue all kinds of handlings and livings [*Hant-ierungen und Nahrungen*] that are honest and do not harm the common good, and trade all kinds of wares, genuine wares, as is everywhere customary and permitted in the Holy Empire, as well as doing penny work, selling cloth by the cubit as well as in great amounts and bales, to trade and sell in their houses and in the open."[129] As the previous generation of Reformed refugees had secured permission to work and sell cloth in their new homes, so too the Reformed seeking to leave Frankfurt for Hanau established the right to practice their trades. The difference between these articles and the general promise that Poullain received in 1554 that his followers would be "provided with houses and workspaces," was again a matter of specificity. The Hanau Capitulation delineated the specific forms of trade the refugees could practice. Even the types of seals they should use to mark their products were noted in the capitulation between newcomers and lord.[130]

The precision of the Hanau Capitulation vis-à-vis previous treaties is particularly stark when read alongside Frankfurt's city council minutes from the intervening decades. Take, for instance, the issue of alcohol production and sale. In 1556, the refugees in Frankfurt had been confronted several times by the city's supervisor of alcohol (*Braumeister*), who ultimately decided that "they brew bad beer." Because they had no written arrangement guaranteeing their right to produce alcohol, the refugees were subject to the whims of the *Braumeister*, who required them to halt any improvements to their beer. The refugees could only continue to brew "as long as they do not brew better beer" than the city's usual standard.[131] The Hanau Capitulation specified that the refugees might "sell beer or wine from the tap as long as the customary wine and beer tax is paid."[132] For every cask of wine stored in a cellar, the refugees agreed to pay two florins to the count's authorities.[133] While on their own, these specifications might appear strangely detailed, they emerged in response to previous conflicts between the Reformed of Frankfurt and the city's authorities. Such detailed provisions sprang not from a litigious inclination on the part of Count Philipp Ludwig but rather from a long history of contention between the Reformed and Frankfurt's council over similar issues. Beer rules, and the exactitude of the Hanau Capitulation in general, were meant to ensure the long-term viability of Reformed life in Hanau. The Hanau Capitulation established refugee accommodation legally and in great detail.

## PRIVATE WORSHIP AND *AUSLAUF*
## AS TOOLS OF EXPULSION

In the last four decades of the sixteenth century, Frankfurt was not a tolerant city, at least according to the Reformed individuals who lived there. In published accounts and letters to nearby princes, the Reformed complained bitterly about Frankfurt's unfair treatment of their community. According to the Dutch minister Datheen and the French minister Caron, Frankfurt's authorities maliciously portrayed the Reformed as heretical even though they were actually in accord with the city's Protestant church.[134] Admittedly, such memoirs and letters were intended to elicit sympathy for the Reformed refugees, either from nearby princes or subsequent generations. Yet the authors of these texts acted upon their disastisfaction. They left the city. And they did so in direct response to Frankfurt's attempts to restrict their religious practices—first in 1561, when the city forced Reformed worship into private houses, and again after 1596, when the city forced all Reformed worship outside the city.

Datheen and his followers so resented the imposition of private worship that they abandoned Frankfurt promptly. What these people wanted was to "hold their church service publicly [*publice*], openly [*sciente*], and permanently [*perennitente*]."[135] To understand what Datheen meant by "publicly" we can further explore his published account of his time in Frankfurt. As Datheen put it: "It is truly a deplorable thing, that the expelled Christians [from the Low Countries] are not permitted to preach the true doctrine of the Word of God and the Augsburg Confession publicly and in their own language, considering that the idolatrous papists and the horrid Jews—who daily blaspheme the Son of God, deride and trample on him as much as they can—are permitted to publicly carry on and preach their damned frightful heresy and blasphemy."[136] Datheen sought a place for his refugee congregation within Frankfurt's legal order, and he reiterated the very first argument marshalled (unsuccessfully) to defend refugee services: the refugees conformed to the Augsburg Confession. By closing the Church of the White Ladies, Frankfurt had relegated the Reformed residents of the city to a place beneath Catholics and Jews, according to the Dutch minister. Public worship was essential, and Datheen and others did not want to wait for the Frankfurt Council to change its mind and permit Reformed services.

Those Reformed who stayed in Frankfurt remembered the year 1561 as a calamitous moment in their history, a time when many of their friends and family began to resettle outside the city, sometimes far away. 1562 witnessed a major exodus of Reformed refugees from the city on the Main, though this was offset by the arrival of many newcomers. Even the ministers of Frankfurt's Reformed community were eager to leave the city after 1561. Many embraced the opportunity to move to the Palatinate, Hanau, or farther afield to cities in the northern Low Countries. In 1575, after the death of Minister Sebastian Matte, the Dutch Reformed community could not find a long-term replacement. The next two ministers both departed for cities in the northern Low Countries within a year of their elections, and the third departed after three years for Frankenthal.[137] Even as new streams of refugees fled Spanish persecution for Frankfurt, they had difficulty recruiting ministers to join them. Frankfurt may have proven more attractive than Habsburg territories, but clerical, governmental, and (occasional) popular hostility to the Reformed ensured that refugees and their ministers frequently moved to other cities when they could. The city did not become the idyllic home-away-from-home that Poullain had advertised to other Reformed in 1554.

By the turn of the century, those Reformed individuals still in Frankfurt recognized that their religious life was steadily worsening. In 1596, the council took further steps to expel the Reformed faith from the city by banning private worship and terminating the Reformed community's lease on the house they used for sermons and the Lord's Supper. Desperate for legal protection for their faith, hundreds of Reformed people embraced the Hanau Capitulation of 1597 and relocated to Count Philipp Ludwig's nearby lands. Those Reformed people who hoped to maintain their spiritual lives while remaining in Frankfurt had to walk outside the city walls for services, first to a nearby chapel and then—after the citizens destroyed the chapel, which we will see in the next chapter—to the lands of the Count of Isenburg, more than eight kilometers away.[138] Frustrated by this practice of *Auslauf* the French Reformed reached out once more to the Palatinate, and after negotiating a new treaty, many resettled in the town of Oppenheim.[139]

Historians have paid a great deal of attention to private worship, *Auslauf*, and other informal arrangements which facilitated minority worship in early modern cities.[140] Worship in private homes and *Auslauf* have been portrayed as solutions, reluctantly instituted, to the problem of religious plurality in early modern cities.[141] But the accounts of the Reformed living in Frankfurt in 1561 and 1596 portray private worship and *Auslauf* as odious restrictions on previously generous terms of accommodation, terms that had been offered in 1554. Datheen, Caron, and others recognized that conditions for the Reformed were worsening, not improving. The broad concessions won by the initial group of refugees in 1554 had eroded, and, by the start of the seventeenth century, the council, the ministers, and the citizenry of Frankfurt were attacking the Reformed refugees with publicly posted flyers. Private worship and then *Auslauf* were arrangements aimed at pushing the Reformed community outside the city, and they heralded the advent of a more intolerant era in Frankfurt.[142]

During the same decades that Frankfurt became more restrictive and less welcoming to Reformed refugees, many other German territories became more welcoming. Territories like the Palatinate emerged as attractive destinations because they offered legal protection for Reformed worship. In the seventeenth century, many more German princes offered formal treaties of accommodation, and at the end of the century, when Huguenots fled France, thousands moved to the up-and-coming provinces of powerful German princes while relatively few settled in imperial cities like Frankfurt.[143] At that time, Frankfurt still refused to offer Reformed residents the right to worship publicly.

Yet the Reformed community in Frankfurt founded by refugees from the Low Countries persisted. Thousands of refugees and their descendants chose to stay in Frankfurt, and they maintained close ties with their brethren who chose to leave the city on the Main. During the final decades of the sixteenth century, the same years when hundreds of Reformed individuals left the city, the Reformed who stayed behind found creative new ways to sustain their spiritual lives in the increasingly hostile city.

# 5

# Preserving Reformed Life
# in Frankfurt

❧

> If the pure evangelical faith still professed by this church is the real
> source of its permanence, its Presbyterian organization is, accord-
> ing to our deep conviction, one of the exterior causes of its suste-
> nance to this day.
>
> —F. Charles Schröder, minister of
> the French Reformed Church, 1854

ALTHOUGH THE FRANKFURT COUNCIL began to severely restrict
Reformed worship in the closing decades of the sixteenth century,
it did not eradicate the Reformed community in the city. Both Dutch
and French Reformed individuals chose to stay in the city on the Main.
The perseverance of the Reformed community through the tragic years
of 1561, when the city banned public worship, and 1596, when private
worship was also banned, became a point of pride among the Reformed
refugees and their descendants. In 1854, the minister of the French Reformed Church in Frankfurt, Charles Schröder, took the occasion of his
congregation's tricentennial to reflect on the fluctuating health of Reformed religious life in Frankfurt over the previous three hundred years.
And while Schröder lamented the years 1561 and 1596, when "painful debates with the Lutheran ministry" caused his congregation to hemorrhage
hundreds of members, he ultimately praised the resilience of Frankfurt's
Reformed.[1] Despite growing local hostility, and despite the allure of other
locations with more generous terms of accommodation, some members
of the Reformed community chose to remain and build their lives in

Frankfurt. Indeed, the Reformed welcomed more and more new members over the course of the late sixteenth and early seventeenth centuries. They preserved their spiritual lives by building strong and sustained connections with allies abroad and, most importantly, by repurposing, renovating, and reinforcing their central religious institution: the consistory.

The consistory as an institution enabled the Reformed in Frankfurt to secure worship space, administer alms, and sustain their bonds with sister communities in exile. These tasks were essential for the survival of their religious community apart from the Lutheran civic congregation, which the city authorities pressured the Reformed to join. The Reformed could not expect the city to support their poor. They were not permitted to hold their own baptisms or marriages. Worst of all, the Reformed could not celebrate the Lord's Supper openly and were forced to surreptitiously find worship space for their celebrations of the Eucharist. The council had withdrawn many of the Reformed community's religious privileges in response to loud intramural conflicts arising within their community. Recognizing the city's concerns about religious conflicts, the Reformed began to rely on the consistory for another, absolutely vital task: the arbitration of conflicts among congregants. By mediating conflicts and preventing such from reaching Frankfurt's rulers, the Reformed consistory helped ensure that Reformed religious life continued to thrive in Frankfurt.

## A Growing Community in Search of Space

In 1562, the departure of Pieter Datheen's group had decreased the Reformed population in Frankfurt to around 1,300.[2] Over the next forty years, this number more than doubled. The rapid growth of the community did not go unnoticed, and in October 1573, at the pressuring of the city ministers, the council agreed to conduct a census of the "foreign residents" in Frankfurt.[3] The council deputized the patrician Karl von Glauburg to visit the households of Reformed families and take count.[4] Karl von Glauburg was the son of Johann von Glauburg, the great patron of Reformed refugees, and he was therefore a man whom the Reformed would have been inclined to trust. Glauburg's census reveals a thriving, rapidly expanding, dual-language Reformed community in Frankfurt. Glauburg counted 321 heads of households and a total of 1,422 Reformed "foreigners" within the city—though he also noted that many "foreigners" were citizens.[5] At the time, Frankfurt was home to approximately 15,000 residents.[6] In most cases, the census also lists the occupation of the head of household, the citizenship status of the head of household, the number of dependents and servants, and the number of years that the head of household—who was always either a man or widow—had lived in Frankfurt.

According to Karl von Glauburg's census, there was a great deal of variance in the length of time Reformed individuals had spent in Frankfurt. The range of residency time spanned from two weeks to eighteen years. There were recent arrivals like Caspar de Vines, from Tournai, who had only been in the city since the Easter Fair and who "lived on rents."[7] Another new arrival was a weaver named Guillaume Scheffroy, also from Tournai, who had been in Frankfurt for the past four months.[8] At the same time, the census included longtime residents like Charles de Loraine of Valenciennes, a day-laborer who had lived in Frankfurt for eighteen years and had even become a citizen.[9] As a day-laborer, Loraine must have secured citizenship very soon upon his arrival in 1555 before the city increased the citizenship fee that year.[10] Another Reformed parishioner, Hamman Köfer, appears in the census as a "longtime citizen," and his name suggests that he may have originated in a German-speaking area before joining the refugee congregation from the Low Countries.[11] The majority of the Reformed refugee members appearing in the 1573 census had lived in Frankfurt for more than three years, while more than a third had been in the city for more than five years. Frankfurt was not purely a turntable redirecting Reformed refugees to other destinations— although it also played that role.[12]

The Reformed individuals who chose to stay in Frankfurt hosted other refugees passing through the city on their way to other destinations in the empire. In this way, the congregation of Low Country refugees in Frankfurt mirrored Reformed churches in Antwerp, which at the time consisted of nuclei of devoted participants who maintained the institutions of worship during times of Spanish persecution and who were joined by less-committed but still sympathetic "middle groups" during times of relative peace.[13] Frankfurt's situation was naturally different in that the permanent core was joined by transient groups instead of locals who may have avoided participation during waves of persecution. Still, Reformed consistory records from the refugees in Frankfurt reveal a clear interplay between permanent members and the vast number of Reformed who lived in Frankfurt only temporarily, either for business or on their way to Hanau or the Palatinate. At times, the Reformed community in Frankfurt played the role of an airport chapel, welcoming to their religious services friends who were passing through or simply visiting the city for its trade fairs. But providing religious services meant securing worship space, and this task became increasingly difficult in the late sixteenth century.

After the closure of the Church of the White Ladies, securing worship space for services in both French and Dutch became the chief task of the Reformed elders and ministers. Initially, the congregation met for sermons in a barn, but more suitable options soon emerged.[14] Augustin Le Grand, the merchant from Bruges who had challenged Valérand Poullain's leadership, volunteered his spacious home.[15] (Le Grand also housed Casiodoro de Reina, who became minister to refugees from the Low Countries who accepted the real presence in the Eucharist and thus fell within the bounds of the civic Lutheran church, though their services were in French.)[16] The Reformed also started offering sermons in a poorhouse they rented from the Hospital of the Holy Spirit.[17] Space was much needed as the Reformed maintained an ambitious schedule of services. Consistory minutes from May 1571 include a summary of the French services conducted by Ministers Théophile de Bannois and Jean Salvard: "The ministers agreed to preach on Sundays in two locations, in the morning and in the afternoon, at the usual time, and to teach the catechism in two locations."[18] Beyond these services, the French-speakers arranged that "the general censor [Bible Study] will take place . . . every three months, and for special cases every eight days."[19] The Dutch Reformed sought to offer the same schedule of services. Space was tight and scheduling competitive.

In late 1570, after almost a decade of private worship in Frankfurt, the Dutch Reformed became convinced that Reformed consistory gave scheduling preference to the French. They decided to break from their French brethren and form their own independent congregation governed by its own consistory. Since the advent of refugee accommodation in Frankfurt, the Reformed Christians from the Low Countries had maintained a single consistory that oversaw communal discipline, a consistory founded under the leadership of Poullain in 1554 and then expanded under John a Lasco, who had appointed Datheen to be preacher to the Dutch-speakers.[20] Now, in 1570, the Dutch wanted more than their own preacher. They wanted direct control over their language services and direct control over their community's discipline, via the election of Dutch-speaking elders by the Dutch-speaking men.

On Friday, 17 November 1570, "several men" of the Dutch-speaking community gathered at the house of Lauwerejns Ackerman and declared their independence from the French-speakers.[21] The group consisted of at least five men, four of whom would become the congregation's first elders: Lauwerejns Ackerman, the host of the gathering and a former iconoclast in Antwerp; Pieter Bisschop, a merchant from Nieuwkerke; Jan de Hossche, from Veurne; and Gillis von Muijsenhole, from Ghent.[22] The fifth founding member was Sebastian Matte, of Ypres, who would be the congregation's first minister and, as such, the leader of its new consistory. Matte, who Latinized his name as Sebastian Storea, had been recommended for the position by Datheen in Heidelberg.

Born into the trade of hat making in Ypres, Matte had embraced religious reform and become a fiery preacher and opponent of Catholicism.[23] His preaching forced him to flee the Low Countries for England in the late 1550s with his wife and children, but he returned in 1566 to incite and lead iconoclastic riots.[24] When Spanish troops arrived to punish the perpetrators, Matte had to escape, and he traveled with his family to Frankfurt. Irrespective of Frankfurt's ban on Reformed services, the city on the Main proved a much safer home for Matte than his native Low Countries. Matte served not only as the Dutch congregation's first minister but also as its first secretary. He recorded the earliest minutes from the Dutch Reformed consistory, minutes which capture almost every aspect of daily life within the Dutch Reformed Congregation.[25]

Two days after the meeting in Ackerman's house, a Sunday, the new Dutch Reformed Congregation gathered at 7:00 a.m. "in the house of Muijsenhole" for the congregation's first sermon.[26] Following the sermon, the men of the community formally elected Ackerman, Bisschop, Hossche, and Muijsenhole as elders. These four were also duly elected as the community's deacons, along with two other men, Atheunus Seedt, from Menen, and Hans Gestens, a wealthy merchant from Antwerp.[27] The elders confirmed Matte's appointment as minister, and the leadership of the Dutch Reformed Congregation was thusly established: a minister, four elder-deacons, and two deacons. The minister and the elders formed the initial consistory—a small group of men to govern a small community. The new Dutch Reformed Congregation of Frankfurt consisted of just sixty-one people "who find themselves prepared for the sermon."[28]

Concerns over worship space, not liturgical disagreement, had inspired the Dutch (whom the French now called Flemish) to break from their French (whom the Dutch called Walloon). According to the earliest

Dutch Reformed Consistory minutes, the French accepted the need for a second Reformed consistory. Minister Matte recorded how his community, after its first sermon that Sunday, sent representatives to announce their new independence to the French: "Gaspar Heyden, Jan de Hossche, Gillis van Muijsenhole and Pieter Bisschop went to the consistory of the Walloons on the advice of the other brethren, in order to announce to them, that the Dutch now desired to have their own congregation.... To this the Walloon brethren all together gave their assent."[29] Yet while the Dutch consistory minutes describe the French assenting to the split, the actions of the French suggest that the divorce was not wholly amicable. The breakaway Dutch hoped to continue using the same poorhouse that the Reformed had been renting from the Hospital of the Holy Spirit, at least for a span, but when they approached the French about the idea, the French replied that "they could not agree to this, for several reasons named by them."[30]

The Dutch now embarked on their own quest to find worship space. Minister Matte's house would serve as the first site of preaching, "until something else is agreed upon."[31] Matte would host two Sunday sermons, and the Dutch Reformed consistory decided it would only be fair to have the weekday sermon somewhere else. They decided on Jan de Hossche's courtyard for Wednesday-afternoon sermons.[32] As the Dutch Reformed Congregation grew, the challenge of finding preaching space became ever more daunting. In the year 1572 alone, Matte described attempts to find new space on 13 January, 18 February, 29 February, 10 August, 17 August, 31 August, and 3 September.[33] The site of religious services moved so frequently that the Dutch Reformed consistory assigned one deacon, Anthoine de Brouckere, the task of moving the community's benches from one location to the next.[34] Reading Matte's minutes, it seems that securing worship space was the chief task of the new Dutch Reformed Consistory, which may also explain why the French—who struggled to find their own space—assented to the formation of a second consistory, a second task force to find private worship space in a city that banned Reformed services in church buildings.

By early 1571, the now separated Dutch and French Reformed had begun quarreling over space. That March, when the Dutch asked again to hold one of their services in the house where the French would meet, the French minister Bannois demurred, "You should not preach there."[35] Matte recorded his own reaction to Bannois's refusal, "I then said, that I cannot understand this [reply] as anything other than that they did us an injustice."[36] Later that year, Bannois still refused access to the house. The French Reformed Consistory recorded these exchanges, though naturally from a different perspective. According to the French, on 29 August 1571, Bannois went to "speak with the Flemish brothers to tell them . . . to have the patience to preach in the Garden of the French."[37] It seems the French had their own space issues. On 25 October two of the French elders began to search for additional space: "Monsieur Le Bailleu and Simon Rousseau advise inspecting the barn that is facing the house of the church . . . to hold and accommodate the church."[38]

The French became concerned that the separatism of the Dutch could imperil the position of both Reformed congregations in the city. The council was known to detest religious controversy and factionalism—like the English refugees' fight over Cranmer's Book of Common Prayer in 1555 or the French feud between ministers Perucel and Houbraque in 1559. The wealthy Le Grand, whose house continued to host French gatherings, had witnessed the Perucel-Houbraque conflict and deemed the Dutch insistence on independence a foolhardy provocation. He also resented Matte and the Dutch for the split because the French thereby lost several of their richest parishioners and thus a great deal of support for their community's poor. At least once, the French Reformed sent a representative to their Dutch brethren to clarify "complaints uttered by Augustin Le Grand . . . that they the French were very worried that the Dutch were beginning to establish a church and collect alms, which would be a detriment to their [French] church."[39] Le Grand's complaints left the Dutch indignant. According to Matte, "they knew themselves to indeed be innocent and had begun their church with the consent of the French."[40]

Soon, the Dutch became aware of letters sent by the French Reformed to communities in Heidelberg and Frankenthal and even to the Frankfurt patricians (or at least those sympathetic to the Reformed) expressing worry that Dutch separatism could endanger all Reformed worship in the city. The French had grown concerned about new rumors of troublemaking and Anabaptism that swirled once again around the entire Reformed community. In a letter from late 1571 or early 1572, the French explained to the council that the French Reformed Congregation had nothing to do with "a certain enthusiastic person from Lower Germany [who] was wandering through this city . . . scattering from this place many impious and most absurd doctrines."[41] As a result of this rambling troublemaker, the French had been treated "as if we are favorers of Anabaptists from whom we have always differed most distantly with respect to both doctrine and customs."[42] Notably, the French did not defend the entire Reformed community in the city but only those "subjects and citizens with the shared name of Belgian living here, who use the French tongue."[43] The French consistory no longer petitioned in the name of all refugees from the Low Countries, as they had previously done.

Minister Matte and the Dutch elders worried about their own position in the city. They wrote to Datheen, their former preacher, who had recently been appointed court preacher to Elector Friedrich in Heidelberg. They asked Datheen to intercede on their behalf with Johann von Glauburg: "Write to Dr. Glauburg, as this man may remember us Dutch, when a hope exists to gain a church."[44] The Dutch hoped the Glauburgs, the long-standing patrician allies of the Reformed in Frankfurt, would help them. Matte suggested to the consistory that any letter to Datheen or Glauburg should implore the recipient to "think about the Dutch, because these people have been expelled in just as great a number as the Walloons."[45] Matte and the Dutch elders, like the French, now formally distinguished between the two Reformed communities from the Low Countries living in Frankfurt, one Dutch and one French. Before this time, the entire Reformed community had employed the terms "Belgian," "Netherlandish," "Walloon," and "foreign" almost interchangeably to refer to their entire community.

Unfortunately for the Dutch, Minister Bannois and the French Reformed had contacted Glauburg first and convinced him that the Dutch "want to make a disturbance and perpetrate something new."[46] Glauburg shared the concerns of the French Reformed—petitions from a new consistory to the council could result in a backlash against the entire Reformed community in the city. Glauburg advised the Dutch against petitioning the council and urged them to acknowledge the "precedence" of the French.[47] The French leaders and Glauburg were worried about the proliferation of Reformed congregations in the city, and with good cause. Minutes from a special advisory committee of the council from 7 December 1569 had expressed exasperation that Reformed refugees "daily arrive in great numbers" and "hold their meetings in three or four places in the city, not without notable suspicion from the citizens."[48] Moreover, the Dutch Reformed could not simply claim to the council that their new consistory was intended to facilitate preaching in their language because the Lutheran ministers of Frankfurt had long dismissed the necessities of language as sufficient grounds for ecclesiastical independence. The Lutheran clergy reminded the council that they could appoint foreign-language preachers of their choosing.[49]

The foundation of a new Reformed consistory in a city which had banned the public practice of Reformed Christianity was a risky proposition. Whatever the benefits of having two Reformed consistories to secure worship space for services in two different languages, the foundation of a new congregation in 1570 was in some senses a foolhardy act. The Frankfurt Council had abandoned its support for the refugees in 1561 precisely because the councilmen had judged the Reformed community to be dissentious. Ironically, though, it had been the council's imposition of private worship in 1561 that necessitated the formation of a separate Dutch consistory by provoking a competition among the Reformed over worship space.

In the decade after the closure of the Church of the White Ladies, the Reformed consistory as an institution became a tool for coordinating worship space in Frankfurt. Minutes from the Reformed consistories in Frankfurt—the dual-language consistory before 1570 as well as the two separate consistories after 1570—reveal a tireless effort by elders and ministers to locate, secure, and prepare private areas for Reformed services. No other matter received such sustained attention in the minutes from 1561 to 1581.

## Searching for Allies outside of Frankfurt

The hunt for private worship space was essential, but the Reformed who stayed in Frankfurt in the second half of the sixteenth century also sought to regain public worship rights or perhaps take part in some of the city's official services. To these ends, the Reformed began to ask nearby princes and nearby Reformed communities for help. From the princes—usually the same princes who had welcomed the Reformed brethren who had left the city—the Reformed in Frankfurt sought political advocacy in their name before the Frankfurt Council. From nearby sister communities, the Reformed sought religious approval for their participation in certain of the city's Lutheran ceremonies. Both the princes and the sister communities responded to letters of supplication, but while princely intervention accomplished little, dialogue with nearby Reformed exile communities helped the French and Dutch Reformed of Frankfurt make peace with the Lutheran city around them.

Treaties of resettlement offered by nearby rulers had inspired many
of the Reformed in Frankfurt to leave the city, as we have seen, and these
treaties also suggested a way forward for the Reformed determined to
stay in the city on the Main. Perhaps neighboring princes would champion the Reformed cause and compel the city to permit Reformed worship publicly. The empire's complex, overlapping jurisdictions provided
room for a powerful prince to exert legal influence even over a nominally
independent imperial city like Frankfurt.[50] Frankfurt remained militarily
vulnerable to the princes of the empire. Residents must have remembered
the city's Schmalkaldic misadventure in 1547 and the siege of Frankfurt
in 1552 by the princes of Saxony, Brandenburg, Hesse, Mecklenburg, and
the Palatinate. Princes armed with cannons could impose their wills on
cities defended by old stone walls.[51] The Reformed refugees in Frankfurt
hoped nearby princes would come to their aid and force the city's rulers
to nullify bans on Reformed worship.

The nearest neighboring prince was the archbishop-elector of Mainz,
but since his seat remained the property of the Catholic Church according to the terms of the Peace of Augsburg, the Reformed could not seriously hope for his support. Archbishop Daniel Brendel von Homburg,
who ruled Mainz from 1555 to 1582, had two main goals vis-à-vis Frankfurt—the return of the church properties in Frankfurt which had been
ceded to the city according to the terms of the Peace of Augsburg and
the expansion of his territorial lands around Frankfurt. Daniel succeeded
in acquiring lands to the west and north of Frankfurt, where he immediately set about implementing the Counter-Reformation.[52] Worse still
for Protestants in the Main River area, the archbishop exercised corule
over several territories belonging to the patrimony of local Protestant
lords, and he could thus frustrate efforts to implement the Reformation.
Clearly, Mainz would never ally itself with the Reformed in Frankfurt.
The French and Dutch Reformed instead wrote to Daniel's chief imperial rival, the Elector of the Palatinate Friedrich III—whose cousin had
been a candidate for the archbishopric of Mainz but lost the cathedral
chapter's election narrowly to Daniel.[53]

Friedrich had already shown his support for the Reformed in 1561,
when he wrote to Frankfurt's rulers to insist they halt clerical denunciations of the Reformed in the city. In 1562, he worked with the Dutch
minister Datheen to craft a treaty that welcomed disaffected Reformed
refugees living in Frankfurt to his lands. Friedrich's blossoming devotion to the Reformed cause attracted Dutch and French refugees to

Frankenthal, and later to Schönau, and other small towns in the Pa-latinate.[54] In 1563, Friedrich issued a new church order and catechism, crafted by his theologians in Heidelberg, prescribing religious practices consistent with those of the refugees in Frankfurt, a document which would guide the refugees' liturgy in future years.[55] In short, the Reformed in Frankfurt knew they had a major ally in Friedrich.

In 1571, the Reformed who chose not to resettle in the Palatinate wrote to the Elector Friedrich asking him to intercede on their behalf with the Frankfurt Council, which Friedrich promptly did. On 29 March, the council minutes refer to a letter from Friedrich that requested "that the honorable council open a church for the foreign, or expelled, Chris-tians where they may preach God's word and receive the Holy Sacra-ment."[56] On 13 September, Friedrich's legate presented another letter to Frankfurt's rulers "on account of the foreign and expelled Christians, who asked and campaigned that a church may be opened to them, which sub-sequently your most gracious elector and lord also asked and campaigned for."[57] One can detect the political impact of the elector's letters by looking at the sheer quantity of council minutes describing efforts to formulate a response. The councilmen were upset that a minority community in the city had begun to seek redress from a nearby prince.

Unfortunately for the Reformed in Frankfurt, the city council had a great deal of experience dealing with aggrieved neighboring princes. Usu-ally, the council decided to postpone any response to the elector, and it is unclear whether the Reformed community in Frankfurt gained knowl-edge of most of the elector's letters.[58] On 29 March, for example, the council reacted with an adjournment: "We should consult about what answer to send to the electoral prince tomorrow."[59] The next day, during their consultation session, the councilmen resolved that "the matter that the honorable council recently discussed will be left alone until the next fair."[60] The next fair occurred two weeks later, and at that time, the coun-cil wrote to the elector and told him to expect an official answer the fol-lowing year. Four days after Easter, the elector wrote to Frankfurt's rulers again. This time, he received a reply relatively quickly—only eight weeks later—complete with an apology that "your lordship was not answered until now."[61] By 1573, Friedrich's tone had become accusatory. He wrote to the council saying, "You intend such unseemly abuses, which are de-signed solely to frustrate and to aggrieve the church of Christ."[62] The cor-respondence between the council and Friedrich lasted until 1576, when Friedrich died and was succeeded by his son Ludwig VI, who favored

Lutheranism and therefore abandoned support for the Reformed of Frankfurt. The council's strategy of delay ultimately worked.

In 1597, the treaty of resettlement drafted between the French Reformed of Frankfurt and Count Philipp Ludwig von Hanau-Münzenberg not only inspired many Reformed to leave the city but also revealed to those staying behind that they had allies in Frankfurt's immediate vicinity. The Reformed in Frankfurt wrote to Philipp Ludwig asking for support. They also reached out to his relative Count Johann Reinhard of Hanau-Lichtenberg, who sued the Frankfurt Council before the Imperial Chamber Court. The case concerned the arrest of "two Hanau subjects" by the city authorities, and the two subjects must have been in Frankfurt on account of the Reformed community as the Reformed later cited the case as evidence of the city's hostility toward Reformed Christians.[63] The counts of Hanau were less powerful than the elector of the Palatinate, but they could still advocate for the religious rights of the Reformed community in Frankfurt and challenge the city at the imperial level. In some ways, they proved more successful in intervening for the Reformed residents of Frankfurt than Friedrich had been.

Indirectly, Count Philipp Ludwig helped the Reformed gain the opportunity for *Auslauf*, the opportunity to walk outside the city to worship on Sundays. The count's treaty of 1597 proved so successful in drawing Reformed people out of Frankfurt that the city's patricians began to worry that the city's industry and trade would suffer.[64] It was the richest, most successful Reformed individuals who were relocating to Hanau. The city council decided to prevent further losses by permitting the Reformed to build a small chapel outside the city wall but still on Frankfurt's territory. The plan was designed and supported by patricians on the first and second benches of the council, including members of the Glauburg and Bromm families.[65] The lowest bench, the guild bench, voted against the idea.[66] The patrician Johann Adolf von Glauburg, son of Adolf von Glauburg who had supported Poullain and the first wave of refugees, volunteered his land for the new chapel.[67] A small wooden chapel was built, and the Reformed celebrated their first Supper in the new building on 12 July 1601, a moment of joy for the Reformed.

The circumstances surrounding the construction of the wooden chapel in Frankfurt reveal the power of neighboring princes and local elites to exploit territorial borders in order to accommodate religious dissent. Yet the new chapel did not herald an era of tacit toleration. Denounced by Frankfurt's ministers, the Reformed chapel outside the wall became a flashpoint for the city's Lutherans. On 29 July 1608, the chapel caught fire and burned to the ground. The Reformed cried arson.[68] They claimed the citizens of Frankfurt had destroyed their church, a building known to Frankfurters as the Church of the Foreign Reformed.[69] Though we lack evidence for who the aggressors were, the burning of the Reformed Chapel epitomizes the hostility this minority congregation faced in early modern Frankfurt after 1561. The council entertained no further plans for chapels outside the city wall. On 8 November 1608, the council voted to reaffirm its ban on all Reformed worship on Frankfurt's territory.[70] More French Reformed individuals fled the city, this time for Oppenheim in the Palatinate.[71] Those remaining began *Auslauf* outside of Frankfurt's territory to Offenbach, a town controlled by Count Wolfgang Ernst of Isenburg, who permitted Reformed worship. This was a two-hour walk.

In March 1613, a collection of the empire's most powerful princes tried to pressure the city to permit Reformed worship. They did so at a crucial moment in Frankfurt's history. The city was experiencing a major revolt against the authority of the patricians, with Lutheran guildsmen and Catholic priests calling for sweeping—though decidedly different— political reforms.[72] During this vulnerable moment, the council received a letter from the leaders of the Protestant Union, a new defensive military alliance founded by the ruler of the Palatinate. The authors included Johann II, guardian of the new elector of the Palatinate; Margraves Christian, Joachim Ernst, and Johann Sigismund von Brandenburg; Duke Johann Friedrich von Württemberg; Margrave Georg Friedrich von Baden; and Prince Christian von Anhalt, who would become a champion of Protestantism during the Thirty Years' War.[73] This august group of men sent the Frankfurt Council a "letter of intercession concerning the practice of religion [*Exercitium Religionis*] by several of the local Dutch and French citizens."[74] Frankfurt's mayors and council together replied that their restrictions on the religious practice of the Reformed emerged out of "highly sensible, well-considered considerations of several political reasons," and that the city had, on the whole, treated the Reformed "without prejudice," and even with "tolerance [*Tollerantz*]."[75] Ultimately, though, in order to "prevent all sorts of coming disturbances" and in order to respect "the familiar, public confession of the city church," the council would not change its stance toward the Reformed minority.[76] In the same letter of reply, Frankfurt's rulers described the potential for Reformed "seduction" of citizens away from the city's Lutheran churches, concluding that the city could not allow the Reformed the practice of their faith.[77] The council stood its ground, and the princes of the empire could not compel it to remove its ban on Reformed services. Soon the violence of the Thirty Years' War prevented the Reformed from continuing their weekly *Auslauf* to Offenbach.[78] Only decades later did they reestablish a stable practice of *Auslauf* when Count Philipp Moritz, the son of Philipp Ludwig, permitted them to build a small church on territory he controlled to Frankfurt's northwest.[79]

Throughout the late sixteenth century and into the early seventeenth, the princes of the empire were not able to compel Frankfurt to permit Reformed worship. The Frankfurt Council refused to reopen the Church of the White Ladies, it proscribed the practice of the Reformed Supper, and it required the Reformed to have their children baptized and their young people married by the Lutheran clergy in the city. But princes were not the only recipients of urgent letters from the Reformed. Very soon after the closure of their church, and parallel to the correspondence with nearby princes, the Reformed minority in Frankfurt wrote letters to other communities in exile regarding the permissibility of taking part in Lutheran ceremonies, specifically Lutheran baptism and marriage ceremonies.[80] The answers they received helped them improve their situation in Frankfurt.

Already in 1562, the Reformed wrote to brethren in exile about Lutheran ceremonies. That October, they received a promising letter from Calvin in Geneva. Calvin offered his approval for their participation in the civic baptism ceremonies of Frankfurt.[81] Calvin's letter is remarkable considering his uncompromising denunciation of Protestants who attended Catholic ceremonies, people he disparagingly called Nicodemites.[82] Calvin saw the situation of the Reformed very differently. Unlike Nicodemites, the Reformed in Frankfurt faced a subtle conundrum. Calvin could appreciate both sides of the debate over whether to leave the city or accept Lutheran baptism and marriage: "Part of you believes that, notwithstanding the closing of the temple, you must nevertheless remain here. . . . [O]thers maintain, on the contrary, that it is wrong to do so, that with very great indignity and opprobrium the truth is being oppressed, as though it is sent into exile."[83] Both responses were acceptable, according to Calvin. It was permissible for the Reformed to either abandon Frankfurt or participate in Lutheran baptism and marriage ceremonies: "For the church to keep standing, we should not consider it illegal for private persons to change places, all the more should it be allowed for those who are deprived of their exercise of piety to move elsewhere. . . . On the other hand, to repute and defame as traitors to the truth those who have been prevented and detained by the domestic necessity of their affairs, unable to go to another place, that would be inhuman."[84] Calvin insisted only on abstention from the Lutheran Supper: "It is another thing with the Holy Supper, which no one can receive from their [the Lutherans'] hand."[85]

Calvin's approval of Lutheran baptism contradicted earlier advice to English refugees in Frankfurt from the Italian reformer Peter Martyr Vermigli. Vermigli recommended abstention from Lutheran ceremonies.[86] He explained his reasoning clearly: "Firstly, we teach that baptism is a sealing of the faith of the person who is being baptized, or if this person is a child and therefore does not yet have the faith, then we understand it as a promise and a commitment upon the faith of the one who brings the child to baptism. Now because our faith and the faith of the Lutherans is not the same in all parts, we cannot permit those who are ours to be sealed by these people."[87] To soften the psychological impact of his position on the Reformed in Frankfurt, Vermigli had reassured them, "Your children's salvation is not endangered, if they die without baptism."[88]

In the years after 1562, the Reformed mostly accepted Calvin's position and rejected Vermigli's. They acquiesced to Lutheran civic control over baptisms and marriages. In this respect, they responded to Lutheran demands similarly to Reformed individuals in other Lutheran cities.[89] Confessional minorities across the empire began to distinguish between those Christian rituals which served a civic function—what one historian of Münster recently titled "rites of passage"—and those pertaining to the salvation of the soul—"rites of community."[90] Baptism and marriage fell squarely in the category of civic rituals; they "filled the gap that confessional differences had opened up."[91] The Eucharist, on the other hand, remained a sacred rite of religious communion for the Reformed in Frankfurt. The Lord's Supper needed to be defended against all human corruption, including the encroachments of the Lutheran clergy. On this matter, the Reformed refugees in Frankfurt again agreed with Reformed communities across Europe.[92]

Still, the Reformed were not confident in their decision to accept Lutheran baptism and marriage ceremonies. Community members disagreed, and the elders continued for decades to reassure themselves of their decision by eliciting statements of approval from nearby sister communities of refugees. The Frankfurt Reformed maintained a close bond with the community in Frankenthal founded by Datheen after the Frankfurt Council locked the Church of the White Ladies. In addition to the Frankenthal community, the Palatinate housed several other Reformed refugee communities including ones in Heidelberg, Lambrecht, and Schönau, which sent representatives to a gathering of Reformed congregations in 1571 in Emden. The Synod of Emden, as this meeting was called, proposed a new system for organizing groups of Reformed churces, with each group called a classis.[93] Frankfurt's Reformed congregations became part of the Palatine classis of refugee congregations.[94] Over the coming years, five other congregations joined the Palatine classis, those in Annweiler, Hanau, Offenbach, Otterberg, and Wetzlar.[95]

The Palatine classis gathered for its first independent meeting in 1578 in Frankenthal. Over the subsequent thirty years, the classis met nineteen times in various locations, according to the French Reformed records in Frankfurt, and the city on the Main played host in 1585, 1588, 1592, and 1599.[96] Frankfurt's Reformed sent representatives with letters detailing the most pressing issues confronting them, and Lutheran baptism remained an issue of debate at all meetings.[97] Frankfurt's Reformed probably believed nearby, smaller congregations would be willing to sanction accommodation with the city's Lutherans. After all, these sister communities benefited greatly from having an established Reformed community in the city on the Main, a position which dominated the trade routes in the area. Frankfurt served as the point of entry and temporary refuge for many Protestants fleeing the Low Countries or France for congregations in the Palatine classis. Frankfurt's Reformed also organized Reformed services during the city's important trade fairs that drew brethren from the nearby communities to Frankfurt twice a year to sell wares on an international market. The hopes of the Reformed in Frankfurt were not in vain; the Palatine congregations proved amenable to the idea of Lutheran baptism. The classis's meeting in 1586 in Heidelberg concluded that baptism by a Lutheran minister was acceptable, justifying its decision via Augustine's ancient argument against the Donatists: "There is only one catholic Church, one body of Christ, one house of the Lord. . . . [O]ur churches and the Lutherans' are true and essential parts of this Church, this body this home."[98] Unfortunately for the Reformed, the city's Lutheran clergy did not share this broad-minded ecclesiological attitude and despite the Reformed giving their children to be baptized by the city clergy, the Lutheran ministers continued to campaign for a complete ban on Reformed services—even those in private.

Baptism was not the only issue of cross-confessional contact troubling the Reformed of Frankfurt. According to the Dutch Reformed Consistory, in 1577 the elder Matthijs Schats asked "whether it was permitted at the burial of the Germans to process behind the cross."[99] A bond still existed between the Reformed refugees and certain Lutheran families like the Glauburgs, and some of the Reformed wanted to join the burial services of Lutherans. The Dutch consistory rejected the idea entirely, insisting that funeral processions were idolatry meant for "papists."[100] The Dutch elders stressed that one could not take part in such idolatry "without a burden of conscience."[101] Lutherans should likewise not attend Reformed burials, the Dutch consistory explained, because Lutherans "refuse to go to our burials if the cross is not brought forth."[102] By excluding burial from the category of civic rituals that all local Christians could join, the Dutch Reformed in Frankfurt distinguished themselves from Christians in other parts of the empire who accepted burials as civic rites of passage.[103] Still, the Reformed questioned their position on burials sufficiently to send delegates to a meeting of the congregations of the Palatine classis in 1578, asking again about partaking in Lutheran ceremonies. The approbation of fellow Reformed Christians mattered immensely, though even this would not satisfy certain individuals. In 1593, the Dutch preacher Gomarus so detested Lutheran marriage that he left the city to marry his wife, thus provoking a serious backlash against the community.[104]

While letters to nearby princes did not gain further privileges for the Reformed in Frankfurt, outreach to other Reformed congregations in exile helped the French and Dutch Reformed navigate life in Frankfurt. Certain accommodations would have to made with the city's Lutheran church, and the sister congregations helped establish what these accommodations would be.

## The Reformed Consistory and the Keeping of Good Order

In addition to organizing worship spaces and coordinating with nearby supporters, the Reformed consistories of Frankfurt served as agents of discipline. Discipline, to the Reformed, meant more than simply controlling the behavior of congregants—though it absolutely included this—it entailed the ordering of all aspects of life within the congregation.[105] When the French Reformed consistory stated in 1571 that it aimed "to keep good order among the foreigners," it included coordinating worship and caring for the poor within this assignment.[106] Frankfurt's rulers had made it very clear in 1554 that the city would not be responsible for the poor of the refugee community. Good order also meant preventing and resolving internal conflicts. Intramural harmony mattered greatly as the Reformed could not make use of the city's judicial systems without exposing their conflicts to the gaze of the council. The city's courts were controlled by judges drawn from the upper bench of the council, and the only other judicial recourse was a mayoral audience, meant for minor civil matters.[107] Unable to rely on the institutions of the city, the Reformed relied on the consistory to manage charity and arbitrate conflict.

Since the founding of the Reformed community in Frankfurt, care for the poor and communal discipline had been the chief tasks of the community's consistory. In 1554, Poullain had explained to the council that it should permit his refugee flock to establish "an earnest church discipline" so that they could care for their own poor and ensure that "nothing unorderly or harmful" occurred within the community.[108] Over the next fifty years, the Reformed consistory created new structures and procedures for caring for the poor. When the Dutch-speakers broke from the broader community from the Low Countries in 1571 and formed their own consistory, the Dutch preacher Matte explained that this new independence did not represent a true break with the French-speakers but only a logical step needed for the distribution of alms: "our church is only separated insofar as it concerns poor and alms; we did not wish to be one with them [the French-speakers] in this matter. For what is more efficient than since we support our poor . . . that we therefore receive our own alms."[109] The Dutch simply wanted to administer charity to their fellow Dutch, in addition to organizing their own church space. After all, the Dutch refugees had fled from different areas than the French and had arrived in Frankfurt at different times. Established refugees like Matte regularly took newly arrived Dutch people into their homes. Now a new consistory would coordinate aid to Dutch Reformed refugees in Frankfurt.

The French Reformed Consistory issued a new Deacon's Ordinance in 1585 in order to better coordinate their community's charity by establishing a communal "deacon's oven" to provide food for those members of the congregation who were deserving, modest, and well-behaved.[110] The Deacon's Ordinance also described the proper comportment of those visiting the oven, excluding anyone who "does not invoke the name of God before and after."[111] Charity was intrinsically tied to good behavior. The same was the case in the Dutch Reformed congregation. All recipients of alms had to be interrogated, often twice. For example, the Dutch consistory recorded: "On December 10 [1570], two widowed women, who sought help from the deacons, were interrogated in the Consistory. Following this examination, it was resolved to help them."[112] Such interrogations embodied the connection between alms and discipline. The minutes of the Dutch consistory specified that only the upright could expect alms or be admitted to the community's religious services. Newcomers would have to provide evidence of good behavior: "Nobody who came here from out of town should be admitted to the gathering or, if he desires alms, be given any if he does not provide secure attestation from the community he most recently left. Attention must also be paid to the author of such letters of attestation and their date."[113] Matte believed that Dutch leaders could do a better job of double-checking references from predominantly Dutch-speaking towns than the French could. This effort to establish and control alms distribution to other Dutch-speakers helped inspire the creation of an independent consistory in the first place. Charity and discipline were bound together. Charity demanded a documented history of good behavior.

Consistorial discipline also entailed care for the sick and dying, two tasks which likewise required the policing of bad behavior. One early crisis within the Dutch congregation exemplified the connection between caring for the ill and admonishing bad behavior. In the fall of 1571, the plague entered Frankfurt, and Hans Gestens—a deacon and rich merchant from Antwerp whose correspondence with Datheen in Heidelberg had won Matte the job as minister—contracted the illness. Gestens had hosted the community's first Sunday-afternoon sermon in his own house, and he had remained a fixture in the community. Now terrified that he would die of plague, Gestens sent for Matte, his minister and friend. Matte dutifully went to Gestens, but when asked to return a second time, he refused.[114] Evidently, the consistory felt Matte's health was too important to risk and recorded, "that because the deacons fear damage to the church, and because several brethren had received reproach that our servant [Matte], who was alone, had been allowed to visit the plague-sick, they resolved, that he should not go thence anymore."[115] (As secretary of the consistory, Matte described this general concern for his well-being himself.) Gestens was enraged. He considered it the minister's duty to care for the dying. He called Matte "a mere hireling, because he runs when he sees the wolf coming."[116] Matte should have tended to plague-sick members of the congregation, according to Gestens. He accused Matte of cowardice and dereliction of his ministerial duties.

Eventually, Gestens recovered from the plague, but the damage was done—the friendship between minister and deacon was at an end, and a furious debate ensued among the Dutch Reformed about the role of the minister in caregiving. The consistory admonished Gestens to end his "great unseemliness" and reconcile with Matte.[117] The conflict between minister and deacon was decidedly unseemly, and the Dutch consistory did not want it to reach the ears of outsiders like the city authorities. The elders decided that the matter "should be left in peace, until Hans is healthy."[118] A few weeks later, Gestens had fully convalesced, but it still took several meetings with the consistory before Gestens "confessed to having been badly informed [about Matte]."[119] The consistory ultimately reconciled the two men on 14 November 1571, and Matte recorded in the minutes: "Together raising their hands as a sign of friendship, they departed."[120]

Caring for the sick and combating unseemliness were part of the same overall project for the Dutch and the French Reformed congregations in Frankfurt. Both tasks were expressions of Christian piety, and both were essential for survival in Frankfurt. The plague might kill individual congregants, but interpersonal controversies could destroy communal harmony and possibly elicit the attention of Frankfurt's authorities. The French Reformed consistory likewise recorded a concerted effort to curtail sinful behavior by admonishing wrongdoers. Admonishments could be directed at a single individual—like one man who Minister Banos "discovered to have been committing salaciousness for two years that was known to his wife and his father"—or at an entire group—like one group that reportedly "danced at a wedding" taking place in a small town nearby.[121] Revelry outside of the city was especially prone to catch the notice of the city's authorities, who monitored the gates.

Overall, the aim of such disciplinary efforts by the Reformed consistories was to ensure that only the repentant could attend the community's services and receive the community's alms. Starting in December 1571, the Dutch congregation separated the office of elder from deacon entirely and elected four deacons to care for the poor and help organize communal prayers. Deacons were tasked with distributing alms to those community members who were not in conflict with other members. Also entitled to aid was any newcomer who received a "recommendation" from a member.[122] Communal harmony mattered.

Troublemakers could also be barred from attending the Supper, which was celebrated twice a year. The story of one congregant in particular, a woman name Mariken Houtcliever, reveals the nature and course of consistorial discipline among the Reformed in Frankfurt. While Mariken appears on the first membership list of the Dutch Reformed Congregation in Frankfurt, she was not originally from the Low Countries. She came from Aachen and probably spoke the Low German of her native city. Due to its proximity to the southern Low Countries, Aachen proved to be a very popular initial destination for Protestants fleeing the Duke of Alba's persecution in Flanders and Brabant. Aachen became a point of entry in the German lands, and Aacheners would have encountered displaced newcomers frequently.[123] Mariken certainly did. Born Mariken Steertmans, she met the refugee Nicholas Houtcliever from Brussels sometime after 1567. The two decided to leave Aachen together and travel upriver to Frankfurt. Matte recorded both the names Mariken and Nicholas on his list of initial members, though they are listed separately, with separate last names.[124] Soon after the congregation's foundation, the couple married and became Nicholas and Mariken Houtcliever. After May 1571, the consistory referred to Mariken as either Mariken Houtcliever or Mariken Steertmans Houtcliever.

We cannot be sure of Mariken's motives for marrying Nicholas or leaving Aachen. Perhaps she married Nicholas for support, as she already had a young child who was not Nicholas's. Perhaps she simply fell in love with this refugee from Flanders and joined his congregation of displaced Christians. Nicholas, for his part, seems to have happily taken in and supported both mother and child. No records indicate any internal Houtcliever family conflicts. Conflicts between the Houtclievers and the leaders of their congregation, on the other hand, fill the consistory minutes. Throughout the 1570s, Mariken Houtcliever repeatedly found herself in front of the Dutch Reformed Consistory, which catalogued her transgressions in detail.

Mariken Houtcliever first ran afoul of her congregation's consistory in the fall of 1571. A woman named Magdalena died in the Houtcliever house on 7 October 1571, and Mariken quickly seized the woman's possessions. This seizure caused consternation within the congregation because the rightful ownership of the items was in dispute. When approached by the elders about the issue, Houtcliever declared that she wanted nothing to do with any of the elders. Minister Matte recorded Houtcliever's defiance in the consistory minutes: "She answered the brothers that she has nothing to do with them."[125]

Perhaps due to her outburst, Houtcliever did not receive alms from the consistory, even though she seems to have needed financial support. One of Houtcliever's friends, a baker from 's-Hertogenbosch named Dierick Franss, berated the elders on her behalf on 30 May 1571. Matte recorded the following in the minutes: "It is reported about Dierick the baker that he berated the deacons on account of Mariken Houtcliever and he said much evil about them, because nobody took care of her and she was allowed to go needy."[126] Later that year, a crisis in her life would further distance her from the elders of the Dutch community. When the plague ravaged Frankfurt in the winter of 1571–72, Houtcliever's youngest child succumbed to the disease.[127] Houtcliever accused the members of the consistory of abandoning their pastoral duties by neglecting to care for the sick and dying, including her child. She joined Gestens in denouncing the congregation's leadership.

Relations between Houtcliever and the consistory worsened, and the consistory met again on 27 January 1572 to decide what should be done about her refusal to cooperate. In the past several months, she had rebuffed inquiries from the deacons about the items Magdalena left behind and, more seriously, scoffed when one of the community's three elders admonished her for behaving badly. She did not attend the weekly sermon. Moreover, it seemed that she had dragged her husband, Nicholas, into her scheme to prey on the dead. Matte described how "it was also reported about her and Nicholas . . . that they do not treat the plague-sick who they have in their care well, and that they are all too quick to count on their deaths and bury them."[128] The consistory decided to proceed gingerly and pursue further action only if the couple continued behaving badly.

This decision by the Dutch leaders to give the Houtclievers another chance can be viewed as a gentle expression of pastoral concern.[129] Still, it should be remembered that the consistory had few other options. The consistory consisted of just five men, and their position in Frankfurt did not provide for civic enforcement of their decrees. Mariken Houtcliever knew this, and she taunted the elders by sarcastically suggesting that they should try to proceed legally against her, to which the elders replied that "they knew much about her and should proceed legally against her."[130] But the consistory never did. Houtcliever knew the elders were reluctant to involve Frankfurt's civic authorities. The consistory could do little about Houtcliever beyond the steps outlined by Jesus in Matthew 18: admonish the sinner, admonish her in the company of others, announce her transgressions to the entire community, and ultimately excommunicate her. Houtcliever had already been admonished, and the consistory deferred further steps until her behavior worsened.

Just one month later, Mariken and Nicholas Houtcliever again angered her Dutch Reformed Consistory. On 17 February 1572, the elders learned that two young people, Balthasar Joppen and a girl named Anna, had "gotten into disrepute with each other."[131] Consistory minutes reveal that this disrepute involved drinking and sleeping together, both of which took place in the Houtcliever house, where the young Anna lived. Witnesses summoned by the consistory described the Houtcliever residence as a den of iniquity, where gossip and profanity reigned and where Joppen had attained a reputation as a lothario. It is unclear whether the Houtclievers ran an inn, a boardinghouse, or whether they simply took in fellow refugees who had just arrived in town—as many households did—but the Houtcliever residence gained an unsavory reputation, which it maintained for years.

Despite their reputation as recidivists, the Houtclievers remained members of the congregation. On 4 May 1572, when the Dutch Reformed Congregation gathered for the first time to celebrate the Supper, the Houtclievers arrived but were turned away for their unwillingness to accept the consistory's admonitions regarding the Balthasar Joppen case.[132] Suddenly, the consistory's admonitions gained force. Before the next Supper in August, Nicholas dutifully appeared and confessed before the consistory, expressing remorse for his disobedience and his unseemly words to the elders.[133] Nicholas and Mariken went to the next Supper, but this time Mariken was turned away becaue she had still not appeared before the consistory. Exclusion from the Lord's Supper seems to have worked well as a disciplinary tool. On 11 January 1573, the consistory minutes describe for the first time a contrite Mariken, reconciling with the elders and apologizing to community members whom she had offended.[134]

Over the next year, Mariken Houtcliever began to participate intermittently in the Dutch religious services. She also fell afoul of the consistory's standards much less frequently, though she still did. On 17 January 1574, two elders admonished Houtcliever again for "frivolously taking unsavory characters into her home."[135] It was Houtcliever's desire to attend the Dutch Reformed Supper that inspired her to change her ways, at least for a spell. A pattern developed whereby Houtcliever would run afoul of the consistory, refuse to comply with its admonitions, consequently lose access to the Supper, and after missing a Supper, eventually submit to admonishment before being admitted to the following celebration. The Supper was generally held twice a year, so one can imagine Houtcliever being out of favor with the elders for half the year and reconciled to them the other half. Throughout the 1570s, Houtcliever returned to the consistory repeatedly to confess, receive her admonition, and thereby gain access to the Lord's Supper. Whether she spoke in earnest or simply recited a script she knew would gain her admission, Houtcliever clearly wanted to attend the Reformed Supper. Houtcliever's frequent appearances before the consistory can be viewed as evidence of either disciplinary success or failure. Unambiguous, though, was her desire to attend the Supper.

Judging by the number of admonitions and summons necessary to make Houtcliever confess before the consistory, her obstinacy lessened over time. She gradually came to accept the consistory's admonitions the first time and without complaints. In December 1576, her reputation had improved to the point that the consistory asked her to help convince Nicholas to come to the sermon, which he had stopped attending out of anger over an accusation of theft. She dutifully impressed upon her husband the importance of the sermon.[136] Furthermore, in the summer of 1577, when the consistory chastised the Houtcliever pair for hosting "whoring" in their house, the couple confessed on the spot, abandoning their earlier tactic of refusing to appear.[137] A year later, the consistory made arrangements for Houtcliever to receive aid from the deacons, generosity reserved for members of the community of impeccable standing.[138] Ultimately, Houtcliever's desire to attend the Supper overcame her resentment of the leaders of the Dutch community. She died reconciled to the congregation in the summer of 1579.[139]

Far from an aberrant case, Houtcliever's story of frequent encounters with the Dutch Reformed Consistory parallels the stories of many fellow congregants. Even elders had to answer for their bad behavior before the consistory. In April and May 1577, for example, the Dutch Reformed Consistory admonished Elder Schats for hitting his servant girl Sibylla. Although the consistory concluded that she deserved to be hit for her verbal disrespect, Schats's force had been excessive. The consistory ordered him to apologize before the entire congregation. He was indignant but ultimately complied when his fellow elders explained that failing to apologize would mean he would have to "stay away from the next Supper."[140]

The Dutch Reformed Consistory was particularly concerned about cases of conflict between community members. If a misbehaving congregant had not hurt or offended anyone, the consistory usually determined that "the matter will be left alone."[141] A major case of intramural conflict emerged in February 1573, when several congregants approached the consistory to complain about the conduct of Pieter Bisschop, one of the original elders of the community who had been reelected in November 1572. In February 1573, Bisschop "caused great offense with an Italian who was here [in Frankfurt] on account of the Duke of Alba, in order to pay the cavalry."[142] Frankfurt and other Rhineland cities were entrepôts for German and Swiss mercenaries, and the Spanish duke had apparently sent a representative to recruit.[143] Bisschop "had served him [the Italian representative of Alba], received the money, distributed it, and for the same Italian (who was arrested here) traveled to Antwerp in order to convey a letter."[144] Another member of the congregation, Fransoijs van Lare, had also "caused great offense on account of his service for an Italian who paid for cavalry for the Duke of Alba."[145]

The help provided to Alba's emissary provoked a scandal among the Dutch Reformed refugees in Frankfurt, and understandably so. The duke remained the most feared and hated man among the Reformed refugees in Frankfurt; he had executed many of their friends and family members. In 1573, the fury of Duke Alba and his son Don Fadrique had reached its climax, with their troops pillaging Dutch cities and massacring citizens.[146] At the time that Alba's representative visited Frankfurt, his troops were besieging the starving city of Haarlem.[147] Alba's massacres became so notorious that they provoked outrage even among Spanish leaders.[148] The Dutch in Frankfurt were aware of these events and refused to attend services attended by Bisschop or Van Lare. Bisschop's fellow elders resolved that he and Van Lare should be "unanimously admonished."[149] Bisschop confessed and submitted to the consistory, but Van Lare lashed out in indignation: "He accused the brothers of the consistory of wrecking his reputation and name, indeed they portrayed him as so evil, that he can hardly dare to step foot out of the city for he must fear being killed."[150] Van Lare evidently left Frankfurt. The Dutch consistory minutes only mention him again when he visited the city's trade fairs.

A less serious instance of intramural discord from 1577 further demonstrates the consistory's quest for congregational peace and amity. That

August, Fransois du Boijs approached the consistory to report that his loom, which he had loaned to Abraham Wateau and his wife, was returned with pieces missing.[151] The consistory summoned all parties involved and after several meetings decided that Wateau had indeed kept pieces of the loom, including some of its weights.[152] He was censured and made to reimburse Du Boijs; only afterward was he admitted to the Supper.

On the surface, the story of the Dutch Reformed in Frankfurt supports the idea that Protestants morphed religious celebrations into moments of instruction and admonition—access to the Lord's Supper provided leverage to promote Christian discipline.[153] The Supper was indeed a service that people like Mariken Houtcliever and Abraham Wateau wanted to attend, and they could only do so after confessing before the consistory. Yet it is unclear that the Dutch Reformed elders intended to use the Supper as a disciplinary tool. Houtcliever's obvious desire to attend the Supper allowed the consistory to demand something of her behavior, but the consistory had not arranged the first celebration of the Lord's Supper with an eye to asserting Christian discipline. On the contrary, congregants had insisted upon the first celebration of the Supper on 31 August 1572. Consistory minutes from the weeks before discuss frustration among the sixty-one members of the Dutch community about the fact that the Supper had not yet been held: "the brothers hear resentful comments passing among the people, because the Lord's Supper is not as well distributed among us as among the Walloons, they therefore rushed to achieve this."[154] While the Dutch consistory controlled the organization and admission to the Supper, the body did so in direct response to the demands or complaints of congregants. Individual congregants prized the Supper and put aside quarrels in order to attend. Elders and congregants alike sought to keep the Supper free from conflict and immorality.[155]

## The Consistory and Reformed Survival in Exile

When the nineteenth-century French Reformed minister Charles Schröder looked back on his community's fraught struggle to survive in sixteenth-century Frankfurt, he credited the community's "Presbyterian organization" for its endurance.[156] By Presbyterian organization, Schröder meant the community's semi-democratic structures of governance from local consistory to regional classis to broader synod.[157] Schröder recognized the consistory as the essential element preserving

Reformed harmony locally and maintaining Reformed connections with allies abroad. Schröder was right—the Reformed faith survived in an increasingly hostile Frankfurt thanks to its consistory. This was true of the French Reformed Congregation and the Dutch Reformed Congregation, both of which survived into the twentieth century (though the Dutch Reformed Congregation had by then embraced the German language and changed its name to German Reformed).

Reformed consistories in Frankfurt located and secured worship space, coordinated charity, corresponded with nearby sister communities in exile, and kept good order within the community by arbitrating conflict. Consistories responded to the desires and complaints of congregants. For example, when the French Reformed consistory was unsure whether to approve of Lutheran baptism in July 1572, it surveyed parishioners "to hear from them their desire on the matter of baptism."[158] The French ultimately accepted Lutheran civic control over baptisms and marriages as their Dutch brethren also did. In all these respects, the Frankfurt consistories mirrored their counterparts in other cities where Reformed religious practices were severely restricted, including Antwerp, Emden, and Wesel.[159] The Frankfurt consistories also shared much with the consistory of Geneva. The French and Dutch elders did not merely police the morals of the refugees in Frankfurt.[160] And admonitions were reserved for those congregants actively harming or offending other community members.

The Reformed refugees in Frankfurt cherished their consistories. After the closure of the Church of the White Ladies, the Reformed feared that the Frankfurt Council might target these institutions. The French Reformed wrote to the council explaining how the French consistory performed an essential duty to the city: it restrained "insolence, lest some kind of uproar be able to arise from this, which would harm the Republic."[161] To further appease the council, the Reformed changed the title of elder to the humbler title of assistant [adjoint].[162] These assistants still oversaw discipline. When the Dutch Reformed formed their own consistory in 1570, they, too, altered the name of their elders, calling them deputies instead.[163] When one Dutch elder protested, Minister Matte explained, "We name them deputies because the name elder is suspect in this city."[164] The Reformed of Frankfurt were determined to preserve their consistories and, through them, sustain their religious lives in Frankfurt.

By the early seventeenth century, the Reformed in Frankfurt had settled into the role of an embattled religious minority. The two Reformed groups, French and the Dutch, relied on their consistories to maintain their religious communities and arbitrate intramural conflicts, important tasks considering that intramural quarrels had motivated the Frankfurt Council to ban Reformed ceremonies in the city. The Reformed did not want to rely on Frankfurt's judicial system. The consistories of Frankfurt also preserved their communities' connections to allies abroad by maintaining regular correspondence and by sending legates to nearby communities. The Dutch and French consistories held their communities together and provided structured religious education to guarantee that the Reformed tradition would be preserved without accretions from the Lutheranism of the city. The consistory as an institution made it possible for the Reformed refugee communities to maintain a vibrant religious community in a city hostile to their religious services.

# Conclusion

In 1944, the church of the White Ladies, the church that Valérand Poullain had won for his refugee congregation in Frankfurt, was destroyed when the British firebombed Frankfurt's inner city.[1] The remaining pieces of the church—which had been built for penitential noblewomen in the thirteenth century, divorced from Catholicism in 1542, and granted to the refugees from the Low Countries in 1554—were removed in 1953 after historians recorded the names and arrangements of the graves that lay within the structure's walls.[2] The Reformed community of Frankfurt survived, but its first church did not.

The Church of the White Ladies had served as a laboratory for a great Reformation experiment in welcoming and sheltering persecuted Protestants from abroad. Over the first fifty years of refugee accommodation, this novel venture altered Frankfurt's religious landscape. The newcomers forced the city to redefine the boundaries of the civic church, dividing the city's Protestant residents into Lutheran and Reformed camps. At the same time, exile in Frankfurt changed the refugees. They began to rethink and reimagine their religious communities. Guests and hosts alike were transformed by the experience of refugee accommodation in sixteenth-century Frankfurt. This book investigated five pivotal transformations resulting from Frankfurt's early modern experiment in refugee accommodation, transformations that impacted Frankfurt, the refugees it housed, and the Holy Roman Empire at large.

First, by admitting the initial group of twenty-four displaced families in 1554, Frankfurt's rulers inaugurated an era of refugee accommodation in the city, one that continues to this day. The first refugees to arrive, led by Minister Poullain, quickly advertised the generous terms of accommodation offered to them. Poullain wrote letters to other Protestants

Figure 7. The Church of the White Ladies (Weißfrauenkirche) in 1911, Gottfried Vömel. (Institut für Stadtgeschichte Frankfurt am Main, S7 Vö Nr. 418)

fleeing England and the Low Countries insisting that Frankfurt was the ideal setting in which to continue the reforming work begun in Lille, London, and other cities lost to Catholic rule. Over the next two years, hundreds more refugees arrived in Frankfurt, and ever more letters of advertisement were sent out from the city. Whittingham's community of Englishmen, who arrived a few months after Poullain's initial group, wrote to their fellow Englishmen in Emden, Strasbourg, Wesel, and Zurich, insisting that they had discovered an idyllic home-away-from-home, filled with supportive brethren: "Everie man helpethe us, no man is againste us."[3] More refugees arrived, including influential figures like John Knox and John a Lasco. Two years after admitting the first group of refugees, Frankfurt housed at least one thousand displaced individuals within its city walls, approximately 10 percent of the city's population.[4]

Figure 8. The Church of the White Ladies (Weißfrauenkirche) in 1953, Historisches Museum. (Institut für Stadtgeschichte Frankfurt am Main, S7C Nr. 1998-57130)

The initial affinity between the city's patricians and Poullain resulted in a flourishing refugee community in the city.

The popularity of Frankfurt as a destination resulted from the efforts of the refugees themselves, men like Poullain and women like Anne Hooper. Their tireless work sustained the vibrancy of refugee life in Frankfurt. It was they who attracted and integrated newcomers. The receptivity of Frankfurt's oligarchical council was not sufficient to bring about the massive influx of displaced individuals into the city. Refugees were drawn to Frankfurt by the established communities of displaced people already there. Established refugees worked to mitigate the horrors of religious persecution in the Low Countries and England by building and advertising a flourishing community in exile. As the Dutch Reformed consistory records reveal, established refugees regularly housed newcomers. Refugees cultivated new bonds with coreligionists they had never met, and in so doing they expanded and diversified the refugee community in the city.

In their effort to survive and thrive in exile, the refugees in Frankfurt competed and coordinated with nearby refugee communities. For example, in late 1554, the English refugees in Frankfurt exchanged letters with the English community in Zurich, and a debate commenced over which city should be the new center of English Protestantism in exile.[5] The English in Zurich refused to come to Frankfurt. Their leaders wrote to Frankfurt's Englishmen in October 1554, "ye will not interrupte oure studies, urge oure removinge, and bringe us thither, feelinge here alreadie the exceadinge goodnesse off god towardes us."[6] Letters from Frankfurt to Strasbourg's English community resulted in a fierce fight over which community's liturgical practices were correct.[7]

At the same time, nearby exile communities could offer consolation, counsel, and financial support. Frankfurt's Reformed consistories recognized this and sought to preserve their bonds to nearby coreligionists. In April 1572, the French Reformed in Frankfurt sent their minister, "accompanied by one of the deacons or deputies [i.e., elders]," to the Reformed congregation of Frankenthal in order to "protect the peace and union between the Churches."[8] In June of that year, they dispatched deacons and elders to Strasbourg to learn whether its refugee community had succeeded in securing access to a city church.[9]

Throughout this new era of displacement, refugees like those in Frankfurt forged their own narratives of exile. Through published accounts— like Whittingham's *Brieff Discours* and Datheen's *Kurtze und warhafftige Erzelung*—they explained why they had fled, how they had been mistreated, and who was to blame.[10] Refugees also endeavored to collect and preserve the most important documents concerning their exile, especially those documents concerning their privileges, or lack thereof. The French Reformed consistory minutes from 27 February 1572 declared that "The papers belonging to this church will be conserved and collected in one place, principally regarding the memories of the restoration of this church."[11] All documents were important, but especially those from the community's struggle to regain worship rights in Frankfurt. The texts the refugees in Frankfurt wrote and preserved construct a tendentious narrative of exile, but taken together with city council minutes and letters from the city ministers, a balanced story of Frankfurt's experience of accommodation emerges, a story in which the city authorities repressed refugee ecclesiastical independence in response to a stream of quarrels and controversies provoked by the newcomers.

Frankfurt's story became a common one in the aftermath of the Reformation. Just as Frankfurt was becoming a haven for displaced Protestants from the Low Countries, so too were dozens of other German cities.[12] Refugees became a nearly ubiquitous feature of sixteenth-century German urban life as persecution emerging from religious fractures led many to flee, while new religious affinities inspired many to welcome these displaced people.

Frankfurt's decision to welcome refugees resulted in a second major transformation. While pan-Protestant sympathies had inspired the city's rulers to welcome the "expelled Christians" who would "rather be chased from their lands than separated from confessing the true religion," the encounter between refugees and native Frankfurters ruptured Protestantism in the city and led to the construction of two distinct confessional camps, Lutheran natives and Reformed foreigners.[13] Frankfurters witnessed the religious ceremonies of the newcomers firsthand and determined that these people understood the Lord's Supper differently. By 1556, the city pastors, led by chief minister Hartmann Beyer, began to denounce the refugees for their "unusual ceremonies," ceremonies that revealed the refugees were "not one with us in their doctrine."[14] The focus of Beyer's concern was the Eucharist: "This disunion concerns, principally, the holy sacrament of the body and blood of our lord Christ."[15] Beyer and his fellow native ministers had obviously witnessed the refugees' services themselves. They complained that the newcomers "bring their young children with them into the church and hold them even though they are unclean, so that there are many bad smells."[16] By 1561, the refugee community complained to the Frankfurt Council that the city's clergy had turned the "common man against us, behaving towards us as though they understood us to be Calvinists, Zwinglians, fanatics, or Sacramentarians."[17] Encounter with refugee rituals had fractured Protestant fraternity and led to a new confessional distinction.

In response to the refugee services, Beyer and most of the other Frankfurt ministers tried to rewrite the history of the refugees' initial admission into Frankfurt as well as the history of the early Reformation in the city. The ministers insisted that they had not been privy to the city council's decision to admit the newcomers: "We, the teachers in our Christian community and teachers of the Gospel of Christ, were not spoken to about it."[18] The council rejected this claim, and its minutes— along with refugee letters and earlier writings by Beyer—prove that the city ministers had indeed approved of the council's decision to welcome displaced Christians from the Low Countries. Beyer and his supporters then claimed that the city's Reformation had been founded upon the Augsburg Confession, a document that the refugees flouted—according to Beyer—by rejecting the real presence of Jesus in the Eucharist. Yet as the refugees replied, and as the city's two oldest ministers corroborated, the city had introduced the Reformation based upon Martin Bucer's *Concordia Buceriana*, a document constructed as a careful compromise between Luther's literal understanding of Jesus's presence in the Supper and Zwingli's symbolic understanding. Beyer replaced his two dissenting colleagues and worked to bring Frankfurt's understanding of the Eucharist in line with the unaltered Augsburg Confession, an effort precipitated by Beyer's encounter with refugees. Frankfurt's civic church became Lutheran, not merely Protestant, and Beyer claimed it had always been thus.

Life in exile also prompted the refugees themselves to erect religious barriers. They began to perceive a religious chasm dividing them from Frankfurt's native Protestants. Lasco, the Polish refugee and first superintendent of the Reformed in Frankfurt, became convinced that the German Christians in Frankfurt and similar cities like Bremen and Hamburg were actually "Luthero-Papists," meaning they were still practicing elements of Catholic idolatry.[19] Lasco's disdain for Lutherans likely resulted from his community's maltreatment by north German cities, a maltreatment that occurred as his community fled from England's Queen Mary.

The English refugees in Frankfurt began to erect religious barriers among themselves, as the French minister Richard Vauville observed firsthand. In April 1555, Vauville wrote to Calvin to describe "the falling apart of the English [community] on account of ceremonies."[20] Should the English liturgy include candles and vestments as prescribed by Archbishop Cranmer's Book of Common Prayer? Different English refugees answered this question differently, and when forced to live together in the same foreign city, English refugees found that friction over liturgical practices morphed into a deep fissure that marred the face of English

Protestantism over the next century.[21] In short, displacement led to new boundaries among Protestants.

A third major transformation resulting from refugee accommodation was a political shift in who controlled Frankfurt's churches. During the first seven years of accommodation (1554–61), Frankfurt's native ministers struggled in vain to rid the city's churches of refugee services. The council controlled the churches—except those reclaimed for Catholicism after the Schmalkaldic War—and patricians like the Glauburgs controlled the council. These men supported the refugee community and refused to curtail refugee access to the Church of the White Ladies.[22] But by 1561, it had become difficult for the patricians to protect refugee access to any city church. A series of fierce quarrels erupted within the Reformed communities of Frankfurt—both the congregation from the Low Countries and the short-lived English one—and these quarrels erupted onto the imperial stage, embarrassing Frankfurt and potentially endangering its relationship with the emperor, whom the refugee minister Knox labeled, "no lesse enemy unto Christe then ever was Nero."[23]

The refugees spent their first seven years in Frankfurt in a nearly constant state of intramural discord. The democratic structures of the Reformed communities—in which all men voted for the elders and ministers—combined with the rapid influx of new members escalated disagreements into partisan rifts as newly arrived refugees disagreed with established groups over fundamental issues like ecclesiastical structures, liturgical practices, and leadership. Frankfurt's patrician rulers feared religious and political upheaval. When the refugee congregations became sources of both, the patricians began to agree with the city's Lutheran ministers: the ecclesiastical independence of the Reformed refugees led to conflict. The patricians ultimately acceded to the demands of the city ministers. Frankfurt's churches were shut to Reformed services, and the Lutheran ministers were given authority over the Reformed community's baptisms and marriages. Frankfurt's ministers replaced the council as the ultimate authority over the city's Protestant churches.

A fourth major transformation took place in and around Frankfurt following the city's ban on Reformed services. Reformed individuals began to depart the city on the Main, an exodus that was part of a broader geographic shift in refugee accommodation across the empire. In the early and mid-sixteenth century, imperial and free cities—places like Aachen, Frankfurt, and Strasbourg—had been the most popular German destinations for Protestant refugees from England, France, and especially the Low Countries.[24] The initial choice of imperial cities seems natural considering that these cities were large metropolitan centers with populations that had embraced the Reformation, much like the cities of the Low Countries. Unlike the cities of the Low Countries, imperial cities were self-governing political entities represented at imperial diets and thus able to sustain Protestant reforms. Frankfurt's patricians were able to shield Protestant refugees from the religious policies of the Catholic emperor. Ironically, though, the very presence of refugees in imperial cities like Frankfurt disintegrated the Protestant fraternity responsible for their welcome in the first place.[25] And while hundreds more refugees arrived in Frankfurt and other imperial cities after the fall of Antwerp in 1585, the territories of German princes began to attract many of the refugees already in the city.[26] By the close of the century, imperial territories like the Palatinate had well-established refugee towns, towns which grew rapidly in the early seventeenth century. The trend toward princely accommodation continued over the next century.

German princes were willing to offer what Reformed refugees eagerly sought: formal legal accommodation in the form of refugee treaties.[27] The emergence of the refugee treaty as a common legal phenomenon in the sixteenth and seventeenth centuries reveals how early modern refugees yearned to be citizens and Reformed Christians at the same time. They sought the same legal protection for their faith as modern people displaced for their religious beliefs, though they certainly did not champion toleration for all—indeed, they sought to repress Catholicism, which they considered an invention of the Antichrist. For displaced people like Datheen and his followers, mere coexistence did not satisfy. They wanted legal sanction for their faith, which territorial rulers like the Count of Hanau-Münzenberg furnished.

The fifth and final transformation studied here involves the repurposing and strengthening of the Reformed community's central religious institution, the consistory. Comprised of elders and ministers, the consistory proved essential for the preservation of Reformed religious life after Frankfurt's closure of the Reformed church in 1561 and the city's total ban on Reformed worship in 1596. Parishioners trusted their consistory to locate and secure space for their many religious services, including Sunday-morning sermons, Sunday-afternoon sermons, and Wednesday-afternoon sermons. Securing worship space proved increasingly difficult as more and more French and Dutch refugees arrived in Frankfurt seeking to participate fully in the spiritual life denied them in their homelands. Consistory minutes describe a frantic effort to find worship space. Convinced that the French-speakers prioritized their own services to an unfair degree, the Dutch-speakers formed their own independent consistory in late 1570, and the new consistory's minutes likewise record an endless search for space. The Dutch consistory deputized one of the community's deacons to carry benches from service to service. The French were also pressed for space, and the French elders recommended "inspecting the barn that is facing the house of the church" to see if it would hold the French congregation.[28] Frankfurt's council fought these efforts by the Reformed to hold services in private spaces. In 1596, the city council terminated the lease on a house where the Reformed were gathering to worship.[29]

The consistory assumed the task of conflict arbitration among the Reformed in Frankfurt, an especially important task considering that the city's own justice system revolved around the patrician judges who comprised the upper bench of the council, men who were no longer convinced the Reformed should even remain in the city. The Reformed realized it was dangerous to allow any intramural conflicts to reach the ears of Frankfurt's authorities since it had been incessant, loud conflicts within the refugee community that had impelled the council to restrict Reformed worship in the first place. When the Dutch founded their own consistory, they explained to their French brethren that they did so in order to better coordinate charity and solve internal feuds within their language community.

The refugees entering Frankfurt, like the hundreds of thousands of other Reformation refugees crossing central Europe, transformed the society they entered.[30] Their arrival in Frankfurt inaugurated a new era in which Frankfurt began to express and define a moral obligation to certain outsiders. At first, this category of Christians deserving protection included any Protestants—besides Anabaptists—fleeing Catholic authorities. Soon, only those refugees who accepted the Augsburg Confession—specifically the unaltered version of 1530, which the city's clergy erroneously claimed to be the foundation of the Reformation in Frankfurt—could expect formal accommodation. The arrival of Poullain and other refugees had recast the Reformation in Frankfurt into a confessional mold, a mold that made it difficult for them to remain in Frankfurt. Refugees also destabilized the power structures in Frankfurt, motivating the city's ministers to wrest more authority over the city churches away from the ruling council.

At the same time, the experience of displacement changed the refugees themselves. Native hostility impelled the refugees to reshape their religious institutions in lasting ways. The consistory became an essential mechanism for organizing charity, finding worship spaces, and arbitrating the community's conflicts. By allowing the Reformed to mediate conflicts and control their communities locally, consistories equipped the Reformed to survive in exile. The experience of refugee accommodation transformed the religion of the refugees.

Sixteenth-century religious refugees, like their twenty-first-century counterparts, were not merely victims of sweeping religious changes taking place around them, although they did suffer tremendously. They were leaders of religious change. They built new churches in new places, churches that continue to this day. They also inspired religious change in the communities they entered. As the case of Frankfurt reveals, refugees helped determine the fate of the Reformation.

# Epilogue

❧

O VER THE COURSE of the seventeenth and eighteenth centuries, the Reformed community in Frankfurt assumed a permanent second-class position within the city's social order. When Frankfurt's most famous son, Johann Wolfgang von Goethe (1749–1832), visited his writing tutor, Heinrich Hüsgen, he noted that Hüsgen's highly educated and capable father was "of the Reformed religion, and therefore incapable of public office."[1] By Goethe's time, the city's restrictions on Reformed worship—which had originally targeted refugees in the sixteenth century—had crystalized into political inequality based on religious affiliation. Any resident of Frankfurt who refused to take part in the city's officially sanctioned religious services was excluded from the central institutions of the city, including the guilds, the citizenry, and the council.[2] Momentous episodes in Frankfurt's history therefore affected the city's Lutheran majority and Reformed minority very differently. Yet as Goethe's observation also makes clear, Reformed individuals like Hüsgen built successful lives for themselves and freely interacted with the Lutheran majority in the city.

Reformed men and women faced repeated waves of local hostility, including occasional calls for expulsion. For example, in the years 1612–14, an urban revolt led by a gingerbread baker named Vincenz Fettmilch reshaped the city's political landscape. Fettmilch and his supporters denounced unchecked patrician control over the city and demanded constitutional reforms that would bring political power out from within the two patrician clubhouses that dominated city government.[3] Initially, wealthy Reformed merchants supported the effort to restructure the city's government, perhaps hoping their wealth would earn them say in Frankfurt's political decisions. Soon though, it became clear that

Fettmilch and his closest confederates also aimed to banish denizens, noncitizens like many Reformed, whose presence in Frankfurt Fettmilch considered an expression of capricious patrician power.[4] (The Reformed constituted the bulk of all denizens.) The Fettmilch Uprising resulted in a new Citizens Compact (*Bürgervertrag*), which included among its seventy-one articles the following demand: "The council should, on account of the glut of denizens, make proper arrangements and plans, so that the citizenry not be further burdened on their [the denizens'] account."[5] Still dissatisfied, Fettmilch and others attacked and plundered the Jewish ghetto. Fettmilch ordered the Jews to leave the city.

Aided by less radical citizens, the Frankfurt Council eventually arrested Fettmilch in 1614 and executed him after a lengthy trial in 1616.[6] The patricians reestablished control, ordered the guilds dissolved, and welcomed the Jews back to Frankfurt.[7] Yet despite Fettmilch's demise, the gingerbread baker's specter loomed over the city, menacing the patricians who ruled and the Reformed who depended on the patricians for protection. Fettmilch's head was impaled along with those of his closest collaborators and mounted on the city's main bridge. As a child, Goethe walked across the city bridge and looked up at Fettmilch's skull. Reading about the man's assault on the patricians, young Goethe began to sympathize with Fettmilch: "I pitied these unfortunate humans, whom one could well regard as sacrifices made for a better constitution in the future."[8] While Goethe venerated Fettmilch's assault on arbitrary patrician rule, it is unlikely that Goethe's Reformed tutor would have admired the xenophobic gingerbread baker.

The eighteenth century began with another urban revolt by the citizenry against the ruling patricians in 1705.[9] This time, the rebels were less violent, more litigious, and more explicit in their denunciation of the Reformed community—though initially the Reformed supported constitutional reforms this time too.[10] Rich Lutherans began denouncing the Reformed and demanded the council restrict their commerce and industry since, the Lutherans argued, the economic and demographic limits of the city had obviously been reached.[11] In 1708, the council implemented the Denizen Ordinance, which went to great lengths to not only limit denizen economic opportunities but also to segregate them from Frankfurt's Lutherans.[12] Article Seven of the new ordinance forbid commercial association between denizens and citizens.[13] Article Eight limited marriage opportunities between denizens and citizens.[14] Outraged, the Reformed community sued the city before the Imperial Aulic Council, presenting a wealth of documentary evidence, tracing back to 1554, of the city's maltreatment of the Reformed. And while this court documentation was printed and remains an invaluable source base for the study of Reformed life in Frankfurt, the Imperial Aulic Council refused to annul the Frankfurt Denizen Ordinance. The Reformed lost their case and succeeded only in binding the Lutheran citizenry and the ruling council together in opposition to Reformed rights.[15]

The watershed moment in the long relationship between the Reformed residents of Frankfurt and the Lutheran city around them came in the late eighteenth century. In 1785, Frankfurt's residents watched from afar as Hamburg—a city whose intransigent hostility toward the Reformed faith had inspired Frankfurt's earliest restrictions on Reformed residents—relented and legalized the Reformed faith.[16] Hamburg earned the applause of Frederick the Great.[17] Encouraged by events in Hamburg, the Reformed of Frankfurt approached Frankfurt's senior mayor, Johann Friedrich Maximilian von Stalburg, and asked him to end the ban on Reformed services.[18] Stalburg belonged to one of the oldest and most influential patrician families in the city. His ancestors Christoph Stalburg and Claus Stalburg had served as mayors several times in the mid-sixteenth century, including the years when the council had first welcomed and defended the budding refugee community.[19] Stalburg's influence notwithstanding, the Reformed still struggled to attain public worship in Frankfurt. Finally, on 15 November 1787, the Reformed gained the right to occupy a church, a right they had last enjoyed in 1561. Two years later, in 1789, the two Reformed congregations in the city, French and German (the Dutch Reformed had embraced the German language in 1636) began constructing churches in the richest quarter of the city, although the city still forbade them from designing their churches with steeples or bells.[20] The new churches were dedicated in 1792 and 1793.

Restrictions on Reformed citizenship remained until Napoleon's armies conquered the city in 1806.[21] On 10 October 1806, the Reformed in the city received full civic equality via a new constitution issued not by Frankfurt's council but rather by the new Prince Primate of the Confederation of the Rhine, an office created as part of Napoleon's reorganization of German satellite states.[22] The Reformed could now add steeples with bells to their churches, though they chose not to as the structures did not allow for such additions.

Following the collapse of the Confederation of the Rhine in 1813, the Reformed and Lutheran communities of Frankfurt grew closer. Together they experienced the Prussian annexation of Frankfurt in 1866, which permanently destroyed the city's proud tradition of self-governance that traced back five centuries. Prussia had already united its Reformed and Lutheran communities into one church, but it did not impose such a union on the newly conquered Frankfurt.[23] In 1899, the Lutheran church and the two surviving Reformed congregations combined their ecclesiastical structures and formed one joint consistory governing Protestantism in the city.[24] The two religious traditions remained separated over matters of theology and ritual, and certain city churches offered Lutheran services while others offered Reformed services.

The twentieth century witnessed the Reformed community further integrate with the Lutheran majority around them and share in the city's calamities and triumphs. In 1916, as the nationalism of World War I raged, the French Reformed congregation in Frankfurt changed its language of worship to German, something the Dutch-speakers had done long before.[25] In the 1930s, the Reformed congregations joined the city's Lutheran congregations as part of a broader territorial church under Nazi leadership, though Reformed resistance to the Führerprinzip and support for the Confessing Church existed.[26] In 1944, American and British airmen destroyed Frankfurt's oldest and most important churches, including the three churches in which the Reformed had worshiped—the Church of the White Ladies that Poullain entered in 1554 and the Dutch and French Reformed Churches built after the city ended its ban on public worship.[27] Yet the Reformed tradition survives in Frankfurt and continues to trace its origins back to March 1554, when Poullain and twenty-four families entered the city on the Main. After World War II, the French Reformed community in Frankfurt built a new church outside of the city center, where services continue to this day. In bustling modern Frankfurt, one can still see the importance and legacy of Reformation refugees.

# NOTES

## ABBREVIATIONS

AFGK    *Archiv für Frankfurts Geschichte und Kunst*

ARG    *Archiv für Reformationsgeschichte*

Auszüge    *Die Eingliederung der niederländischen Glaubensflüchtlinge in die Frankfurter Bürgerschaft: Auszüge aus den Frankfurter Ratsprotokolle.* Edited by Hermann Meinert. Frankfurt a. M.: Waldemar Kramer, 1981.

Bmb    Bürgermeisterbücher

CO    *Ioannis Calvini Opera quae supersunt omnia.* Edited by G. Baum, E. Cunitz, and E. Reuss. 59 vols. Brunswick, 1863–1900. Also published as vols. 29–87 of *Corpus Reformatorum.*

FRG    Französisch-Reformierte Gemeinde, Bestand H.13.63.

FRH    *Franckfurtische Religions-Handlungen [. . .].* 2 vols. Frankfurt a. M., 1735.

IfSG    Institut für Stadtgeschichte, Frankfurt

OL    *Original Letters Relative to the English Reformation, Written during the Reigns of King Henry VIII, King Edward VI, and Queen Mary.* Edited by Hastings Robinson. 2 vols. Cambridge: Cambridge University Press, 1846–47.

PNRG    *Das Protokollbuch der Niederländischen Reformierten Gemeinde zu Frankfurt am Main, 1570–1581.* Edited by Hermann Meinert and Wolfram Dahmer. Frankfurt a. M.: Waldemar Kramer, 1977.

Rp    Ratsprotokolle

Rsl    Ratschlagungsprotokolle

## NOTES ON NAMES AND TERMINOLOGY

1. Stollberg-Rilinger, *The Holy Roman Empire,* 25.
2. *Centre National de Ressources Textuelles et Lexicales,* s.v. "réfugier," www .cnrtl.fr/definition/réfugié.
3. The displaced people in Frankfurt referred to themselves with the Latin word *peregrini* (foreigners, strangers, or pilgrims). In German, the refugees used the words *die Verjagten* (the chased or expelled), *die Vertriebenen* (the expelled), or simply *Fremde* (strangers or foreigners). The Frankfurt city council used the labels *Fremde, Welsche* (foreigners or Walloons), and *die*

*Vertriebenen* (the expelled). For a detailed consideration of Reformation refugee self-perceptions, see Veen, "'Wir sind ständig unterwegs'"; and Müller, *Exile Memories*.

4. Although it was coined in 1572, the term *réfugié* came into common usage in the seventeenth century, when Englishmen and Prussians needed a word to describe the Protestants fleeing Louis XIV's France following the Edict of Fontainebleau in 1685. See note 2; see also Zolberg, *Escape from Violence*, 5.

5. UN General Assembly, *Draft Convention Relating to the Status of Refugees*, 14 December 1950, A/RES/429, www.refworld.org/docid/3b00f08a27.html.

6. Leaman, "'Count Every Step,'" 18.

7. Soen, *Geen pardon zonder Paus!*; Janssens, *Brabant in Verweer*; Marnef, "Protestant Conversions," 35.

8. Waite, "Conversos and Spiritualists," 158. The concept of inner exile originated in twentieth-century Germany as a way to describe and exonerate literary figures who had remained in Nazi Germany despite feeling detached from the regime's politics. For a discussion of the concept of *innere Emigration*, see the many works in Kroll, *Schriftsteller und Widerstand*.

9. Cerutti, *Étrangers*, 12.

10. Malkii, "Speechless Emissaries."

11. Eire, "Calvin and Nicodemism"; Eire, *War against the Idols*, 235–38; Gunther, *Reformation Unbound*, 99, 104–5; Woo, "Nicodemism and Libertinism."

## INTRODUCTION

1. Valérand Poullain, "Bittschrift," in *FRH*, vol. 1, Beilage I, 1–2; reprinted in Ebrard, *Die französisch-reformierte Gemeinde*, 156–58.

2. Bmb, 18 March 1554, in *Auszüge*, 172.

3. Terpstra, *Religious Refugees*, 1–7.

4. *Centre National de Ressources Textuelles et Lexicales*, s.v. "réfugier," www.cnrtl.fr/definition/réfugié; cf. Janssen, "The Legacy of Exile," 230.

5. Norwood, *The Reformation Refugees*; Schilling, *Niederländische Exulanten*; Denis, *Les Églises d'étrangers*; Schilling, *Early Modern European Civilization*; Dölemeyer, *Aspekte zur Rechtsgeschichte*; Bahlcke, ed., *Glaubensflüchtlinge*; Trivellato, *The Familiarity of Strangers*; Schätz, *Die Aufnahmeprivilegien*; Grell, *Brethren in Christ*; Cerutti, *Étrangers*; Carvalho and Paras, "Sovereignty and Solidarity"; Janssens, "The Republic of Refugees"; Kaplan, "The Legal Rights of Religious Refugees."

6. Schilling, *Niederländische Exulanten*, 127.

7. Denis, *Les Églises d'étrangers*, 323.

8. Dietz, *Frankfurter Handelsgeschichte*, 2:37–45; 3:255–65.

9. Malkii, "Speechless Emissaries."

10. Pettegree, *Foreign Protestant Communities*; Prestwich, ed., *International Calvinism*; Pettegree, *Emden and the Dutch Revolt*; Grell, "Merchants and Ministers"; Pettegree, *Marian Protestantism*; Benedict, *Christ's Churches Purely Reformed*; Oberman, *John Calvin and the Reformation of the Refugees*; Müller, *Exile Memories*. See "Notes on Names and Terminology" for a discussion of the term "Reformed."

11. Veen, "Wir sind ständig unterwegs."

12. Grell, *Brethren in Christ*.

13. Brady, *German Histories*, 252.

14. Veen, "Wir sind ständig unterwegs."

15. Terpstra, *Religious Refugees*; Lachenicht, "Refugees and Refugee Protection."

16. Fehler et al., eds., *Religious Diaspora*; Spohnholz and Waite, eds., *Exile and Religious Identity*; Terpstra, *Religious Refugees*. These authors build upon the confessionalization paradigm of the late twentieth century. For a discussion of confessionalization historiography, see Zeeden, "Grundlagen und Wege"; and Reinhard, "Reformation, Counter-Reformation"; cf. Lotz-Heumann, "Confessionalization." Seminal works on confessionalization include Schilling, *Konfessionskonflikt und Staatsbildung*; Hsia, *Society and Religion*; and Nischan, *Prince, People, and Confession*.

17. Ozment, *The Age of Reform*; Kittelson, "The Confessional Age"; Chaunu, *Le temps des Réformes*; cf. Ehrenpreis and Lotz-Heumann, *Reformation und konfessionelles Zeitalter*; Cohn, "The Territorial Princes." For a recent critical summary of the periodization of Reformation historiography, see Hamm, "Farewell to Epochs."

18. Whaley, *Religious Toleration and Social Change*; Pettegree, *Foreign Protestant Communities*; Volk, "Peuplierung und religiose Toleranz"; Dölemeyer, *Aspekte zur Rechtsgeschichte*; Spohnholz, *The Tactics of Toleration*; Veen and Spohnholz, "Calvinists vs. Libertines"; Fehler et al., *Religious Diaspora*; Christman, *Pragmatic Toleration*; Kaplan, "The Legal Rights of Religious Refugees."

19. Lecler, *Toleration and the Reformation*, 475; cf. Schwartz, *All Can Be Saved*, 3–8; Walzer, *On Toleration*.

20. Luria, *Sacred Boundaries*, xxviii; Kaplan, *Divided by Faith*; Spohnholz, *The Tactics of Toleration*; Pietsch and Stollberg-Rilinger, *Konfessionelle Ambiguität*; Blum, *Multikonfessionalität im Alltag*; Christman, *Pragmatic Toleration*; Luebke, *Hometown Religion*, 5–6.

21. Spohnholz, *The Tactics of Toleration*, 13.

22. Christman, *Pragmatic Toleration*, 131.

23. Luebke, *Hometown Religion*, 5; Turchetti, "Religious Concord and Political Tolerance," 18; Benedict, "Un roi, une loi, deux fois," 65; cf. Walsham, *Charitable Hatred*, 1–5.

24. Te Brake, *Religious War and Religious Peace*.

25. Schwartz, *All Can Be Saved*, 6; Walzer, *On Toleration*, 1–7. On the distinction between freedom of worship and freedom of conscience, see Benedict, "Un roi, une loi, deux fois," 67–68; and Tol, *Germany and the French Wars of Religion*, 149.

26. Datheen [Dathenus], *Kurtze und warhafftige Erzelung*, under "Das acht Capitel"; French Reformed Church to the Frankfurt City Council, 17 November 1561, in *FRH*, vol. 1, Beilage XLI, 76.

27. See David Nirenberg's distinction between repression aimed at reinforcing hierarchy and repression aimed at expulsion (Nirenberg, *Communities of Violence*). Te Brake, *Religious War and Religious Peace*.

28. Spohnholz, *The Convent of Wesel*, 106.

29. The first document to include this suffix was Maximilian I's preamble to the conclusion of the Imperial Diet in Cologne in 1512 (see Schulze, *Grundstrukturen*).

30. Stollberg-Rilinger, *The Holy Roman Empire*, 39; Hardy, *Associative Political Culture*, 14.

31. Moeller, *Reichsstadt und Reformation*; Blickle, *From the Communal Reformation*; Brady, *German Histories*.

32. Holborn, *A History of Modern Germany*, 38. For a discussion of Frankfurt's special importance in imperial politics in the late 1550s, see Leeb, *Der Kurfürstentag*. For an overview of comparable imperial and free cities in the sixteenth century, see the works of Heinrich R. Schmidt and Thomas A. Brady, especially Schmidt, *Reichsstädte, Reich und Reformation*, 30; and Brady, *Turning Swiss*.

33. Dietz, *Frankfurter Handerlsgeschichte*, 3:316–32.

34. Dietz, *Frankfurter Handelsgeschichte*, 1:17–25; Weidhass, *A History*.

35. Poullain, "Bittschrift," in *FRH*, vol. 1, Beilage I, 1–2.

36. Luther, "On Commerce and Usury," in *Werke*, Weimarer Ausgabe, 15:294.

37. Schembs, "Die Alte Brücke"; Jahns, *Frankfurt, Reformation und Schmalkaldischer Bund*, 109.

38. Tol, *Germany and the French Wars of Religion*, 100.

39. Stollberg-Rilinger, *The Holy Roman Empire*, 17; Hardy, *Associative Political Culture*, 12.

40. Bothe, *Geschichte der Stadt*, 49.

41. *Bund, 1436–1986: 550 Jahre*.

42. Soliday, *A Community in Conflict*, 224–30; Stollberg-Rilinger, *The Holy Roman Empire*, 51.

43. Dingel, "Religionssupplikationen," 282.

44. Dingel, "Religionssupplikationen," 282.

45. Veen, "Wir sind ständig unterwegs."

46. Strype, *Memorials*; Schroeder, *Troisième Jubilé Séculaire*; Jung, ed., *Frankfurter Chroniken*; Ebrard, *Die französisch-reformierte Gemeinde*; Jung, *Die englische Flüchtlings-Gemeinde*; Bauer, *Valérand Poullain*.

47. Herminjard, ed., *Correspondance des Réformateurs*; G. Baum, E. Cunitz, and E. Reuss, eds., *Ioannis Calvini Opera quae supersunt omnia*, 59 vols. (1863–1900), published as part of the *Corpus Reformatorum*, vols. 29–87, hereafter *CO*.

## 1. New Dangers, New Allies, and the Emergence of Refugee Accommodation in Frankfurt

1. Stollberg-Rilinger, *The Holy Roman Empire*, 58, 69; Brady, *German Histories*, 207–28; Hardy, *Associative Political Culture*, 243–49; Christman, *Pragmatic Toleration*, 16; Gregory, *Salvation at Stake*, 222.
2. Mauersberg's *Wirtschafts- und Sozialgeschichte*, 49. For a helpful overview of competing estimates, see Soliday, *A Community in Conflict*, 35n1.
3. Dietz, *Frankfurter Handelsgeschichte*, 1:26.
4. Jahns, *Frankfurt, Reformation und Schmalkaldischer Bund*, 19.
5. Dietz, *Stammbuch*, 433; cf. Kasper-Holtkotte, *Die jüdische Gemeinde*.
6. H. Schmidt, *Reichsstädte, Reich und Reformation*, 30.
7. Hardy, *Associative Political Culture*, 243; cf. Isenmann, "Reichsfinanzen," 1–76, 129–218.
8. This number may not have reflected political reality as several of the cities were still claimed by lords (Close, *The Negotiated Reformation*, 23; Stollberg-Rilinger, *The Holy Roman Empire*, 39).
9. Frankfurt paid 17,600 gulden for its confirmation of independence (Bund, "Frankfurt am Main im Spättmittelalter," 54–65; Bothe, *Geschichte der Stadt*, 48).
10. Close, *The Negotiated Reformation*, 27–28.
11. Close, *The Negotiated Reformation*, 27.
12. Johann, *Kontrolle mit Konsens*, 262; H. Schmidt, *Reichsstädte, Reich und Reformation*, 20–21; Bücher, *Die Bevölkerung*, 87–88.
13. Bund, "Frankfurt am Main im Spättmittelalter," 77; Johann, *Kontrolle mit Konsens*, 262.
14. H. Schmidt, *Reichsstädte, Reich und Reformation*, 20–21.
15. Wolff and Jung, eds., *Baudenkmäler* 2:235–40; Moger, "Wolfgang Königstein," 57.
16. Jahns, *Frankfurt, Reformation und Schmalkaldischer Bund*, 19, 283.
17. Eltis, *The Military Revolution*; G. Parker, *The Military Revolution*, 6–10, 24–26.
18. Brady, *German Histories*, 114–15; Stollberg-Rilinger, *The Holy Roman Empire*, 54–55; Hardy, *Associative Political Culture*.
19. Stollberg-Rilinger, *The Holy Roman Empire*, 38–40; Pohl, "Die ständische Gesellschaft," 254; cf. Scott, *The City-State*; and Isenmann, *Die deutsche Stadt*.
20. Stollberg-Rilinger, *The Holy Roman Empire*, 17; Hardy, *Associative Political Culture*, 12.

21. Matthäus, *Hamman von Holzhausen*, 167.

22. G. Parker, *Emperor*, 94; Matthäus, *Hamman von Holzhausen*, 169.

23. Kohler, introduction to *Karl V*; G. Parker, *Emperor*.

24. G. Parker, *Emperor*, 383.

25. G. Parker, *Emperor*, 94; Matthäus, *Hamman von Holzhausen*, 169.

26. Jahns, "Frankfurt am Main in Zeitalter der Reformation," 161; Matthäus, *Hamman von Holzhausen*, 173.

27. Matthäus, *Hamman von Holzhausen*, 175.

28. Telschow, *Die alte Frankfurter Kirche*, 1.

29. Buck, "The Reformation, Purgatory, and Perpetual Rents," 23–33; Moger, *Priestly Resistance*, 42, 50.

30. Bothe, *Gechichte des St. Katharinen- und Weißfrauenstifts*, 21.

31. Buck, "The Reformation, Purgatory, and Perpetual Rents," 25.

32. Jahns, "Frankfurt am Main in Zeitalter der Reformation," 162.

33. Dechent, *Kirchengeschichte*, 1:75. See also Steitz, "Die Melanchthons- und Lutherherbergen zu Frankfurt"; and Moger, *Priestly Resistance*, 41–56.

34. Luther, "To the Christian Nobility of the German Nation," in *Werke*, Weimarer Ausgabe, 6:409.

35. Luther, "To the Christian Nobility of the German Nation," in *Werke*, Weimarer Ausgabe, 6:408.

36. Jahns, "Frankfurt am Main in Zeitalter der Reformation," 162; Matthäus, *Hamman von Holzhausen*, 175; Führ and Telschow, eds., *Die Evangelische Kirche*, 3.

37. Dechent, *Kirchengeschichte*, 1:69–73; Steitz, "Der Humanist Wilhelm Nesen"; Matthäus *Hamman von Holzhausen*, 188.

38. Moger, *Priestly Resistance*, 44–45.

39. Dechent, *Kirchengeschichte*, 1:75–76.

40. Dechent, *Kirchengeschichte*, 1:75–76; Moger, *Priestly Resistance*, 46.

41. Moger, *Priestly Resistance*, 46.

42. Moger, *Priestly Resistance*, 44, 47.

43. Moger, *Priestly Resistance*, 47.

44. Bund, *Frankfurt am Main im Spätmittelalter*, 102.

45. Dechent, *Kirchengeschichte*, 1:18; Bothe, *Geschichte des St. Katharinen- und Weißfrauenstifts*, 50–62.

46. Dechent, *Kirchengeschichte*, 1:84–85; Moger, *Priestly Resistance*, 47–51; Schwarzlose, "Hartmann Ibach und die Reformation"; Bothe, *Geschichte des St. Katharinen- und Weißfrauenstifts*, 62.

47. Moger, *Priestly Resistance*, 49–51.

48. Dienst, "Die Barfüßerkirche," 125, 133–35.

49. Matthäus, *Hamman von Holzhausen*, 281–96.

50. Moger, *Priestly Resistance*, 63–65.

51. Moger, *Priestly Resistance*, 68; Telschow, *Die alte Frankfurter Kirche*, 5; Dechent, *Kichengeschichte*, 1:110–16.

52. Dechent, *Kirchengeschichte*, 1:129.

53. Dechent, *Kirchengeschichte*, 1:124; Moger, *Priestly Resistance*, 49.

54. Remling, *Der Retscher in Speyer*, 3:97; Stollberg-Rilinger, *The Holy Roman Empire*, 64.

55. Dechent, *Kirchengeschichte*, 1:138–39, 142; Moeller, *Imperial Cities*, 91.

56. Dechent, *Kirchengeschichte*, 1:140–45; Denis, *Les Églises d'étrangers*, 308. The *Concordia Buceriana* was included as evidence in the eighteenth-century court case before the Imperial Aulic Council, and it can therefore be found in *Franckfurtische Religions-Handlungen*, vol. 2; cf. also vol. 1:15.

57. Führ and Telschow, eds., *Die Evangelische Kirche*, 3; Bothe, *Geschichte der Stadt Frankfurt*, 113.

58. Telschow, *Die alte Frankfurter Kirche*, 8.

59. Telschow, *Die alte Frankfurter Kirche*, 8; G. Parker, *Emperor*, 191–94.

60. Telschow, *Die alte Frankfurter Kirche*, 10; Moger, *Priestly Resistance*, 98.

61. Gordon, *Calvin*, 85; Close, *The Negotiated Reformation*, 95–97.

62. Martin Bucer et al., *Concordia Concionatorum Francofordiensium* (1542), in *FRH*, vol. 2, Beilage XI, 41; Benedict, *Christ's Churches Purely Reformed*, 43.

63. Bucer et al., *Concordia*, 42.

64. For an overview of these fundamental Protestant conceptions of the Eucharist, see Wandel, *The Eucharist in the Reformation*; and Burnett, *Debating the Sacraments*.

65. Dechent, *Kirchengeschichte*, 1:138.

66. G. Parker, *Emperor*, 268.

67. G. Parker, *Emperor*, 237–40, 273–74; Kohler, *Karl V*, 242.

68. Stollberg-Rilinger, *The Holy Roman Empire*, 66–69; cf. Close, *The Negotiated Reformation*, 58; Brady, *German Histories*, 214–15.

69. P. Wilson, *Heart of Europe*, 114, 564–65; Stollberg-Rilinger, *The Holy Roman Empire*, 68; Close, *The Negotiated Reformation*, 196–97; cf. Haug-Mortiz, *Der Schmalkaldische Bund*.

70. Stollberg-Rilinger, *The Holy Roman Empire*, 68; G. Parker, *Emperor*, 228–29.

71. Jahns, *Frankfurt, Reformation und Schmalkaldischer Bund*, 9.

72. Jahns, "Frankfurt am Main im Zeitalter der Reformation," 175; cf. Jahns, *Frankfurt, Reformation und Schmalkaldischer Bund*, 29.

73. Kohler, *Karl V*, 222. The electors of the empire would later gather in Frankfurt to confirm their decision to elect Ferdinand, though only in 1558.

74. Konzept-Bücher, 1533–34, 139r–139v; cf. Jahns, *Frankfurt, Reformation und Schmalkaldischer Bund*, 283.

75. Bothe, *Geschichte der Stadt Frankfurt*, 121.

76. Bothe, *Geschichte der Stadt Frankfurt*, 118–21; Jahns, *Frankfurt, Reformation und Schmalkaldischer Bund*, 283.

77. Jahns, *Frankfurt, Reformation und Schmalkaldischer Bund*, 283.

78. Jahns, *Frankfurt, Reformation und Schmalkaldischer Bund*, 9.

79. Stollberg-Rilinger, *The Holy Roman Empire*, 68; G. Parker, *Emperor*, 228–29.

80. Brady, *German Histories*, 225.
81. Stollberg-Rilinger, *The Holy Roman Empire*, 69; Brady, *German Histories*, 225–27.
82. Laurentiis, "La collezione," 680, 683.
83. Ambach, "Chronik," in Jung, ed., *Frankfurter Chroniken* (1888): 326–27.
84. Close, *Negotiated Reformation*, 249.
85. Ambach, "Chronik," in Jung, ed., *Frankfurter Chroniken* (1888): 379.
86. Ritter, *Evangelisches Denckmahl*, 406.
87. Ritter, *Evangelisches Denckmahl*, 396–97.
88. Ritter, *Evangelisches Denckmahl*, 396; Moger, "Wolfgang Königstein," 45, 301.
89. Moger, "Wolfgang Königstein," 118, 244–99.
90. Ritter, *Evangelisches Denckmahl*, 406.
91. Wolfgang Königstein, qtd. in translation in Moger, "Wolfgang Königstein," 34n50. Königstein's diary was reproduced in 1888 by Rudolf Jung and recently used by Moger to illuminate the experience of those Frankfurters opposed to the Reformation (Jung, ed., *Frankfurter Chroniken*, 27–173; cf. Steitz, ed., *Tagebuch des Canonicus Wolfgang Königstein*).
92. Ritter, *Evangelisches Denckmahl*, 397.
93. Ritter, *Evangelisches Denckmahl*, 397.
94. Ritter, *Evangelisches Denckmahl*, 408.
95. Hartmann Beyer, "Frage ob beyde Religionen Evangelische und Papistische in einer Kirche unter einem Dach fast zu einer Zeit mit gutem Gewissen können gehandelt warden," in Ritter, *Evangelisches Denckmahl*, 409.
96. Beyer, "Frage ob beyde Religionen," 409.
97. Beyer, "Frage ob beyde Religionen," 409.
98. Beyer, "Frage ob beyde Religionen," 409.
99. Ritter, *Evangelisches Denckmahl*, 407.
100. Seuffert, *Konstanz*, 87, 91; cf. Mauer, *Der übergang der Stadt Konstanz*.
101. Seuffert, *Konstanz*, 87, 91; cf. Mauer, *Der übergang der Stadt Konstanz*.
102. Dietz, *Frankfurter Handelsgeschichte*, 1:294–95; Dechent, *Kirchengeschichte*, 1:167.
103. Dietz, *Frankfurter Handelsgeschichte*, 1:295. One gulden equaled one florin.
104. Dietz, *Frankfurter Handelsgeschichte*, 1:295.
105. Bothe, *Geschichte der Stadt Frankfurt*, 118–21.
106. Bothe, *Geschichte der Stadt Frankfurt*, 118–21; Stollberg-Rilinger, *The Holy Roman Empire*, 71.
107. Bothe, *Geschichte der Stadt Frankfurt*, 118–21.
108. Hieronymus zum Lamb, "Chronik des Stadtadvokaten Dr. Hieronymus zum Lamb über die Belagerung von 1552," in Jung, ed., *Frankfurter Chroniken*, 378.
109. Melchior Ambach, "Chronik des Prädikanten Melchior Ambach über die Belagerung von 1552," in Jung, ed., *Frankfurter Chroniken*, 379–80.

110. Dietz, *Frankfurter Handelsgeschichte*, 1:82–83; Bücher, *Die Bevölkerung*.
111. "Sechs Lieder über die Belagerung von 1552," in Jung, ed., *Frankfurter Chroniken*, 473; Jahns, "Frankfurt am Main im Zeitalter der Reformation," 198.
112. "Sechs Lieder," 473.
113. "Keiser Carle hielt die stat in hut, / versamlet da ein haufen gut / von reutern und landsknechten, / die waren stets ganz wolgemut, / mit umbs blut zu fechten" ("Sechs Lieder," 473).
114. "Konrad von Hanstein to Hesse and other neighboring estates, 1552," in A. Kirchner, *Geschichte der Stadt*, vol. 2, appendix XIV, 549.
115. Bund, "Frankfurt am Main im Spättmittelalter," 54–65.
116. Lamb, "Chronik," 377.
117. Lamb, "Chronik," 360.
118. "Jüdischer Bericht über die Belagerung von 1552," in Jung, ed., *Frankfurter Chroniken*, 431.
119. Ambach, "Chronik," 401.
120. Druffel, ed., *Beiträge zur Reichsgeschichte*, 3:340–41; cf. Close, "Empires of Alliances."
121. Bmb, 13 March 1554, in *Auszüge*, 3; Dietz, *Frankfurter Handelsgeschichte*, 1:296; Bauer, *Valérand Poullain*, 177.
122. Dietz, *Frankfurter Handelsgeschichte*, 1:296.
123. *FRH*, vol. 1, Beilage I, 1–2; *FRH*, vol. 1, Beilage II, 4; *FRH*, vol. 1 Beilage LVII, 92; Rp, 15 March 1554, in *Auszüge*, 3.
124. Je suis gentilhomme, je m'appelle Valerandus Pollanus et Lille en Flandre est ma patrie Poullain quoted in "Bulletin de la société de l'historie du Protestantisme français" (XIII), 281; cf. Bauer, *Valérand Poullain*, 19.
125. Bauer, *Valérand Poullain*, 20–21.
126. Heinz Schilling described the southern Low Countries as "an economically further-developed area," with cities like Antwerp being "the most fully developed of Europe" (next to those of northern Italy, he admits) (Schilling, *Niederländische Exulanten*, 19, 24).
127. I maintain the distinction used by D. C. Coleman between "old" and "new" draperies, with the sometimes-independent category of "light" draperies falling into the category of "new" (Coleman, "An Innovation and Its Diffusion," 417–29).
128. DuPlessis, *Lille and the Dutch Revolt*, appendix A, 322–23.
129. Dietz, *Frankfurter Handelsgeschichte* 1:82–83; cf. Bücher, *Die Bevölkerung*.
130. Tracy, *Holland under Habsburg Rule*, 3; G. Parker, *Emperor*, 3–4.
131. Kooi, *Liberty and Religion*, 2.
132. Christman, *Pragmatic Toleration*, 16.
133. Moreau, *Histoire du Protestantisme*; Duke, *Reformation and Revolt*; Benedict, *Christ's Churches Purely Reformed*, 174. On the general affinity between burghers and Luther, see the scholarship of Bernd Moeller and

180     

Christopher Close: Moeller, *Reichsstadt und Reformation;* Close, *The Negotiated Reformation.* For an overview of historiography on the Reformation in Dutch cities, see Kooi, *Liberty and Religion.*

134. Gordon, *Calvin,* 33.
135. Bauer, *Valérand Poullain,* 21.
136. Poullain qtd. in Bauer, *Valérand Poullain,* 21–22.
137. Poullain qtd. in Bauer, *Valérand Poullain,* 22.
138. Christman, *Pragmatic Toleration,* 19–22.
139. Musculus, *The Temporysour,* first dialogue; cf. Gunther, *Reformation Unbound,* 104, 106.
140. Poullain's French translation, titled *Le temporiseur,* appeared in London in 1550 (Bauer, *Valérand Poullain,* 16).
141. Poullain to Guillaume Farel, 6 October 1543, in CO 11:623; cf. Bauer, *Valérand Poullain,* 34.
142. Poullain to Calvin, 26 May 1544, in CO 11:712.
143. Abray, *The People's Reformation,* 93, 42; Gordon, *Calvin,* 85–86; Denis, *Les Églises d'étrangers,* 35, 62.
144. Poullain to Farel, 6 October 1543, in CO 11:622; cf. Bauer, *Valérand Poullain,* 41–42, 47–48.
145. Poullain to Farel, 6 October 1543, in CO 11:622; cf. Bauer, *Valérand Poullain,* 41–42, 47–48.
146. Poullain to Farel, 6 October 1543, in CO 11:621–22; cf. Bauer, *Valérand Poullain,* 41–42, 47–55.
147. Bauer, *Valérand Poullain,* 44–45.
148. Poullain to Calvin, 28 November 1544, in CO 11:779; cf. Bauer, *Valérand Poullain,* 45.
149. Bauer, *Valérand Poullain,* 44–47.
150. Badea, *Kurfürstliche Präeminenz;* Simon, *Die Geschichte.*
151. Bauer, *Valérand Poullain,* 48–51; Denis, *Les Églises d'étrangers,* 166–67; cf. Pettegree, *Emden and the Dutch Revolt,* 19; Benedict, *Christ's Churches Purely Reformed,* 178.
152. Pastors of Strasbourg to Pastors of Neuchâtel, 29 December 1544, in Herminjard, ed., *Correspondance des Réformateurs,* 9:443.
153. Poullain to Calvin, 13 October 1544, in CO 11:756–57; cf. Denis, *Les Églises d'étrangers,* 72.
154. Poullain to Calvin, 13 October 1544, in CO 11:756–57; cf. Denis, *Les Églises d'étrangers,* 72.
155. Bauer, *Valérand Poullain,* 55.
156. Denis *Les Églises d'étrangers,* 73; Bornert, *La réforme protestante,* 194.
157. Denis *Les Églises d'étrangers,* 73.
158. Bauer, *Valérand Poullain,* 54–55; Denis, *Les Églises d'étrangers,* 74.
159. Bauer, *Valérand Poullain,* 65.

160. Poullain to Calvin, 3 December 1545, in CO 12:226; Albers, *Geschichte der Stadt Metz*, 77–78. France would soon recapture the city (Kamen, *The Duke of Alba*, 39–40).

161. Poullain to Calvin, Wesel, 16 November 1545, in CO 12:216–17; cf. Bauer, *Valérand Poullain*, 66.

162. Spohnholz, *Tactics of Toleration*, 42.

163. Bauer, *Valérand Poullain*, 74; Spohnholz, *Tactics of Toleration*, 42.

164. Bauer, *Valérand Poullain*, 76.

165. Abray, *The People's Reformation*, 116–17; Brady, *Ruling Class*, 275–86.

166. Poullain to Calvin, 15 February 1549, in CO 13:192; cf. Bauer, *Valérand Poullain*, 117–18.

167. Erichson, *Martin Butzer*, 63–64. Friedrich Clemens Ebrard incorrectly dates Poullain and Bucer's departure as 6 April 1548. Internet sources say Poullain arrived in England in 1547, but we know from Poullain's dated letter from Strasbourg that he remained in the city until at least February 1549. Abray and Pettegree confirm the year of Bucer's departure as 1549. Ebrard, *Die franzosisch-refomierte Gemeinde* 33. Abray, *The People's Reformation*, 89; Pettegree, *Foreign Protestant Communities*, 26; cf. Brady, *Ruling Class*, 286.

168. Bauer, *Valérand Poullain*, 132, 148–49; Pettegree, *Foreign Protestant Communities*, 43; Ebrard, *Die franzosisch-refomierte Gemeinde*, 33.

169. Ebrard, *Die franzosisch-refomierte Gemeinde*, 38.

170. Dietz, *Frankfurter Handelsgeschichte*, 2:18.

171. Pettegree, *Marian Protestantism*, 69.

172. Pettegree, *Foreign Protestant Communities*, 114; Pettegree, *Marian Protestantism*, 58. Garrett asserts that the departure occurred 13–15 September, based on Privy Council records. Pettegree's dates are based upon Utenhove's account which seems more reliable regarding the date of departure. Micron confirms Utenhove's date. Garrett, *The Marian Exiles*, 329; Utenhove, *Simplex et fidelis narratio*, 21; Bauer, *Valérand Poullain*, 170.

173. Bauer, *Valérand Poullain*, 170; Pettegree, *Foreign Protestant Communities*, 116; Pettegree, *Marian Protestantism*, 69; Ebrard, *Die franzosisch-refomierte Gemeinde*, 50–51. Garrett mistakenly dates Poullain's departure as 16 September (Garrett, *The Marian Exiles*, 329).

174. Pettegree, *Foreign Protestant Communities*, 118; Bauer, *Valérand Poullain*, 172–84.

175. Denis, *Les Églises d'étrangers*, 183–84; Spohnholz, *Tactics of Toleration*, 42.

176. Melanchthon, *Corpus Reformatorum*, 8:753; Schofield, *Philip Melanchthon*, 181.

177. Poullain, "Bittschrift," in *FRH*, vol. 1 Beilage I, 2; reprinted in Ebrard, *Die französisch-reformierte Gemeinde*, 156–58.

178. Körner, *Frankfurter Patrizier*, 41–43; cf. the new edition of this book: Kröner and Hansert, *Frankfurter Patrizier*, 95.

179. Traut, "Dr. Adolf von Glauburg," 6.

180. Traut, "Dr. Adolf von Glauburg," 13.

181. Traut, "Dr. Adolf von Glauburg," appendix.

182. Bothe, *Geschichte der Stadt Frankfurt*, 121–22.

183. Bothe, *Geschichte der Stadt Frankfurt*, 122.

184. Besser, *Geschichte*, 8; cf. *Frankfurter Biographie*; Lersner, *Der Weitberühmten*, 273.

185. Denis, *Les Églises d'étrangers*, 311.

186. Humbracht and Bromm were mayors at the time of the exile admission. Fichard was Syndic (Lersner, *Der Weit-berühmten*, 273).

187. "Gegenbericht," in *FRH*, vol. 2, Beilage XIV, 51.

188. Kröner and Hansert, *Frankfurter Patrizier*, 95.

189. Whittingham, *A Brieff discours*, 6. This work has been reprinted in several editions. For a discussion of its various version, see Collinson, "The Authorship." All citations here are from the 1574 edition.

190. Poullain to Calvin, 2 December 1555, in *CO* 15:875.

191. Denis, *Les Églises d'étrangers*, 308.

192. Dechent, *Kirchengeschichte*, 1:153; Ritter, *Evangelisches Denckmahl*, 261–62.

193. Gordon, *Calvin*, 234; Benedict, *Christ's Churches Purely Reformed*, 204–5.

194. Denis, *Les Églises d'étrangers*, 308.

195. Close, *The Negotiated Reformation*, 96.

196. *FRH*, vol. 2, Beilage XIII, 46.

197. Besser, *Geschichte der Frankfurter Flüchtlingen*, 6, 44; Dechent, *Kirchengeschichte*, 1:213–14.

198. Bmb, 18 March 1554, in *Auszüge*, 3.

199. Bothe, *Geschichte des St. Katharinen- und Weißfrauenstifts*, 24; Scharff, "Die Niederländischen und die Französische Gemeinde," 245–46; Besser, *Geschichte der Frankfurter Flüchtlingsgemeinden*, 9–10.

200. Schilling, *Niederländische Exulanten*, 19, 24; Norwood *The Reformation Refugees as an Economic Force*.

201. Poullain, "Bittschrift," in *FRH*, vol. 1, Beilage I, 2.

202. Coleman, "An Innovation and Its Diffusion"; Harte, ed., *The New Draperies in the Low Countries and England*; Bauer, *Valérand Poullain*, 177; Breustedt, "Die rechtspolitische Steuerung," 600.

203. Favresse, "Les Débuts"; Aerts and Munro, eds., *Textiles of the Low Countries*; Schilling, *Niederländische Exulanten*, 24.

204. Coleman, "An Innovation and Its Diffusion," 417.

205. *PNRG*, 333.

206. *FRH*, vol. 1, Beilage I, 1. I have translated *Fürsichtigen* here as "caring," though the word also connotes a religious providence not out of place in this context.

207. Datheen [Dathenus], *Kurtze und warhafftige Erzelung* (Heidelberg, 1563), chap. 1.

208. Poullain's supporters insisted his petition include economic advantage for the council at large, which drew fifteen of its forty-three members from the city's "electorally eligible" guilds, which included the weavers, butchers, smiths, bakers, cobblers, furriers, gardeners, tanners, fishermen, and shopkeepers (Bücher, *Die Bevölkerung,* 87).

209. Geltner et al. to the Frankfurt Council, Frankfurt, 5 September 1555, *FRH,* vol. 1, Beilage III, 5.

210. Peter Geltner et al. to the Frankfurt Council, Frankfurt, 29 October 1555, *FRH,* vol. 1, Beilage V, 8.

211. "Gegenbericht," in *FRH,* vol. 2, Beilage XIV, 50.

212. "Gegenbericht," in *FRH,* vol. 2, Beilage XIV, 50. The "passport" likely refers to a letter of reference, possibly from the late Duke of Somerset Edward Seymour. Poullain mentions his community's "eherlichen Abschiedsbriefen" which they had carried with them from England.

213. "Gegenbericht," in *FRH,* vol. 2 Beilage XIV, 50.

214. "Gegenbericht," in *FRH,* vol. 2 Beilage XIV, 50.

215. Valérand Poullain to Hartmann Beyer, ca. 1556, MS-242, Nachlass Beyer, Stadt- und Universitätsbibliothek Frankfurt A1, Universitätsbibliothek Johann Christian Senckenberg.

216. John Calvin to Poullain, qtd. in Schroeder, *Troisième Jubilé Séculaire,* 9–10.

217. Kooi, *Liberty and Religion,* 2.

218. Utenhove, *Simplex et fidelis narratio,* 233: "à pientissimo Senatu humanissimè excipitur."

## 2. Refugee Arrivals and the Advent of Confessionalism

1. Anne Hooper to Henry Bullinger, 20 April 1554, in *OL,* 1:111; cf. Ebrard, *Die französisch-reformierte Gemeinde,* 54; Bauer, *Valérand Poullain,* 184–85.

2. Poullain, *Liturgia sacra* (1551); cf. "Calvins Confession des péchés in Poullains Liturgie für Glastonbury von 1552," appendix 1 of Ebrard, *Die französisch-reformierte Gemeinde,* 154.

3. "Panis quem frangimus, communicatio est corporis Christi"; Poullain, *Liturgia sacra* (1551).

4. Bauer, *Valérand Poullain,* 16.

5. Poullain, *Liturgia sacra* (1551).

6. Bmb, 26 April 1554, in *Auszüge,* 4; Denis, *Les Églises d'étrangers,* 314; Besser, *Geschichte der Frankfurter Flüchtlingsgemeinden,* 13.

7. Poullain, *Liturgia sacra* (1551).

8. Bothe, *Geschichte des St. Katharinen- und Weißfrauenstifts*, 8–9, 22–23; Dechent, *Kirchengeschichte*, 1:13.

9. Bothe, *Geschichte des St. Katharinen- und Weißfrauenstifts*, 22–23.

10. Bothe, *Geschichte des St. Katharinen- und Weißfrauenstifts*, 22–23.

11. For a consideration of the motives behind refugee accounts, see Veen, "Wir sind ständig unterwegs," 442–58; and Müller, *Exile Memories*, 37–40.

12. Brady, *German Histories*, 231.

13. Pettegree, *Foreign Protestant Communities*, 121; Hovda, *The Controversy*; Jürgens, "Benedict Morgenstern." Of the many works on confessionalism, the following continue to prove influential studies of the phenomenon in German-speaking lands: Zeeden, "Grundlagen und Wege"; Schilling, *Die reformierte Konfessionalisierung*; Raitt, *The Colloquy of Montbéliard*; Nischan, *Prince, People and Confessions*; and Ehrenpreis and Lotz-Heumann, *Reformation und konfessionelles Zeitalter*.

14. Poullain to Calvin, Frankfurt, 8 February 1555, in CO 15:424.

15. IfSG, FRG, 101, 20r–23v; cf. Abeele, "Nederlandse vluchtelingen te Frankfort," 8.

16. Pettegree, *Foreign Protestant Communities*, 117.

17. Whittingham, *A Brieff discours*. I have chosen to accept the traditional attribution of *A Brieff discours* to Whittingham, although Patrick Collinson suggests that Thomas Wood could have been the real author (Collinson, "The Authorship of *A Brieff Discours*").

18. Cameron, "Frankfurt and Geneva"; Collinson, "The Authorship;" cf. Garrett, *The Marian Exiles*; Gunther, *Reformation Unbound*, 158–88.

19. Whittingham, *A Brieff discours*, 5.

20. Whittingham, *A Brieff discours*, 5.

21. Whittingham, *A Brieff discours*, 5.

22. Whittingham, *A Brieff discours*, 5.

23. Whittingham, *A Brieff discours*, 6.

24. Bmb, 3 July 1554, in *Auszüge*, 6. Cf. Jung, *Die englische Flüchtlings-Gemeinde*, 11.

25. Rp, 2 July 1554, in *Auszüge*, 5.

26. Garrett, *The Marian Exiles*, 300; Jung, *Die englische Flüchtlings-Gemeinde*, 24.

27. Whittingham, *A Brieff discours*, 5.

28. Garrett, *The Marian Exiles*, 1. While Garrett's work remains important, more recent studies of Marian refugees include Pettegree, *Marian Protestants*; Danner, *Pilgrimage to Puritanism*; and Harkrider, *Women, Reform and Community*, chap. 5.

29. John Foxe, *The Unabridged Acts and Monuments Online or TAMO* (1563 edition) (The Digital Humanities Institute, Sheffield, 2011), Book 5, 1123–24. Available at www.dhi.ac.uk/foxe.

30. Anne Hooper to Henry Bullinger, in *OL*, 110. For an analysis of the connection between John Hooper and the Swiss Reformation, see Gordon,

*The Swiss Reformation* (Manchester, UK: Manchester University Press, 2002), 301.

31. Hooper to Bullinger, in *OL*, 111. Hooper probably only heard of the baptism of Poullain's son secondhand, as she describes it taking place on the Rhine.

32. Foxe, *The Unabridged Acts and Monuments Online*, Book 5, 1118. Available at www.dhi.ac.uk/foxe.

33. Hooper to Bullinger, in *OL*, 108; Jung, *Die englische Flüchtlings-Gemeinde*, 52; cf. Garrett, *The Marian Exiles*, 187.

34. Hooper to Bullinger, in *OL*, 111. For an analysis of the connection between John Hooper and the Swiss Reformation, see Gordon, *The Swiss Reformation*, 301.

35. Hooper to Bullinger, in *OL*, 111.

36. Hooper to Bullinger, in *OL*, 112.

37. Hooper to Bullinger, in *OL*, 114.

38. Rp, 26 April 1554 and 5 June 1554, in *Auszüge*, 4–5.

39. Rp, 8 May 1554, in *Auszüge*, 4; cf. Pettegree, *Marian Protestantism*, 71.

40. Rp, 8 May 1554, in *Auszüge*, 4; cf. Jung, *Die englische Flüchtlings-Gemeinde*, 11.

41. Jung, *Die englische Flüchtlings-Gemeinde*, 11–12.

42. Dietz, *Frankfurter Handelsgeschichte*, 2:27.

43. John Stanton et al. to the congregations of Strasbourg, Zurich, Wesel, Emden, etc., Frankfurt, 2 August 1554, in Whittingham, *A Brieff discours*, 8.

44. Stanton et al., in Whittingham, *A Brieff discours*, 8.

45. Stanton et al., in Whittingham, *A Brieff discours*, 8.

46. Stanton et al., in Whittingham, *A Brieff discours*, 8.

47. Stanton et al., in Whittingham, *A Brieff discours*, 11.

48. Stanton et al., in Whittingham, *A Brieff discours*, 9.

49. Stanton et al., in Whittingham, *A Brieff discours*, 8.

50. The travails of this group, led by John a Lasco, were recorded by Utenhove (Utenhove, *Simplex et fidelis narratio*). For a modern study of this community, see Norwood, "The London Dutch Refugees"; cf. Pettegree, *Emden and the Dutch Revolt*, 24–25; Pettegree, *Marian Protestantism*, 58–63; and Veen, "Wir sind ständig unterwegs."

51. Utenhove, *Simplex et fidelis narratio*, 233.

52. Ebrard, *Die französisch-reformierte Gemeinde*, 74; Besser, *Geschichte der Frankfurter Flüchtlingsgemeinden*, 41; Smid, "Reisen und Aufenthaltsorte," 194; Pettegree, *Marian Protestantism*, 16. Regarding the weather during the winter odyssey, see Mirjiam van Veen's work including "Wir sind ständig unterwegs."

53. Pettegree, *Emden*, 26–28.

54. Besser, *Geschichte der Frankfurter Flüchtlingsgemeinden*, 24.

55. Lasco to Calvin, 19 September 1555, in *CO* 15:773; Dalton, *Johannes a Lasco*, 453.

56. Bartel, *Jan Laski*, 171–73.
57. Lasco to Bullinger, 19 September 1555, in *Joannis a Lasco opera*, ed. Kuyper, 2:714; cf. Bartel, *Jan Laski*, 171–72; cf. also Springer, *Restoring Christ's Church*, 52; and Denis, *Les Églises d'étrangers*, 331.
58. Pettegree, *Marian Protestantism*, 71.
59. Ebrard, *Die französich-reformierte Gemeinde*, 75; Meinert, introduction to *Auszüge*, xiv; Mortiz, *Versuch einer Enleitung in die Staatsverfassung*, 1:206–7; Soliday, *A Community in Conflict*, 199.
60. Utenhove, *Simplex et fidelis narratio*, 233.
61. Ebrard, *Die französich-reformierte Gemeinde*, 74; Meinert, introduction to *Auszüge*, xiv.
62. Pettegree, *Foreign Protestant Communities*, 49.
63. Smid, "Reisen und Aufenthaltsorte," 195; Ebrard, *Die französisch-reformierte Gemeinde*, 74–75.
64. Ebrard, *Die französich-reformierte Gemeinde*, 76; Jung, *Die englische Flüchtlings-Gemeinde*, 10.
65. Utenhove, *Simplex et fidelis narratio*, 233–34.
66. Besser, *Geschichte der Frankfurter Flüchtlingsgemeinden*, 25. Cf. Ebrard, *Die französisch-reformierte Gemeinde*, 75.
67. IfSG, FRG, 101, 20r.
68. IfSG, FRG, 101, 20r.
69. Bauer, *Valérand Poullain*, 206–7; Ebrard, *Die französisch-reformierte Gemeinde* 75; Denis, *Les Églises d'étrangers*, 331; Pettegree, *Marian Protestantism*, 71.
70. Pettegree, *Marian Protestantism*, 71; Spohnholz, *The Convent of Wesel*, 53; Smid, "Reisen und Aufenhaltsorte," 196.
71. Datheen [Dathenus], *Kurtze und warhafftige Erzelung*; Spohnholz, *The Convent of Wesel*.
72. Datheen [Dathenus], *Kurtze und warhafftige Erzelung*, chap. 1, bIII.
73. Pettegree, *Emden and the Dutch Revolt*, 179–80.
74. Theodorus Ruys, *Petrus Dathenus* (Utrecht: Ruys, 1919).
75. Spohnholz, *The Convent of Wesel*; Pettegree, *Foreign Protestant Communities*, 306.
76. Springer, *Restoring Christ's Church* 2; cf. Becker, *Gemeindeordnung und Kirchenzucht*, 1–21.
77. Pettegree, *Foreign Protestant Communities*, 58–62; cf. Becker, *Gemeindeordnung und Kirchenzucht*, 23–106; Springer, *Restoring Christ's Church*, 89–90.
78. Lasco, *Joannis a Lasco opera*, 2:51.
79. Lasco, *Joannis a Lasco opera*, 2:51.
80. Lasco, *Joannis a Lasco opera*, 2:52.
81. Pettegree, *Marian Protestantism*, 40.
82. Hooper and Lasco, *Whether Christian faith maye be kepte secret in the heart*. For a discussion of the mysteries surrounding the printer of this text, see

Evenden, "The Michael Wood Mystery"; King, "John Day"; and Fairfield, "The Mysterious Press."

83. Lasco and Hooper, *Whether Christian faith maye be kepte secret in the heart* (1553).

84. Musculus, *Temporysour,* translated as *Temporisour* by Valérand Poullain (London, 1550), Early English Books Online: https://quod.lib.umich.edu /e/eebo2/A07942.0001.001?rgn=main;view=fulltext.

85. Eire, "Calvin and Nicodemism"; Eire, *War against the Idols,* 235–38; Gunther, *Reformation Unbound,* 99, 104–5; Woo, "Nicodemism and Libertinism."

86. Bauer, *Valérand Poullain,* 56.

87. Eire, *War against the Idols,* 236n9; Gunther, *Reformation Unbound,* 97–130.

88. "ecclesie Germanobelgie Francoforthi," IfSG, FRG, 101, 24r–24v; cf. Abeele, "Nederlandse vluchtelingen te Frankfort," 2–3.

89. Dietz, *Frankfurter Handelsgeschichte,* 2:27.

90. IfSG, FRG, 101, 24v–27r.

91. Dietz, *Frankfurter Bürgerbuch,* 188–90; cf. Dietz, *Frankfurter Handelsgeschichte,* vol. 2.

92. Meinert, introduction to *Auszüge,* xiv.

93. "Gegenbericht," in *FRH,* vol. 2, Beilage XIV, 55; cf. Denis, *Les Églises d'étrangers,* 314; Besser, *Geschichte der Frankfurter Flüchtlingsgemeinden,* 13.

94. Peter Geltner et al. to the Frankfurt Council, 5 September 1555, in *FRH,* vol. 1, Beilage III, 4.

95. Rp, 5 September 1555, in *Auszüge,* 13.

96. Geltner et al. to the Frankfurt Council, 5 September 1555, 4.

97. Dechent, *Kirchengeschichte,* 1:84–85; Moger, *Priestly Resistance,* 47; Schwarzlose, "Hartmann Ibach," 83–86; Bothe, *Gechichte des St. Katharinen- und Weißfrauenstifts,* 62.

98. Dechent, *Kirchengeschichte,* 1:18; Bothe, *Gechichte des St. Katharinen- und Weißfrauenstifts,* 50–62.

99. Geltner et al. to the Frankfurt Council, 5 September 1555, 4.

100. Bücher, *Die Bevölkerung,* 87.

101. H. Schmidt, *Reichsstädte, Reich und Reformation,* 20–21; Moger, "Wolfgang Königstein," 43.

102. Bmb, 5 September 1555, in *Auszüge,* 13.

103. Geltner et al. to the Frankfurt Council, 5 September 1555, 5.

104. Geltner et al. to the Frankfurt Council, 5 September 1555, 5.

105. Geltner et al. to the Frankfurt Council, 5 September 1555, 5.

106. Geltner et al. to the Frankfurt Council, 5 September 1555, 4.

107. Geltner et al. to the Frankfurt Council, 5 September 1555, 4.

108. Brady, *German Histories,* 231–32.

109. Pettegree, *Marian Protestantism,* 72–73.

110. Rp, in *FRH*, vol. 1, Beilage IV, 6.
111. Petition of the English foreigners to the Frankfurt Council, 29 October 1555, in *FRH*, vol. 1, Beilage II, 3.
112. Petition of the English foreigners to the Frankfurt Council, 29 October 1555, 3.
113. Petition of the English foreigners to the Frankfurt Council, 29 October 1555, 4; cf. Jung, *Die englische Flüchtlings-Gemeinde*, 16–17.
114. Jung, *Die englische Flüchtlings-Gemeinde*, 16–17.
115. Pettegree, *Foreign Protestant Communities*, 59.
116. Petition of the English foreigners to the Frankfurt Council, 29 October 1555, 3.
117. Dechent, *Kirchengeschichte* 1:214.
118. Peter Geltner et al. to the Frankfurt Council, 29 October 1555, in *FRH*, vol. 1, Beilage V, 7. For a discussion of Eucharistic debates in the period, see Burnett, *Debating the Sacraments*.
119. Geltner et al. to the Frankfurt Council, 29 October 1555, 7.
120. Geltner et al. to the Frankfurt Council, 29 October 1555, 7.
121. Geltner et al. to the Frankfurt Council, 29 October 1555, 7.
122. Geltner et al. to the Frankfurt Council, 29 October 1555, 7.
123. Geltner et al. to the Frankfurt Council, 29 October 1555, 7.
124. Geltner et al. to the Frankfurt Council, 29 October 1555, 7.
125. Hartmann Beyer, "Frage ob beyde Religionen Evangelische und Papistische in einer Kirche unter einem Dach fast zu einer Zeit mit gutem Gewissen können gehandelt warden," in Ritter, *Evangelisches Denckmahl*, 409.
126. Geltner et al. to the Frankfurt Council, 29 October 1555, 7–8.
127. Wandel, "Fragmentation and Presence," 55–76.
128. Geltner et al. to the Frankfurt Council, 29 October 1555, 8–9.
129. Geltner et al., to the Frankfurt Council, 29 October 1555, 8.
130. Geltner et al. to the Frankfurt Council, 29 October 1555, 8; Sandl, "Here I Stand," 77–98.
131. Rp, 29 October 1555, in *FRH*, vol. 1, Beilage VII, 9.
132. Scharff, "Die Niederländische und die Französische Gemeinde," 249.
133. For a study of a similar generational divide, see Burnett, "A Generational Conflict."
134. Bmb, 31 October 1555, in *Auszüge*, 18.
135. *FRH*, vol. 1, Beilage VI, 10.
136. *FRH*, vol. 1, Beilage V, 8.
137. Glauburg to Calvin, 1 December 1555, in *CO* 15:871; cf. Ebrard, *Die französisch-reformierte Gemeinde*, 83n.
138. Glauburg qtd. in Traut, "Dr. Adolf von Glauburg und seine Bibliothek," 10.
139. Dechent, *Kirchengeschichte*, 1:200; Besser, *Geschichte der Frankfurter Flüchtlingsgemeinden*, 44.

140. Dechent, *Kirchengeschichte*, 1:214.

141. Denis incorrectly asserts that Glauburg's age at death was "trente-trois" (Denis, *Les Églises d'étrangers*, 351). Adolf von Glauburg was born in March 1524, although the exact day of his birth seems unclear (Klötzer, *Frankfurter Biographie*, 1:252; Körner, *Frankfurter Patrizier*, 113; Traut, "Dr. Adolf," 5).

142. Besser, *Geschichte der Frankfurter Flüchtlingsgemeinden*, 44–45; Denis, *Les Églises d'étrangers*, 311.

143. Besser, *Geschichte der Frankfurter Flüchtlingsgemeinden*, 45; Denis, *Les Églises d'étrangers*, 311.

144. 5 September 1555, in *FRH*, vol. 1, Beilage III.

145. 4 February 1556, in *FRH*, vol. 1, Beilage IX.

146. "Gegenbericht," in *FRH*, vol. 2, Beilage XIV, 50.

147. Frankfurt ministers to the Frankfurt Council, 19 March 1556, in *FRH*, vol. 1, Beilage XII, 27.

148. Geltner et al. to the Frankfurt Council, 5 September 1555, 5.

149. Bauer, *Valérand Poullain*, 293.

150. Soliday, *A Community in Conflict*, 224–30.

151. Valérand Poullain to Hartmann Beyer, ca. 1556, MS-242, Nachlass Beyer, Stadt- und Universitätsbibliothek Frankfurt, Universitatsbibliothek A1, Frankfurt am Main.

152. Poullain to Beyer, circa 1556.

153. Poullain to Beyer, circa 1556.

154. Poullain to Beyer, circa 1556.

155. Poullain to Beyer, circa 1556.

156. Poullain to Beyer, circa 1556.

157. Poullain to Beyer, circa 1556.

158. Poullain to Beyer, circa 1556.

159. See Nischan, *Lutherans and Calvinists*.

160. "Joachim Westphal an Hartmann Beyer," November 8, 1557, in Schade, *Joachim Westphal*, 230.

161. Frankfurt ministers to the Frankfurt Council, 19 March 1556, in *FRH*, vol. 2, Beilage XII, 27–28.

162. "Supplication vom 7. Aug. 1561," *FRH*, vol. 1, Beilage XLII, 77.

163. Spohnholz, *Tactics of Toleration*, 63; see also 136–42, 146.

164. *FRH*, vol. 1, Beilage I, 1.

165. Brady, *German Histories*, 252.

166. Pettegree, *Foreign Protestant Communities*, 121.

167. Van Tol, *Germany and the French Wars of Religion*, 129–33.

168. Pettegree, "The London Exile Community," 223–51.

169. Pettegree, *Foreign Protestant Communities*, 121.

170. Dietz, *Frankfurter Handelsgeschichte* 2:67.

171. Lehnemann, *Historische Nachricht;* Steitz and Dechent, *Geschichte;* Bund, *400 Jahre.*

## 3. REFUGEE CONTROVERSIES AND THE END OF ACCOMMODATION

1. Frankfurt's ministers to the Frankfurt Council, 7 November 1555, in *FRH,* vol. 1, Beilage VI, 11.
2. Bothe, *Geschichte der Stadt,* 137–39.
3. Schilling, *Niederländische Exulanten,* 28, 52.
4. Denis, *Les Églises d'étrangers,* 308.
5. H. Schmidt, *Reichsstädte, Reich und Reformation,* 20–21.
6. H. Schmidt, *Reichsstädte, Reich und Reformation,* 21; cf. Bücher, *Die Bevölkerung,* 87.
7. Rp, 23 August 1554, in *Auszüge,* 6.
8. Rp, 13 September 1554, in *Auszüge,* 7.
9. Besser, *Geschichte der Frankfurter Flüchtlingsgemeinden,* 18.
10. Peter Geltner et al. to the Frankfurt Council, 5 September 1555, in *FRH,* vol. 1, Beilage III, 5.
11. Geltner et al. to the Frankfurt Council, 5 September 1555, 6.
12. Richard Vauville to Calvin, Frankfurt, 10 April 1555, in *CO,* 15:2181, 558.
13. Frankfurt's ministers to the Frankfurt Council, 19 March 1556, in *FRH,* vol. 2, Beilage XII, 28.
14. Frankfurt's ministers to the Frankfurt Council, 19 March 1556, 28.
15. Beyer, "Gegenbericht," 88.
16. Whittingham, *Brieff discours,* 8–9.
17. Whittingham, *Brieff discours,* 14.
18. Benedict, *Christ's Churches Purely Reformed,* 72; Springer, *Restoring Christ's Church,* 70; cf. Becker, *Gemeindeordnung und Kirchenzucht,* 23–106.
19. Lasco, *Forma ac ratio,* 52.
20. Garrett, *The Marian Exiles,* 329.
21. Garrett, *The Marian Exiles,* 168, 253–58.
22. Garrett, *The Marian Exiles,* 253.
23. Gunther, *Reformation Unbound,* 158–88.
24. Whittingham, *A Brieff discours,* 23.
25. Whittingham, *A Brieff discours,* 23–24.
26. Whittingham, *A Brieff discours,* 24.
27. Cameron, "European Context of Knox," 60; Gunther, *Reformation Unbound,* 158–88.
28. Procter, *A History of the Book of Common Prayer,* 53.
29. Cummings, introduction to *The Book of Common Prayer,* xxxiii.

30. Whittingham, *Brieff discours*, 48.
31. Whittingham, *Brief discours*, 48.
32. Whittingham, *Brief discours*; cf. Cuming, A History of Anglican Liturgy, 88.
33. Cameron, "European Context of Knox," 60.
34. Whittingham, *Brieff discours*, 27.
35. Cuming, *A History of Anglican Liturgy*, 88–89.
36. Calvin to the English in Frankfurt, 31 May 1555, in Whittingham, *Brieff discours*, 52.
37. Denis, *Les Églises d'étrangers*, 323.
38. Garrett, *The Marian Exiles*, 134; Denis, *Les Églises d'étrangers*, 323.
39. Garrett, *The Marian Exiles*, 134.
40. Garrett, *The Marian Exiles*, 134; Denis, *Les Églises d'étrangers*, 323.
41. Whittingham, *Brieff discours*, 43.
42. Whittingham, *Brieff discours*, 45.
43. Whittingham, *Brieff discours*, 46.
44. Anne Hooper to Henry Bullinger, 20 April 1554, in *OL*, 1:111.
45. Anne Hooper to Henry Bullinger, 12 November 1554, in *OL*, 1:113.
46. Duffy, *Fires of Faith*, 92, 98, 116.
47. John Hooper to Henry Bullinger, 27 March 1550, in *OL*, 1:79. Cf. Cuming, *A History of Anglican Liturgy*, 71; Benedict, *Christ's Churches Purely Reformed*, 237–38.
48. Benedict, *Christ's Churches Purely Reformed*, 238.
49. Foxe, *The Unabridged Acts and Monuments*, 5:1548.
50. Cameron, "Frankfurt and Geneva," 60.
51. Knox, *Works*, 3:308.
52. Knox to Anne Locke, 9 December 1556, in *Works*, 4:240; Dawson, *John Knox*, 150–54.
53. Valérand Poullain, "Bittschrift," in *FRH*, vol. 1, Beilage I, 2; reprinted in Ebrard, *Die französisch-reformierte Gemeinde*, 156–58.
54. Stanton et al., in Whittingham, *A Brieff discours*, 8.
55. Shachar, *Multicultural Jurisdictions*, 2; Kymlicka, *Multicultural Citizenship*; Cover, "The Supreme Court," 4–68.
56. Whittingham, *Brieff discours*, 48.
57. Calvin to Richard Cox and the English in Frankfurt, Geneva 1555, reproduced in Whittingham's *Brieff discours*, 53. This letter is not in the *Corpus Reformatorum* (CO).
58. Calvin to Richard Cox and the English in Frankfurt, Geneva 1555, 52.
59. Calvin to Richard Cox and the English in Frankfurt, Geneva 1555, 52.
60. Besser, *Geschichte der Frankfurter Flüchtlingsgemeinden*, 14
61. Poullain to Frankfurt Church, Frankfurt, 14 September 1554, in *FRH*, vol. 1, Beilage XXXIV, 60.

62. Poullain to Frankfurt Church, 14 September 1554, 60.

63. Ebrard, *Die französisch-reformierte Gemeinde*, 62–65; Bauer, *Valérand Poullain*, 13; Pettegree, *Marian Protestantism*, 120.

64. Peter Geltner et al. to the Frankfurt Council, 29 October 1555, in *FRH*, vol. 1, Beilage V, 7.

65. Geltner et al. to the Frankfurt Council, 29 October 1555, 7.

66. Benedict, *Christ's Churches Purely Reformed*, 71. Benedict incorrectly lists Emden as the site of publication for the *Forma ac ratio*.

67. Benedict, *Christ's Churches Purely Reformed*, 7.

68. Pettegree, *Marian Protestantism*, 32–34; cf. Rodgers, *John a Lasco in England*; Springer, *Restoring Christ's Church*, 1–11; and Becker, *Gemeindeordnung und Kirchenzucht*, 1–21.

69. Geltner et al. to the Frankfurt Council, 29 October 1555, 9; cf. Scharff, "Die Niederländischen und die Französische Gemeinde," 248.

70. Pettegree describes the entire text as "a work of polemic" (Pettegree, *Foreign Protestant Communities*, 57).

71. Lasco, *Joannis a Lasco opera*, 2:22.

72. Lasco, *Joannis a Lasco opera*, 2:22.

73. Lasco, *Joannis a Lasco opera*, 2:22.

74. Lasco, *Joannis a Lasco opera*, 2:51; Benedict, *Christ's Churches Purely Reformed*, 71.

75. Geltner et al. to the Frankfurt Council, 29 October 1555, 8. For a discussion of how religious controversy intersected with civic authority and the material interests of printers, see Creasman, *Censorship and Civic Order*; and Burnett, *Debating the Sacraments*.

76. Geltner et al. to the Frankfurt Council, 29 October 1555, 8.

77. *FRH*, vol. 1, Beilage I, 1–2.

78. Rp, 11 November 1555, in *Auszüge*, 18.

79. Rp, 11 November 1555, in *Auszüge*, 19.

80. Rp, 11 November 1555, in *Auszüge*, 19.

81. Besser, *Geschichte der Frankfurter Flüchtlingsgemeinden*, 48.

82. Dietz, *Frankfurter Handelsgeschichte*, 2:27.

83. Jean de Poix to Farel, August 1554, in Denis, *Les Églises d'étrangers*, appendix 17, 663.

84. Denis, *Les Églises d'étrangers*, 327; Dietz, *Frankfurter Handelsgeschichte*, 2:27.

85. Denis, *Les Églises d'étrangers*, 327.

86. Dietz, *Frankfurter Handelsgeschichte*, 2:27, 64.

87. Ebrard, *Die französisch-reformierte Gemeinde*, 93.

88. Poullain to Calvin, Frankfurt, 8 February 1555, in *CO* 15:422; Denis, *Les Églises d'étrangers*, 326.

89. Poullain to Calvin, Frankfurt, 8 February 1555, in *CO* 15:422; Denis, *Les Églises d'étrangers*, 326.

90. Denis, *Les Églises d'étrangers*, 328.

91. Pettegree, *Foreign Protestant Communities*, 49.

92. Ebrard, *Die französisch-reformierte Gemeinde*, 94; cf. Denis, *Les Églises d'Etrangers*, 329; Pettegree, *Foreign Protestant Communities*, 53; Bauer, *Valérand Poullain*, 186, 238–41. The travails of this group, led by Johannes a Lasco and Jan Utenhove, were recorded by Utenhove in his *Simplex et fidelis narratio* (1560); cf. Norwood, "The London Dutch Refugees."

93. Denis, *Les Églises d'étrangers*, 329.

94. Lasco to Calvin, Frankfurt, 14 October 1555, in CO 15:820.

95. Poullain qtd. in Pettegree, *Foreign Protestant Communities*, 53.

96. Denis, *Les Églises d'étrangers*, 329.

97. Besser, *Geschichte der Frankfurter Flüchtlingsgemeinden*, 34.

98. Vauville to Calvin, Frankfurt, 10 April 1555, in CO 15:559.

99. Vauville to Calvin, Frankfurt, 10 April 1555, in CO 15:559.

100. Lasco to Calvin, Frankfurt, 14 October 1555, in CO 15:819.

101. Denis, *Les Églises d'Étrangers*, 336.

102. Calvin to French Church of Frankfurt, 26 Decemeber 1555, in CO 15:895.

103. Johann von Glaburg to Calvin, Frankfurt, 1 December 1555, in CO 15:872.

104. Ebrard, *Die französisch-reformierte Gemeinde*, 97.

105. Pettegree, *Marian Protestantism*, 75–76; Gordon, *Calvin*, 242–43.

106. Calvin, "Procès-Verbal de l'interrogatoire d'Augustin Legrand," in CO 16:291.

107. Ebrard, *Die französisch-Reformierte Gemeinde*, 95.

108. Poullain to Calvin, Frankfurt, 2 December 1555, in CO 15:875.

109. Utenhove, *Simplex et fidelis narratio*, 234.

110. Utenhove, *Simplex et fidelis narratio*, 234.

111. Utenhove, *Simplex et fidelis narratio*, 235.

112. Bmb, 20 October 1556, in *Auszüge*, 36.

113. Denis, *Les Églises d'étrangers*, 349.

114. Denis, *Les Églises d'étrangers*, 349.

115. Valérand Poullain, "Antidotus," in *FRH*, vol. 2, Beilage XVIII, 217.

116. Pettegree, *Marian Protestantism*, 78.

117. Poullain, "Antidotus," 217.

118. Poullain, "Antidotus," 217.

119. Poullain, "Antidotus," 234.

120. Poullain, "Antidotus," 239.

121. Poullain, "Antidotus," 246.

122. Denis, *Les Églises d'étrangers*, 349; Bauer, *Valérand Poullain*, 300; Ebrard, *Die französisch-reformierte Gemeinde*, 95. Denis disagrees with both Bauer and Ebrard on the date of Poullain's death, and as Denis examined evidence not seen by the other two authors, his estimate of autumn 1557 appears correct.

123. Denis, *Les Églises d'étrangers*, 352–54; Besser, *Geschichte der Frankfurter Flüchtlingsgemeinden*, 71–73.
124. Pettegree, *Foreign Protestant Communities*, 49.
125. Spohnholz, *Tactics of Toleration*, 44–47.
126. Pettegree, *Marian Protestantism*, 66.
127. Denis, *Les Églises d'étrangers*, 336.
128. Bauer, *Valérand Poullain*, 261.
129. Ebrard, *Die französisch-reformierte Gemeinde*, 98.
130. Noe du Fay et al. to Frankfurt, 7 February 1559, in *FRH*, vol. 1, Beilage XXIV, 49.
131. Bmb, 7 February 1559, in *Auszüge*, 62.
132. Rp, 9 March 1559, in *Auszüge*, 63.
133. Schilling, *Niederländische Exulanten*, 126–31; Pettegree, *Marian Protestantism*, 81.
134. Ebrard, *Die französisch-reformierte Gemeinde*, 98.
135. Bmb, 18 March 1561, in *Auszüge*, 87.
136. Rsl, 22 April 1561, *FRH*, vol. 1, Beilage XXXI, 59.
137. Smid, "Reisen und Aufenthaltsorte a Lascos," 196.
138. Spohnholz, *Tactics of Toleration*, 257.
139. Beyer, "Gegenbericht," in *FRH*, vol. 2, Beilage XIV, 88.
140. Beyer, "Gegenbericht," 88.
141. Steitz, *Der Lutherische Prädicant Hartmann Beyer*, 121.
142. Datheen, *Kurtze und warhafftige Erzelung*, chap. 5, p. b2.

## 4. The Quest for Legal Protection outside of Frankfurt

1. Schilling, *Niederländische Exulanten*, 176.
2. Dutch Supplication to the Frankfurt Council, 7 August 1561, in *FRH*, vol.1, Beilage XLII, 77.
3. Bmb, 28 August 1561, in *FRH*, vol. 1, Beilage XLV, 78; cf. *Auszüge*, 100; and Ebrard, *Die französisch-reformierte Gemeinde*, 99.
4. "Fest-gegründete Gegen-Information," in *FRH*, vol. 1, 31; cf. Ebrard, *Die französisch-reformierte Gemeinde*, 103.
5. IfSG, FRG, 101, 24v–27r.
6. *FRH*, vol. 1, sec. 1, 5; Ebrard, *Die französisch-reformierte Gemeinde*, 103; PNRG, 230.
7. *FRH*, vol. 1, sect. 1, 5.
8. Whittingham, *A Brieff discours*, 59; Dickens, *The English Reformation*, 309–16.
9. Bmb, 23 March 1559, in *Auszüge*, 64. While the Bürgermeisterbuch and the Ratsprotokolle refer to the gilded gift as a "vergülten credentz," we know that the item was actually a column because it remains to this day

in the Historisches Museum Frankfurt. Cf. Jung, *Die englische Flüchtlings-Gemeinde*, 19–21; Fischer, "Niederländische Glaubensflüchtlinge," 7–8; and Fischer, "Die Gründung," 28–29.

10. French Reformed Church to the Frankfurt Council, 17 November 1561, in *FRH*, vol. 1, Beilage XLI, 76.

11. French Reformed Church to the Frankfurt Council, 17 November 1561, in *FRH*, vol. 1, Beilage XLI, 76.

12. *FRH*, vol. 1, Beilage XLIII, 77–78.

13. *FRH*, vol. 1, Beilage XLVI, 79.

14. Ebrard, *Die französisch-reformierte Gemeinde*, 98–99.

15. Steitz, *Der Lutherische Prädicant Hartmann Beyer*, 139–40.

16. *FRH*, vol. 1, sec. 1, 5.

17. This was the case in the prince-bishopric Münster, where marriage and baptism were considered "rites of passage" that bound all Christians together (Luebke, *Hometown Religion*, 50–51).

18. Luebke, *Hometown Religion*, 51. Jesse Spohnholz has shown how in other cities, the Eucharist itself could be deemed a malleable signifier of confessional unity (Spohnholz, "Multiconfessional Celebration," 705–30).

19. Ebrard, *Die französisch-reformierte Gemeinde*, 101.

20. Ebrard, *Die französisch-reformierte Gemeinde*, 112.

21. Steitz, *Der Lutherische Prädicant Hartmann Beyer*, 140; Ebrard, *Die französisch-reformierte Gemeinde*; cf. Bothe, "Fürstliche Wirtschaftspolitiker"; Maus, *Die Geschichte der Stadt*; Kaller, "Die Anfänge," 393–403; and Ehrmantraut and Martin, eds., *Das Protokollbuch*.

22. Roosbroeck, *Emigranten*, 16; cf. Kaller "Wallonische und niederländische Exulantensiedlungen," 329; and Spohnholz, *The Convent of Wesel*, 53–54.

23. For a comprehensive description of Frankfurt and its environs, see Wolff and Jung, eds., *Die Baudenkmäler*.

24. Denis, *Les Églises d'étrangers*, 393.

25. Scheible, *Kurfürst Ottheinrich*, 36; Kuby, "Gründe, Wege und Folgen"; Ellrich, *Die Wittelsbacher*.

26. Benedict, *Christ's Churches Purely Reformed*, 211; Denis, *Les Églises d'étrangers*, 392.

27. Kluckhohn, "Wie ist Kurfürst Friedrich III"; Press, *Calvinismus und Territorialstaat*; Chadwick, "The Making of a Reforming Prince," 56; cf. Benedict, *Christ's Churches Purely Reformed*, 211; Tol, *Germany and the French Wars of Religion*, 67.

28. Götz, *Die erste Einführung*; Vogler, "Le role des électeurs Palatins"; Benedict, *Christ's Churches Purely Reformed*, 211–14; Thomas, "A House Divided"; Tol, *Germany and the French Wars of Religion*, 68–73, 77; Eire, *Reformations*, 313.

29. Denis, *Les Églises d'étrangers*, 392–93.

30. Benedict, *Christ's Churches Purely Reformed*, 212–13; Tol, *Germany and the French Wars of Religion*, 68–69.

31. Tol, *Germany and the French Wars of Religion*, 66–69; Spohnholz, *The Convent of Wesel*, 53.

32. Friedrich to the Frankfurt Council, 15 August 1561, *FRH*, vol. 1, Beilage XLVII, 79.

33. Friedrich to the Frankfurt Council, 15 August 1561, 79.

34. Bmb, 19 August 1561, in *Auszüge*, 100.

35. Calinich, *Der Naumburger Furstentag*, 224–28; Koch, "Striving for the Union," 112; Horie, "The Lutheran Influence," 535; Tol, *Germany and the French Wars of Religion*, 125–29.

36. Datheen also wrote to the German city of Emden (Roosbroeck, *Emigranten*, 190).

37. Christmann, "Die Kapitulation"; cf. Kaller, "Die Anfänge," 395.

38. Christmann, "Die Kapitulation"; Hürkey, ed., *Kunst, Kommerz, Glaubenskampf*; Denis, *Les Églises d'étrangers*, 394.

39. A. Schäfer, "Wallonische und niederländische Exulantensiedlungen," 329; Thomas, "A House Divided," 159–60; Denis, *Les Églises d'étrangers*, 394.

40. IfSG, FRG, 108, 71v–90r; Maus, ed., *Die Geschichte der Stadt*, 156; Denis, *Les Églises d'étrangers*, 395.

41. Denis, *Les Églises d'étrangers*, 394–95.

42. Frankenthal Capitulation, Stadtarchiv Frankenthal, I, 1; reproduced in IfSG, FRG, 108, 73r. Printed versions of the Capitulation exist in the *Monatschrift der Frankenthaler Altertumsvereins* 1 (1894): 9–11; (1897): 6–7; Hildenbrand, *Quellen zur Geschichte*, 4–12; cf. Bütfering, "Niederländische Exulanten in Frankenthal," 37–47.

43. "Soll man inen wilfaren," Bmb, 18 March 1554, in *Auszüge*, 3.

44. Frankenthal Capitulation, IfSG, FRG, 108, 71v; cf. Kuby, "Gründe, Wege und Folgen," 22–25.

45. Frankenthal Capitulation, IfSG, FRG, 108, 71v.

46. Frankenthal Capitulation, IfSG, FRG, 108, 71v.

47. Frankenthal Capitulation, IfSG, FRG, 108, 71v.

48. Frankenthal Capitulation, IfSG, FRG, 108, 71v; cf. Denis, *Les Églises d'étrangers*, 395.

49. Frankenthal Capitulation, IfSG, FRG, 108, 71v; cf. Maus, ed., *Die Geschichte der Stadt*, 156.

50. Frankenthal Capitulation, IfSG, FRG, 108, 71v.

51. Frankenthal Capitulation, IfSG, FRG, 108, 72v; Kaller, "Wallonische und niederländische Exulantensiedlungen," 339.

52. Frankenthal Capitulation, IfSG, FRG, 108, 71v

53. Denis, *Les Églises d'étrangers*, 395.

54. Denis, *Les Églises d'étrangers*, 395; Benedict, *Christ's Churches Purely Reformed*, 214.

55. Frankenthal Capitulation, IfSG, FRG, 108, 71v–72r.
56. There is some disagreement among historians over the exact number of families. Sixty is the number offered by Bütfering, Hildenbrand, Georg Franz, and Hermann Meinert, though Meinert offers the number as the total of all individuals. Kaller suggests that the actual number of families was sixty-two (see Bütfering, "Niederländische Exulanten," 38, 45n14; Hildenbrand, Quellen, 4–11; Franz, Aus der Geschichte der Stadt, 66; Meinert, introduction to Auszüge, xxix; and Kaller, "Wallonische und niederländische Exulantensiedlungen," 329).
57. Kaller, "Wallonische und niederländische Exulantensiedlungen," 329; Bütfering, "Niederländische Exulanten," 37; Maus, ed., Die Geschichte der Stadt, 156. For a discussion of the linguistic backgrounds of the Reformed leaving for Frankenthal, see Kaller, "Die Anfänge," 394; Roosbroeck, "Die niederländischen Glaubensflüchtlinge," 11–15; and Denis, Les Églises d'étrangers, 395.
58. Kaller "Wallonische und niederländische Exulantensiedlungen," 329.
59. Kaller "Wallonische und niederländische Exulantensiedlungen," 329; Denis, Les Églises d'étrangers, 395.
60. Frankenthal Capitulation. There has been a surprising amount of variance in the spelling of these names. I have given preference to the German forms, with the exception of Datheen. These conform more to the spelling in Maus than in Kaller. Kaller mistakenly spells Gillis's name "Billis" (Maus, ed., Die Geschichte der Stadt, 156). Kaller, "Wallonische und niederländische," 329; Cuno, "Geschichte der wallonisch-reformirten Gemeinde," 5.
61. Maus, ed., Die Geschichte der Stadt, 156.
62. Frankenthal Capitulation, IfSG, FRG, 108, 72v.
63. Kaller, "Die Anfänge," 395.
64. Bütfering, "Niederländische Exulanten," 38.
65. Maus, ed., Die Geschichte der Stadt, 154.
66. Maus, ed., Die Geschichte der Stadt, 154; Kaller, "Wallonische und niederländische Exulantensiedlungen," 338
67. Benedict, "Un roi, une loi, deux fois," 67–68; Tol, Germany and the French Wars of Religion, 149.
68. Bütfering, "Niederländische Exulanten," 38; cf. Kaller, "Wallonische und niederländische Exulantensiedlungen," 329; Denis, Les Églises d'étrangers, 394.
69. Kiefner, Die Privilegien.
70. Kaplan, "The Legal Rights of Religious Refugees."
71. Schilling, "Religion, Politik und Kommerz"; cf. Bahlcke, ed., Glaubensflüchtlinge.
72. On the lasting importance of the displacement in the communal identities of these groups, see Müller, Exile Memories; and Kamp, "Ein frühes reformiert-pietistisches Netzwerk," 182–208.
73. IfSG, Repertorien Nr. 657, "Ergänzungsfindbuch zum Bestand Inquisitionsamt," ed. Ernst Roediger (1911).

74. Schelven, *De Nederduitsche vluchtelingenkerken*, 26–29, 34; G. Parker, *The Dutch Revolt*, 119; Arnade, *Beggars, Iconoclasts*, 166–211; Spohnholz, *Tactics of Toleration*, 71; Kamen, *The Duke of Alba*, 75–105

75. Kamen, *The Duke of Alba*, vii; Edelmayer, "The Duke of Alba."

76. G. Parker, *The Dutch Revolt*, 177.

77. Pettegree, *Emden and the Dutch Revolt*, 148; Spohnholz, *Tactics of Toleration*, 71.

78. Kamen, *The Duke of Alba*.

79. IfSG, Repertorien Nr. 657, "Ergänzungsfindbuch," sub. Gorgette, 11.

80. IfSG, Repertorien Nr. 657, "Ergänzungsfindbuch," sub. Gorgette, 11.

81. IfSG, Repertorien Nr. 657, "Ergänzungsfindbuch," sub. Gorgette, 11.

82. IfSG, Repertorien Nr. 657, "Ergänzungsfindbuch," 31.

83. On early modern toleration as an enduring of unpleasantness, see Luebke, *Hometown Religion*, 5; Turchetti, "Religious Concord," 18; and Benedict, "Un roi, une loi, deux fois," 65; cf. Walsham, *Charitable Hatred*, 1–5.

84. Dietz, *Frankfurter Handelsgeschichte* 2; cf. Ebrard, *Die französisch-reformierte Gemeinde*, 112.

85. *FRH* 1, sec. 2, 31; Dietz, *Frankfurter Handelsgeschichte* 2:26, 67.

86. Ebrard, *Die französisch-reformierte Gemeinde*, 103.

87. Dietz, *Frankfurter Handelsgeschichte* 2:67.

88. Magdelaine, "Frankfurt am Main: Drehscheibe"; Dölemeyer, *Die Hugenotten*, 37–40.

89. Magdelaine, "Frankfurt am Main: Drehscheibe"; Dölemeyer, *Die Hugenotten*, 37–40.

90. *FRH*, vol. 1, Beilage LXIII, 100.

91. Dietz, *Frankfurter Handelsgeschichte* 2:67

92. Meinert, introduction to *Auszüge*, xxxxii–xxxxiii; Ebrard, *Die französisch-reformierte Gemeinde*, 111.

93. Meinert, introduction to *Auszüge*, xxxxii–xxxxii.

94. Meinert, introduction to *Auszüge*, xxxxii–xxxxii.

95. Rp in *Auszuge*, 515; cf. Meinert, introduction to *Auszüge*, xxxxii.

96. Rp, 27 July 1596, in *Auszüge*, 576; cf. Meinert, introduction to *Auszüge*, xxxxiii; Fischer, "Die Gründung"; Ebrard, *Die französisch-reformierte Gemeinde*, 111; and Bott, *Gründung und Anfänge*.

97. Ebrard, *Die französisch-reformierte Gemeinde*, 111.

98. Rp, 27 July 1596, in *Auszüge*, 576.

99. Bmb, 5 August 1596, in *Auszüge*, 577; and *FRH*, vol. 1, Beilage 86, 132–36; cf. Fischer, "Die Gründung," 36.

100. Fischer, "Die Gründung," 36; Meinert, introduction to *Auszüge*, xxxxiii–xxxxiv.

101. Bmb, 26 August 1596, in *Auszüge*, 579; cf. Meinert, introduction to *Auszüge*, xxxxiv; Fischer, "Die Gründung," 36.

102. Meinert, introduction to *Auszüge*, xxxxii–xxxxii; Fischer, "Die Gründung," 36.
103. Kaplan, *Divided by Faith*, 145.
104. Fischer, "Die Gründung," 36.
105. IfSG, FRG, 99, 30r; Kaplan, "The Legal Rights of Religious Refugees," 91; Fischer, "Die Gründung," 36.
106. "in Haften und nemlich auf S. Catharinen Thurn gefänglich eingezogen warden," "Memorial diejenige Reformirte," 1597, in *FRH*, vol. 1, sec. 1, 56.
107. "Memorial diejenige Reformirte," 1597, in *FRH*, vol. 1, sec. 1, 56.
108. "Memorial diejenige Reformirte," 1597, in *FRH*, vol. 1, sec. 1, 56.
109. "Memorial diejenige Reformirte," 1597, in *FRH*, vol 1, sec. 1, 56.
110. "Memorial diejenige Reformirte," 1597, in *FRH*, vol. 1, sec. 1, 56.
111. Diefendorf, *Beneath the Cross*, 140.
112. Fischer, "Die Gründung," 37.
113. Hanau Capitulation, Hessisches Staatsarchiv Marburg, Slg 15 No. 240/11. This was reproduced in IfSG, FRG, 99, 30r, and also in the appendix to Bothe, "Fürstliche Wirtschaftspolitiker," 107.
114. Friedrich Bothe compiled their professions in the appendix to his article "Fürstliche Wirtschaftspolitiker," 113.
115. "von wegen der reformierten Religion," Hanau Capitulation, Hessisches Staatsarchiv Marburg, Slg 15, No. 240/11.
116. Hanau Capitulation, Hessisches Staatsarchiv Marburg, Slg 15, No. 240/11.
117. Strohm, *Johannes Calvin*, 24; Benedict, *Christ's Churches Purely Reformed*.
118. Hanau Capitulation, Hessisches Staatsarchiv Marburg, Slg 15, No. 240/11; Kaplan, "The Legal Rights of Religious Refugees," 91.
119. Kaplan, "The Legal Rights of Religious Refugees," 92; Bott, *Gründung und Anfänge*, 103.
120. Kaplan, "The Legal Rights of Religious Refugees," 92–94.
121. Hanau Capitulation, Hessisches Staatsarchiv Marburg, Slg 15, No. 240/11.
122. "Gegenbericht," *FRH*, vol. 2, Beilage XIV, 50.
123. Hanau Capitulation, Hessisches Staatsarchiv Marburg, Slg 15, No. 240/11.
124. Hanau Capitulation, Hessisches Staatsarchiv Marburg, Slg 15, No. 240/11.
125. "Rotten oder Sekten." Hanau Capitulation, Hessisches Staatsarchiv Marburg, Slg 15, No. 240/11; cf. Bothe, "Fürstliche Wirstschaftspolitiker," 108.
126. Hanau Capitulation, Hessisches Staatsarchiv Marburg, Slg 15, No. 240/11.
127. Hanau Capitulation, Hessisches Staatsarchiv Marburg, Slg 15, No. 240/11.
128. Hanau Capitulation, Hessisches Staatsarchiv Marburg, Slg 15, No. 240/11.
129. Hanau Capitulation, Hessisches Staatsarchiv Marburg, Slg 15, No. 240/11.
130. Hanau Capitulation, Hessisches Staatsarchiv Marburg, Slg 15, No. 240/11.
131. Bmb, 16 April 1556, in *Auszüge*, 27.
132. Hanau Capitulation, Hessisches Staatsarchiv Marburg, Slg 15, No. 240/11.
133. Hanau Capitulation, Hessisches Staatsarchiv Marburg, Slg 15, No. 240/11.

134. Datheen [Dathenus], *Kurtze und warhafftige Erzelung.*
135. *FRH*, vol. 1, sec. 1, 5–6.
136. Datheen [Dathenus], *Kurtze und warhafftige Erzelung,* under "Das acht Capitel."
137. Meinert, introduction to *PNRG,* 9–10, 342.
138. Ebrard, *Die französisch-reformierte Gemeinde,* 113–14.
139. Oppenheim Capitulation, Hessisches Staatsarchiv Darmstadt, A2, 197/368; cf. Bothe, "Fürstliche Wirschaftspolitik," 115–16.
140. Luebke, *Hometown Religion,* 107–8; Kaplan, *Divided by Faith,* 144–71; Whaley, *Religious Toleration and Social Change,* 36–37. On other informal arrangements of toleration, see also Pettegree, *Foreign Protestant Communities;* Volk, "Peuplierung und religiose Toleranz," 205–31; Luria, *Sacred Boundaries;* Walsham, *Charitable Hatred;* Spohnholz, *The Tactics of Toleration;* Pietsch and Stollberg-Rilinger, eds., *Konfessionelle Ambiguität;* Blum, *Multikonfessionalität im Alltag;* and Christman, *Pragmatic Toleration.*
141. Luebke, *Hometown Religion,* 107–8; Kaplan, *Divided by Faith,* 144–97; Whaley, *Religious Toleration and Social Change,* 36–37.
142. In this respect, Frankfurt's restrictions fit into a category of repression aimed at expulsion, a category David Nirenberg describes in *Communities of Violence.* See also Te Brake, *Religious War and Religious Peace.*
143. Magdelaine, "Frankfurt am Main: Drehscheibe."

## 5. Preserving Reformed Life in Frankfurt

1. Schröder, *Troisième Jubilé Séculaire,* 12.
2. Schilling, *Niederländische Exulanten,* 176.
3. IfSG, Repertorien Nr. 657, "Ergänzungsfindbuch."
4. Körner, *Frankfurter Patrizier,* 43.
5. IfSG, Repertorien Nr. 657, "Ergänzungsfindbuch."
6. This estimate is based upon both Dietz and Mauersberg (Dietz, *Frankfurter Bürgerbuch,* 189; Mauersberg, *Wirtschafts- und Sozialgeschichte,* 48–55).
7. IfSG, Repertorien Nr. 657, "Ergänzungsfindbuch," 5.
8. IfSG, Repertorien Nr. 657, "Ergänzungsfindbuch," 12.
9. IfSG, Repertorien Nr. 657, "Ergänzungsfindbuch," 5.
10. Dietz, *Frankfurter Bürgerbuch,* 189.
11. IfSG, Repertorien Nr. 657, "Ergänzungsfindbuch," 13.
12. Magdelaine, "Frankfurt am Main: Drehscheibe," 26–37.
13. Marnef, *Antwerp in the Age of Reformation,* 206–8.
14. Ebrard, *Die französisch-reformierte Gemeinde,* 103.
15. *FRH*, vol. 1, sec. 2, 31; cf. Dietz, *Frankfurter Handelsgeschichte* 2:26, 67.
16. See chap. 1. Cf. Lehnemann, *Historische Nachricht;* Steitz and Dechent, *Geschichte;* and Bund, *400 Jahre.*

17. *FRH*, vol. 1, sec. 1, 5; Ebrard, *Die französisch-reformierte Gemeinde*, 103.

18. IfSG, FRG, 1, 1.

19. IfSG, FRG, 1, 1.

20. Bauer, *Valérand Poullain*, 206–7; Ebrard, *Die französisch-reformierte Gemeinde* 75; Denis, *Les Églises d'étrangers*, 331; Pettegree, *Marian Protestantism*, 71.

21. *PNRG*, 61, 227.

22. *PNRG*, 61, 228; Meinert, introduction to *PNRG*, 51n13; IfSG, Repertorien Nr. 657 "Ergänzungsfindbuch," sub. "Peter Bischof." Regarding Pieter Bisshop's origins, Frankfurt's Inquisitionsamt listed him as being from Antwerp, whereas the internal Dutch consistory records his hometown as Nieuwkerke. The latter seems more trustworthy.

23. Meinert, introduction to *PNRG*, 43–45.

24. Meinert, introduction to *PNRG*, 43–45.

25. Hermann Meinert explains that the minutes of the Dutch Reformed Consistory were much more detailed than other consistory minutes, constituting "an elaborate record to the point of minutiae" of life within the Dutch Reformed Congregation in Frankfurt (Meinert, introduction to *PNRG*, 7). For a discussion of the limitations of consistory minutes, see Pollman, "Off the Record."

26. *PNRG*, 62, 228.

27. *PNRG*, 62, 228.

28. *PNRG*, 62, 228.

29. *PNRG*, 62, 228.

30. *PNRG*, 62, 228.

31. *PNRG*, 64, 230.

32. *PNRG*, 65, 231.

33. *PNRG*, 98–115, 262–79.

34. *PNRG*, 114, 278.

35. *PNRG*, 73, 238.

36. *PNRG*, 73, 238–39.

37. IfSG, FRG, 1.

38. IfSG, FRG, 1, "Verfassung der Gemeinde."

39. *PNRG*, 68, 234.

40. *PNRG*, 68, 234.

41. *FRH*, vol. 1, Beilage LXIII, 100.

42. *FRH*, vol. 1, Beilage LXIII, 100.

43. *FRH*, vol. 1, Beilage LXIII, 101.

44. *PNRG*, 67, 233.

45. *PNRG*, 67, 233.

46. *PNRG*, 73, 239.

47. *PNRG*, 69, 234.

48. "Ratschlagung 7 December 1569," in *FRH*, vol. 1, Beilage LXXIII, 118.

49. "Ratschlagung 7 December 1569," in *FRH*, vol. 1, Beilage LXXIII, 118.

50. Friedrichs, "Urban Conflicts," 98–125.

51. G. Parker, *The Military Revolution*, 7–10.

52. Bothe, "Erzbischof Johan Schweikart," 9.

53. Brück, "Pfalzgraf Reichart," 10.

54. Kaller, "Die Anfänge."

55. Benedict, *Christ's Churches Purely Reformed*, 212.

56. Bmb, 29 March 1571, in *Auszüge*, 183.

57. Bmb, 13 September 1571, in *Auszüge*, 189.

58. Bmb, 13 September 1571, in *Auszüge*, 189.

59. Bmb, 29 March 1571, in *Auszüge*, 183.

60. Rsl, 30 March 1571, in *Auszüge*, 66.

61. Bmb, 12 June 1571, in *Auszüge*, 187.

62. Friedrich Pfalzgraf an der Stadt FfM, 19 March 1573, in *FRH*, vol. 1, 120–21.

63. *FRH*, vol. 1, Beilage XCV, 149.

64. Scharff, "Die niederländische und die französische Gemeinde," 284–85; Fischer, "Die Gründung," 38.

65. Scharff, "Die niederländische und die französische Gemeinde," 284.

66. Scharff, "Die niederländische und die französische Gemeinde," 284.

67. Ebrard, *Die französisch-reformierte Gemeinde*, 113.

68. IfSG, FRG, 171, Bl. 673Rff; Ebrard, *Die französisch-reformierte Gemeinde*, 113; Fischer, "Die Gründung," 39.

69. "Gegenbericht," *FRH*, vol. 2, Beilage XIV, 50.

70. Ebrard, *Die französisch-reformierte Gemeinde*, 114.

71. Oppenheim Capitulation, Hessisches Staatsarchiv Darmstadt, A2, 197/368; cf. Bothe, "Fürstliche Wirtschaftspolitik," 115–16.

72. Bothe, "Erzbischof Johan Schweikart," 21; Friedrichs, "Politics or Pogrom?," 187–88.

73. *FRH*, vol. 1, Beilage CXVII, 179–81.

74. *FRH*, vol. 1, Beilage CXVII, 179.

75. *FRH*, vol. 1, Beilage CXVII, 181.

76. *FRH*, vol. 1, Beilage CXVII, 181.

77. *FRH*, vol. 1, Beilage CXVII, 182.

78. Ebrard, *Die französisch-reformierte Gemeinde*, 114–15.

79. Ebrard, *Die französisch-reformierte Gemeinde*, 115–17.

80. *FRH*, vol. 1, sec. 1, 5; Ebrard, *Die französich-reformierte Gemeinde*, 106.

81. A. Kirchner, *Geschichte der Stadt*, 2:434–35; cf. Ebrard, *Die französisch-reformierte Gemeinde*, 107.

82. Eire, "Calvin and Nicodemism," 45–69; Eire, *War against the Idols*, 235–38; Gunther, *Reformation Unbound*, 99, 104–5; Woo, "Nicodemism and Libertinism," 287–96.

83. John Calvin to the Church of Frankfurt, 27 October 1562, in *CO* 19:566.

84. Calvin to the Church of Frankfurt, 27 October 1562, 566.
85. Calvin to the Church of Frankfurt, 27 October 1562, 567.
86. Christian Moser, *A Companion to Peter Martyr Vermigli* (Leiden: Brill, 2009), 450–51.
87. Peter Martyr Vermigli to Frankfurt, April 1562, qtd. in Bauer, *Die Beziehung Calvins*, 67.
88. Vermigli to Frankfurt, April 1562, 67.
89. Spohnholz, *Tactics of Toleration*, 42–47; Luebke, *Hometown Religion*, 50–59.
90. Luebke, *Hometown Religion*, 12–13, 50–63.
91. Luebke, *Hometown Religion*, 51. Jesse Spohnholz has shown how in other cities, the Eucharist itself could be deemed a malleable signifier of confessional unity (Spohnholz, "Multiconfessional Celebration of the Eucharist," 705–30).
92. C. Parker, "The Moral Agency," 44; cf. Mentzer, "Disciplina nervus ecclesiae"; and Kaplan, "Dutch Particularism."
93. Spohnholz, *Convent of Wesel*, 45–46; Benedict, *Christ's Churches*, 283–85.
94. Freudenberg and Siller, eds., *Emder Synode 1571*.
95. Kaller, "Die Anfänge."
96. IfSG, FRG, 99, 9v.
97. IfSG, FRG, 99, 105v–106r.
98. "Arrêté de la Classe de Heidelberg sur le baptême 1586," in appendix B to Schröder, *Troisième Jubilé Séculaire*, 69.
99. *PNRG*, 163, 327.
100. *PNRG*, 163, 327.
101. *PNRG*, 163, 328.
102. *PNRG*, 163, 328.
103. Luebke, *Hometown Religion*, 13.
104. Meinert, introduction to *Auszüge*, xxxxii–xxxxiii; Ebrard, *Die französisch-reformierte Gemeinde*, 111.
105. Meinert, introduction to *PRNG*, 7.
106. IfSG, FRG, 1, 1571.
107. Johann, *Kontrolle mit Konsens*, 262.
108. Valérand Poullain, "Bittschrift," in *FRH*, vol. 1, Beilage I, 1–2; reprinted in Ebrard, *Die französisch-reformierte*, 156–58.
109. *PNRG*, 72, 238.
110. "pasle des diacres," Diakonieordnung von 1585, in Ebrard, *Die französisch-reformierte*, 159.
111. Diakonieordnung von 1585, in Ebrard, *Die französisch-reformierte*, 159.
112. *PNRG*, 64, 230.
113. *PNRG*, 64, 230.
114. *PNRG*, 87, 252.
115. *PNRG*, 87–88, 252.

116. *PNRG*, 88, 252

117. *PNRG*, 88, 253.

118. *PNRG*, 88, 253.

119. *PNRG*, 88–89, 254.

120. *PNRG*, 89, 254.

121. IfSG, FRG, 1, 2, 31 October 1571, 13 December 1571.

122. *PNRG*, 94, 258.

123. T. Kirchner, *Katholiken, Lutheraner und Reformierte.*

124. *PNRG*, 196–97, 362.

125. *PNRG*, 98, 263.

126. *PNRG*, 77, 242.

127. *PNRG*, 208, 373.

128. *PNRG*, 98, 263.

129. Spijker, *The Ecclesiastical Offices*, 170.

130. *PNRG*, 98, 263.

131. *PNRG*, 101, 265.

132. *PNRG*, 109, 273.

133. *PNRG*, 113, 277.

134. *PNRG*, 121, 285.

135. *PNRG*, 128, 293.

136. *PNRG*, 151, 315.

137. *PNRG*, 164–65, 329–30.

138. *PNRG*, 184, 349.

139. *PNRG*, 211, 376.

140. *PNRG*, 162, 326.

141. *PNRG*, 110, 274.

142. *PNRG*, 123, 287.

143. Tol, *Germany and the French Wars of Religion*, 100.

144. *PNRG*, 123, 287.

145. *PNRG*, 123–24, 288.

146. Stensland, *Habsburg Communication*, 58; G. Parker, *The Dutch Revolt*, 99.

147. Kamen, *The Duke of Alba*, 114–15.

148. Kamen, *The Duke of Alba*, 115–17.

149. *PNRG*, 123, 287.

150. *PNRG*, 123–24, 288.

151. *PNRG* 169, 333.

152. *PNRG*, 169, 333.

153. Karant-Nunn, *Reformation and Ritual*, 127.

154. *PNRG*, 109, 273.

155. C. Parker, "The Moral Agency," 44–45.

156. Schröder, *Troisième Jubilé Séculaire*, 12.

157. Schröder, *Troisième Jubilé Séculaire*, 12; Spohnholz, *Convent of Wesel*, 44; Benedict, *Christ's Churches*, 283–85

158. IfSG, FRG, 1, 6.
159. Marnef, *Antwerp in the Age of Reformation;* Fehler, *Poor Relief and Protestanntism;* Spohnholz, *Tactics of Toleration.*
160. Kingdon, *Adultery and Divorce.*
161. *FRH,* vol. 1, Beilage LXIII, 100.
162. Ebrard, *Die französich-reformierte Gemeinde,* 104.
163. *PNRG,* 92–93, 257.
164. *PNRG,* 93, 257.

## Conclusion

1. Atzert, "Die Ausgrabungen," 13; Görcke, "Das Bauen," 247; Bothe, *Geschichte des St. Katharinen- und Weißfrauenstifts,* 8–9, 22–23; E. Schäfer, *Die Kirche,* 84; Bund, *1436–1986: 550 Jahre.*
2. Atzert, "Die Ausgrabungen," 13; Dechent, *Kirchengeschichte,* 1:155.
3. Stanton et al. in Whittingham, *A Brieff discours,* 8.
4. Dietz, *Frankfurter Bürgerbuch,* 189; Mauersberg, *Wirtschafts- und Sozialgeschichte,* 48–55.
5. Whittingham, *A Brieff discours,* 8–19.
6. Robert Horne et al. to the English in Frankfurt, Zurich 13 October 1554, in Whittingham, *A Brieff discours,* 15.
7. Whittingham, *A Brieff discours,* 23–24.
8. IfSG, FRG, 1, 5.
9. IfSG, FRG, 1, 6.
10. Müller, *Exile Memories,* 1–17, 37–38.
11. IfSG, FRG, 1, 5.
12. Denis, *Les Églises d'étranger,* Schilling, *Niederländische Exulanten.*
13. IfSG, *FRH,* vol. 1, Beilage I, 1.
14. Peter Geltner et al. to the Frankfurt Council, 5 September 1555, in *FRH,* vol. 1, Beilage III, 5.
15. Peter Geltner et al. to the Frankfurt Council, 29 October 1555, in *FRH,* vol. 1, Beilage IV, 7.
16. Geltner et al. to the Frankfurt Council, 5 September 1555, 5.
17. "Extract Niederlender Supplication vom 7. Aug. 1561," *FRH,* vol. 1, Beilage XLII, 77.
18. Geltner et al. to Frankfurt Council, 5 September 1555, 4.
19. Lasco, *Joannis a Lasco opera,* 2:22.
20. Richard Vauville to Calvin, Frankfurt, 10 April 1555, in CO 15:2181:558.
21. Molen, "Anglican against Puritan," 50; Garrett, *The Marian Exiles,* 59; Lim, *In Pursuit of Purity,* 213–14. For a reassessment of the impact of the Frankfurt conflicts on Elizabethan Christianity, see Gunther, *Reformation Unbounded,* 158–88.
22. Datheen [Dathenus], *Kurtze und warhafftige Erzelung,* chap. 8, 2.

23. Knox, *Works*, 3:308.

24. Denis, *Les Églises d'étrangers*, 47–122, 147–60.

25. On the tensions between refugees and Cologne, see Schilling, *Niederländische Exulanten*, 152–54.

26. Pettegree, *Emden and the Dutch Revolt*, 148.

27. Kaplan, "The Legal Rights"; Dölemeyer, *Die Hugenotten*.

28. IfSG, FRG, 1, "Verfassung der Gemeinde."

29. Rp, 27 July 1596, in *Auszüge*, 576; cf. Meinert, introduction to *Auszüge*, xxxxiii; and Fischer, "Die Gründung;" Bott, *Gründung*.

30. Terpstra, *Religious Refugees*, 2–3.

## Epilogue

1. Goethe, *Werke* 9:160.

2. Ebrard, *Die französisch-reformierte Gemeinde*, 100–101.

3. Friedrichs, "Politics or Pogrom?," 186–228; Bothe, ed., *Frankfurts wirtschaftlich-soziale Entwicklung*; Bothe, "Erzbischof Johann Schweikart," 14–17; cf. Brunner, "Souveranitatsproblem und Sozialstruktur," 329–60.

4. Bothe, "Erzbischof Johann Schweikart," 14–17.

5. Bürgervertrag, 1612, in Bothe, ed., *Frankfurts wirtschaftlich-soziale Entwicklung*, 32.

6. Soliday, *A Community in Conflict*, 15.

7. Soliday, *A Community in Conflict*, 15–16.

8. Goethe, *Werke*, 9:148.

9. Soliday, *A Community in Conflict*, 16–21.

10. Soliday, *A Community in Conflict*, 16–21.

11. Soliday, *A Community in Conflict*, 225.

12. Soliday, *A Community in Conflict*, 206–10.

13. Soliday, *A Community in Conflict*, 209. A reprinting of the Denizen Ordinance of 1708 exists in *FRH*, vol. 1, Lit. B, 15–25.

14. Soliday, *A Community in Conflict*, 209.

15. Soliday, *A Community in Conflict*, 228–29.

16. Ebrard, *Die französisch-reformierte Gemeinde*, 128–30; Whaley, *Religious Toleration and Social Change*, 167–68.

17. Whaley, *Religious Toleration and Social Change*, 168.

18. Ebrard, *Die französisch-reformierte Gemeinde*, 130.

19. Lersner, *Der Weit-berühmten* 273.

20. Telschow, *Die alte Frankfurter Kirche*, 24; Ebrard, *Die französisch-reformierte Gemeinde*, 115.

21. Telschow, *Die alte Frankfurter Kirche*, 24.

22. Ebrard, *Die französisch-reformierte Gemeinde*, 140–41; Telschow, *Die alte Frankfurter Kirche*, 29–30.

23. Telschow, *Die alte Frankfurter Kirche*, 59–61.

24. Telschow, *Die alte Frankfurter Kirche*, 66.

25. Telschow, *Die alte Frankfurter Kirche*, 79; cf. Telschow, *Evangelische Kirche*; Telschow, *Ringen um den rechten Weg*.

26. Telschow, *Die alte Frankfurter Kirche*, 153–60; cf. Telschow, *Evangelische Kirche*; Telschow, *Ringen um den rechten Weg*.

27. Telschow, *Die alte Frankfurter Kirche*, 130–59; Telschow, *Ringen um den rechten Weg*.

# BIBLIOGRAPHY

## ARCHIVES

Hessisches Staatsarchiv Darmstadt
Hessisches Staatsarchiv Marburg
Institut für Stadtgeschichte Frankfurt
Universitätsbibliothek Johann Christian Senckenberg, Frankfurt

## PUBLISHED PRIMARY SOURCES

Beyerbach, Johann Conradin. *Sammlungen der Verordnungen der Reichsstadt Frankfurt, 1530–1806.* 11 parts. Frankfurt, 1798–1818.

Bothe, Friedrich, ed. *Frankfurts wirtschaftlich-soziale Entwicklung vor dem Dreißigjährigen Kriege und der Fettmilchaufstand, 1612–1616.* Vol. 2. Frankfurt a. M.: Joseph Baer, 1920.

Bucer, Martin. *Deutsche Schriften.* Edited by Robert Stupperich and Gottfried Seebass. 10 vols. Gütersloh: Gerd Mohn, 1960–87.

———. *Von der waren Seelsorge, unnd dem rechten Hirten dienst.* Strasbourg: Wendel Rihel, 1538.

Calvin, John. *Ioannis Calvini Opera quae supersunt omnia.* Edited by Guilielmus Baum, Eduardus Cunitz, and Eduardus Reuss. 59 vols. Brunswick, Germany, 1863–1900. Also published as volumes 29–87 of *Corpus Reformatorum.*

Cummings, Brian, ed. *The Book of Common Prayer: The Texts of 1549, 1559, and 1662.* Oxford: Oxford University Press, 2011.

Datheen [Dathenus], Peter. *Kurtze und warhafftige Erzelung, welcher massen, den Frantzösischen unnd Niderländischen verjagten Christen, in der Statt Franckfurt am Meyn [. . .].* Heidelberg, 1563. Reprint, Christoff Löw und Johan Lancelot, 1598.

Foxe, John. *The Acts and Monuments of John Foxe.* Edited by George Townsend and Stephen Reed Cattley. 8 vols. London, 1837.

———. *The Unabridged Acts and Monuments Online or TAMO (1563 edition).* The Digital Humanities Institute. Sheffield, 2011. Available from http://www.dhi.ac.uk/foxe.

*Franckfurtische Religions-Handlungen [. . .].* 2 vols. Frankfurt a. M.: Frantz Varrentrapp, 1735.

Goethe, Johann Wolfgang von. *Goethes Werke: Hamburger Ausgabe*. 14 vols. Hamburg: Wegner, 1948.

Herminjard, Aimé Louis, ed. *Correspondance des Réformateurs dans les pays de langue Française*. 9 vols. Geneva, 1866–97.

Hildenbrand, Johann Friedrich, ed. *Quellen zur Geschichte der Stadt Frankenthal*. Vol. 1, *Kapitulation von 1562 und 1573; Bauordnung 1569 und Festungsverträge 1620, 1622. Mit 4 Abbildungen* (1894).

Hooper, John, and John a Lasco. *Whether Christian faith maye be kepte secret in the heart, without confession thereof openly to the worlde as occasion shal serve*. London, 1553. https://quod.lib.umich.edu/e/eebo/A18644.0001.001/1:1?rgn =div1;view=fulltext.

Jung, Rudolf, ed. *Frankfurter Chroniken und annalistische Aufzeichnungen der Reformationszeit*. Vol. 2 of *Quellen zur Frankfurter Geschichte*, edited by Hermann Grotefend. Frankfurt a. M.: Carl Jügel, 1888.

Kiefner, Theo. *Die Privilegien der nach Deutschland gekommenen Waldenser* 2 vols. Stuttgart: W. Kohlhammer, 1990.

Knox, John. *The Works of John Knox*. Edited by David Laing. 6 vols. Edinburgh: Bannatyne Club, 1846–64.

Lasco, John a. *Joannis a Lasco opera [. . .]: Recensuit vitam auctoris*. Edited by Abraham Kuyper. Amsterdam: F. Muller, 1866.

Luther, Martin. *D. Martin Luthers Werke: Kritische Gesamtausgabe*. Weimarer Ausgabe. 127 vols. Weimar: Böhlau, 1883–2009.

Meinert, Herman, ed. *Die Eingliederung der niederländischen Glaubensflüchtlinge in die Frankfurter Bürgerschaft, 1554–1596: Auszüge aus den Frankfurter Ratsprotokollen*. Frankfurt a. M.: Waldemar Kramer, 1981.

Meinert, Hermann, and Wolfram Dahmer, eds. *Das Protokollbuch der Niederländischen Reformierten Gemeinde zu Frankfurt am Main, 1570–1581*. Frankfurt a. M.: Waldemar Kramer, 1977.

Melanchthon, Philip. *Corpus Reformatorum: Philippi Melanchthonis opera quae supersunt omnia*. 28 vols. 1834–1960.

Musculus, Wolfgang. *The Temporysour*. Translated from Valérand Poullain's French by Robert Pownall. [Wesel?], 1555.

Poullain, Valérand. *Liturgia sacra, seu ritus ministerii in ecclesia peregrinorum profugorum propter Evangelium Christi Argentinae*. London, 1551.

———. *Valerandus Pollanus: Liturgia sacra*. Edited by A. C. Honders. Leiden: Brill, 1970.

Robinson, Hastings, ed. *Original Letters Relative to the English Reformation, Written during the Reigns of King Henry VIII, King Edward VI, and Queen Mary: Chiefly from the Archives of Zurich*. 2 vols. Cambridge: Cambridge University Press, 1846–47.

Schade, Herwarth von, ed. *Joachim Westphal und Peter Braubach: Briefwechsel zwischen dem Hamburger Hauptpastor, seinem Drucker-Verleger und ihrem*

*Freund Hartmann Beyer in Frankfurt am Main über die Lage der Kirche und die Verbreitung von Büchern.* Hamburg: Friedrich Wittig, 1981.

Schroeder, F. C. *Troisième Jubilé Séculaire de la Fondation de L'Église Réformée Française de Francfort s/M: Discours prononcés a cette occasion, le 18 Mars 1854 par les pasteurs de cette église.* Frankfurt a. M., 1854.

Strype, John. *Memorials of the Most Reverend Father in God, Thomas Cranmer sometime Lord Archbishop of Canterbury wherein the history of the Church, and the reformation of it, during the primacy of the said archbishop, are greatly illustrated: and many singular matters relating thereunto: now first published in three books: collected chiefly from records, registers, authentick letters, and other original manuscripts.* London: Richard Chiswell, 1694.

Utenhove, Jan. *Simplex et fidelis narratio.* Basel, 1560.

Whittingham, William. *A Brieff discours off the troubles begonne at Franckford in Germany anno domini 1554 aboute the booke off off [sic] common prayer.* Heidelberg, 1574.

## SECONDARY SOURCES

Abeele, Robert M. van den. "Nederlandse vluchtelingen te Frankfort in de XVIde eeuw." In *Onze Stam: Familienkundige Bijlage van "Ons Heem,"* 8. Antwerp, 1950.

Abray, Lorna Jane. *The People's Reformation: Magistrates, Clergy, and Commons in Strasbourg, 1500–1598.* Ithaca, NY: Cornell University Press, 1985.

Aerts, Erik, and John Munro, eds. *Textiles of the Low Countries in European Economic History.* Leuven, Belgium: Leuven University Press, 1990.

Albers, Johann Heinrich. *Geschichte der Stadt Metz: Nach den zuverlässigsten Chroniken und auf Grund von Einzeldarstellungen bis auf die Gegenwart.* Metz: G. Scriba, 1902.

Arnade, Peter. *Beggars, Iconoclasts, and Civic Patriots: The Political Culture of the Dutch Revolt.* Ithaca, NY: Cornell University Press, 2008.

Atzert, Walther. "Die Ausgrabungen in der Weißfrauenkirche zu Frankfurt am Main." *Archiv für Frankfurts Geschichte und Kunst* 47 (1960): 11–31.

Backhaus, Fritz et al., eds. *Die Frankfurter Judengasse: Jüdisches Leben in der Frühen Neuzeit.* Frankfurt a. M.: Societäts-Verlag, 2006.

Bade, Klaus J., ed. *Deutsche im Ausland, Fremde in Deutschland: Migration in Geschichte und Gegenwart.* Munich: Beck, 1992.

Badea, Andrea. *Kurfürstliche Präeminenz, Landesherrschaft und Reform: Das Scheitern der Kölner Reformation unter Hermann von Wied.* Münster: Aschendorff Verlag, 2009.

Bahlcke, Joachim, ed. *Glaubensflüchtlinge: Ursachen, Formen und Auswirkungen frühneuzeitlicher Konfessionsmigration in Europa.* Berlin: Lit Verlag, 2008.

Bartel, Oskar. *Jan Laski.* Warsaw: Państwowe Wydawn Naukowe, 1955.

Battonn, Johann Georg. *Oertliche Beschreibung der Stadt Frankfurt am Main.* Edited by L. H. Euler. 7 vols. Frankfurt a. M.: Verein für Geschichte und Altertumskunde, 1861–75.

Bauer, Karl. "Der Bekenntnisstand der Reichsstadt Frankfurt a. M. im Zeitalter der Reformation." *ARG* 19 (1922): 194–251; *ARG* 20 (1923): 127–74; *ARG* 21 (1924): 1–36, 206–38; *ARG* 22 (1925): 39–101.

——. *Die Beziehungen Calvins zu Frankfurt a. M.* Leipzig: Vermittlungsverlag von Heinsius Nachfolger, 1920.

——. "Die Einstellung des reformierten Gottesdienstes in der Reichstadt Frankfurt a. M. im Jahre 1561." Ph.D. diss., University of Münster, 1925.

——. *Valérand Poullain: Ein kirchengeschichtliches Zeitbild aus der Mitte des sechzehnten Jahrhunderts.* Elberfeld: Buchhandlung des Erziehungsvereins, 1927.

Beck, Kurt. *Rat und Kirche: Der Rat der Freien Reichsstadt Frankfurt am Main und des Evangelisch-lutherische Predigerministerium.* Frankfurt a. M.: Evangelischer Regionalverband, 1981.

Becker, Judith. *Gemeindeordnung und Kirchenzucht: Johannes a Lascos Kirchenordnung für London (1555) und die reformierte Konfessionsbildung.* Leiden: Brill, 2007.

Beik, William. *A Social and Cultural History of Early Modern France.* Cambridge: Cambridge University Press, 2009.

Benedict, Philip. *Christ's Churches Purely Reformed: A Social History of Calvinism.* New Haven, CT: Yale University Press, 2002.

——. "Un roi, une loi, deux fois: Parameters for the History of Catholic-Reformed Co-existence in France, 1555–1685." In *Tolerance and Intolerance in the European Reformation,* edited by Ole Peter Grell and Bob Scribner, 65–93. Cambridge: Cambridge University Press, 1996.

Besser, Gustav Adolf. *Geschichte der Frankfurter Flüchtlingsgemeinden, 1554–1558.* Halle a. S.: Max Niemeyer, 1906.

Bischoff, Johannes. *Lexikon deutscher Hugenotten-Orte: Mit Literatur- und Quellen-Nachweisen für ihre evangelisch-reformierten Réfugiés-Gemeinden von Flamen, Franzosen, Waldensern und Wallonen.* Bad Karlshafen: Verlag des Deutschen Hugenotten-Vereins, 1994.

Bleicher, Heinrich. *Statische Beschreibung der Stadt Frankfurt am Main und ihrer Bevölkerung.* 2 vols. Frankfurt a. M.: Sauerländer in Komm, 1892–95.

Blickle, Peter. *From the Communal Reformation to the Revolution of the Common Man.* Translated by Beat Kümin. Leiden: Brill, 1998.

Blum, Daniela. *Multikonfessionalität im Alltag: Speyer Zwischen politischem Frieden und Bekenntniszwang, 1555–1618.* Münster: Aschendorff, 2015.

Boes, Maria R. *Crime and Punishment in Early Modern Germany: Court and Adjudicatory Practices in Frankfurt am Main, 1562–1696.* Surrey, UK: Ashgate, 2013.

Bonney, Richard, and D. J. B. Trim, eds. *Persecution and Pluralism: Calvinists and Religious Minorities in Early Modern Europe, 1550–1700.* Oxford: Peter Lang, 2006.

Bornert, René. *La réforme protestante du culte à Strasbourg au XVIe siècle, 1523–1598.* Leiden: Brill, 1981.

Bothe, Friedrich. "Beiträge zur Wirtschafts- und Sozialgeschichte der Reichsstadt Frankfurt." In *Beilage zum Jahresbericht der Liebig-Realschule Fr. a. M.* Altenburg: Ostern, 1906.

———, ed. *Die Entwicklung der direkten Besteuerung in der Reichsstadt Frankfurt bis zur Revolution 1612–1614.* Leipzig: Duncker and Humbolt, 1906.

———. "Erzbischof Johan Schweikart vom Mainz." In *Archiv für Frankfurts Geschichte und Kunst,* 9–40. Frankfurt a. M.: Waldemar Kramer, 1951.

———. *Frankfurter Patriziervermögen im 16. Jahrhungert: Ein Beitrag zur Charakteristik der bürgerlichen Vermögen und der bürgerlichen Kultur.* Berlin: A. Duncker, 1908.

———. *Frankfurts wirtschaflich-soziale Entwicklung vor dem Dreißigjährigen Krlege und der Fettmilchaufstand.* Part 2: *Statistische Bearbeitungen und urkundliche Belege.* Frankfurt a. M.: Historische Kommission der Stadt Frankfurt a. Main, 1920.

———. "Fürstliche Wirschaftspolitik und die Reichsstadt Frankfurt vor dem Dreißigjährigen Krieg." *Archiv für Frankfurts Geschichte und Kunst* 4, Folge 2 (1929): 103–23.

———. *Geschichte der Stadt Frankfurt a. M. in Wort und Bild.* 3rd ed. Frankfurt a. M.: Englert Schlosser, 1929.

———. *Geschichte des St. Katharinen- und Weißfrauenstifts zu Frankfurt am Main.* Frankfurt a. M.: Waldemar Kramer, 1950.

Bott, Heinrich. *Gründung und Anfänge der Neustadt Hanau, 1596–1620.* 2 vols. Marburg: Historische Kommission für Hessen und Waldeck, 1970–71.

Brady, Thomas A. *Community, Politics and Reformation in Early Modern Europe.* Leiden: Brill, 1998.

———. "A Crisis Averted: Jacob Sturm and the Truce of Frankfurt, 1539." In *Krisenbewusstsein und Krisenbewältigung in der frühen Neuzeit: Festschrift für Hans-Christoph Rublack,* edited by Monika Hagenmaier and Sabine Holtz, 47–60. Frankfurt a. M.: Peter Lang, 1992.

———. *German Histories in the Age of Reformations, 1400–1650.* Cambridge: Cambridge University Press, 2009.

———. *Ruling Class, Regime and Reformation at Strasbourg, 1520–1555.* Leiden: Brill, 1978.

———. *Turning Swiss: Cities and Empire, 1450–1550.* Cambridge: Cambridge University Press, 1985.

Brandt, Robert, Olaf Cunitz, Jan Ermel, and Michael Graf, eds. *Der Fettmilch-Aufstand: Bürgerunruhen und Judenfeindschaft in Frankfurt am Main, 1612–1616*. Frankfurt a. M.: Historisches Museum Frankfurt, 1996.

Braun, Guido, and Susanne Lachenicht, eds. *Hugenotten und deutsche Territorialstaaten: Immigrationspolitik und Integrationsprozesse = Les Etats allemands et les Huguenots: Politique d'immigration et processus d'integration*. Munich: Oldenbourg, 2007.

Breustedt, Sonja. "Die rechtspolitische Steuerung der Immigration im frühneuzeitlichen Frankfurt am Main." *Zeitschrift für Historische Forschung* 44, no. 4 (2017): 597–633.

Brück, Anton Philipp. "Pfalzgraf Reichart von Simmern als Kandidat für den Mainzer Erzstuhl 1555." *Blätter für pfälzische Kirchengeschichte und religiöse Volkskunde* 21 (1954): 2, 11.

Brunner, Otto. "Souveranitatsproblem und Sozialstruktur in den deutschen Reichsstadten der früheren Neuzeit." *Vierteljahrschriftfiir Sozial- und Wirtschaftsgeschichte* 50 (1963): 329–60.

Bücher, Karl. *Die Bevölkerung von Frankfurt am Main im XIV. und XV. Jahrhundert*. Tübingen, 1886.

Buck, Lawrence. "The Reformation, Purgatory, and Perpetual Rents and the Revolt of 1525 at Frankfurt am Main." In *Pietas et Societas: New Trends in Reformation Social History: Essays in Memory of Harold J. Grimm*, edited by Grimm, Kyle C. Sessions, and Philip N. Bebb, 23–33. Kirksville, MO: Sixteenth Century Journal, 1985.

Bund, Konrad. "Frankfurt am Main im Spätmittelalter." In *Frankfurt am Main: Die Geschichte der Stadt in neun Beiträgen*, edited by Frankfurter Historischen Kommission, 53–149. Sigmaringen: Jan Thorbecke, 1994.

———. *400 Jahre Niederländische Gemeinde Augsburger Konfession zu Frankfurt am Main 1585–1985*. Frankfurt: Stadtarchiv, 1985.

———. *1436–1986: 550 Jahre Stadtarchiv Frankfurt am Main: Eine Kurzübersicht über seine Bestände*. Frankfurt a. M.: Waldemar Kramer, 1986.

Burn, John Southerden. *The History of the French, Walloon, Dutch and Other Foreign Protestant Refugees Settled in England from the Reign of Henry VIII to the Revocation of the Edict of Nantes; with Notices of Their Trade and Commerce, Copious Extracts from the Registers, Lists of the Early Settlers, Ministers, &c., and an Appendix Containing Copies of the Charter of Edward VI, &c*. London: Longman, Brown, Green, and Longmans, 1846.

Burnett, Amy Nelson. *Debating the Sacraments: Print and Authority in the Early Reformation*. Oxford: Oxford University Press, 2018.

———. "A Generational Conflict in the Late Reformation: The Basel Paroxysm." *Journal of Interdisciplinary History* 32, no. 2 (Autumn 2001): 217–42.

———. *The Yoke of Christ: Martin Bucer and Christian Discipline*. Kirksville, MO: Truman State University Press, 1994.

Bütfering, Elisabeth. "Niederländische Exulanten in Frankenthal: Gründungs-geschichte, Bevölkerungsstruktur und Migrationsverhalten." In *Kunst, Kommerz, Glaubenskampf: Frankenthal um 1600,* edited by Edgar Hürkey, 37–47. Worms: Wernersche Verlagsgesellschaft, 1995.

Calinich, Robert. *Der Naumburger Fürstentag 1561: Ein Beitrag zur Geschichte des Lutherthums und des Melanchthonismus aus den Quellen des Königlichen Hauptstaatsarchivs zu Dresden.* Gotha: Perthes, 1870.

Cameron, Euan. "Frankfurt and Geneva: The European Context of John Knox's Reformation." In *John Knox and the British Reformation,* edited by Roger Mason, 51–73. Aldershot, UK: Ashgate, 1998.

Canny, Nicholas P., ed. *Europeans on the Move: Studies in European Migration, 1500–1800.* Oxford: Oxford University Press, 1994.

Carvalho, Benjamin de, and Andrew Paras. "Sovereignty and Solidarity: Moral Obligations, Confessional England, and the Huguenots." *International History Review* 37, no. 1 (February 2015): 1–21.

Cavaciocchi, Simonetta, ed. *Le migrazioni in Europa secc. XIII–XVLLL.* Florence: Le Monnier, 1994.

Cerutti, Simona. *Étrangers: Étude d'une condition d'incertitude dans une société d'Ancien Régime.* Paris: Bayard, 2012.

Chadwick, Owen. "The Making of a Reforming Prince: Frederick III, Elector Palatine." In *Reformation, Conformity and Dissent: Essays in Honour of Geoffrey Nuttall,* edited by R. Buick Knox, 44–69. London: Epworth, 1977.

Chaunu, Pierre. *Le temps des Réformes: Histoire religieuse et système de civilization.* Brussels: Éditions Complexe, 1984.

Christman, Victoria. *Pragmatic Toleration: The Politics of Religious Heterodoxy in Early Reformation Antwerp, 1515–1555.* Rochester, NY: University of Rochester Press, 2015.

Christmann, Volker. "Die Kapitulation zwischen Kurpfalz und den Einwohnern von Frankenthal, 1562 und 1571." *Frankenthal einst und jetzt* 2 (1962): 16–20.

Close, Christopher W. "Empires of Alliances: Shared Sovereignty and State Formation in Early Modern Europe, 1488–1686." Manuscript. November 22, 2019.

———. *The Negotiated Reformation: Imperial Cities and the Politics of Urban Reform, 1525–1550.* Cambridge: Cambridge University Press, 2009.

Cohn, Henry J. "The Territorial Princes in Germany's Second Reformation, 1559–1622." In *International Calvinism, 1541–1715,* edited by Menna Prestwich, 135–66. Oxford: Clarendon, 1985.

Coleman, D. C. "An Innovation and Its Diffusion: The 'New Draperies.'" *Economic History Review* 22 (1969): 417–29.

Collinson, Patrick. "The Authorship of *A Brieff Discours off the Troubles Begonne at Franckford.*" *Journal of Ecclesiastical History* 9, no. 2 (October 1958): 188–208.

Cottret, Bernard. *The Huguenots in England: Immigration and Settlement, 1550–1700.* Translated by Peregrine Stevenson and Adriana Stevenson. Cambridge: Cambridge University Press, 1991.

Cover, Robert. "The Supreme Court 1982 Term, Forward: Nomos and Narrative." *Harvard Law Review* 97 (1983): 4–68.

Cowell, H. J. "The Sixteenth-Century, English-Speaking Refugee Churches at Geneva and Frankfort." In *Proceedings of the Huguenot Society of London* 14 (1933): 62–95.

Creasman, Allyson. *Censorship and Civic Order in Reformation Germany, 1517–1648: "Printed Poison and Evil Talk."* Aldershot, UK: Ashgate, 2012.

Cuming, G. J. *A History of Anglican Liturgy.* 2nd ed. Houndmills, UK: Macmillan, 1988.

Cuno, Friedrich Wilhelm. "Geschichte der wallonisch-reformirten Gemeinde zu Frankenthal." *Geschichtsblätter des Deutschen Hugenotten-Vereins* 3, no. 3 (Magdeburg, 1894).

Dalton, Hermann. *Johannes A Lasco: Beitrag zur Reformationsgeschichte Polens, Deutschlands und Englands.* Gotha, 1881.

Danner, Dan. *Pilgrimage to Puritanism: History and Theology of the Marian Exiles at Geneva, 1555–1560.* New York: Peter Lang, 1999.

Davis, Natalie Zemon. *The Return of Martin Guerre.* Cambridge, MA: Harvard University Press, 2001.

———. *Society and Culture in Early Modern France: Eight Essays.* Stanford, CA: Stanford University Press, 1975.

Dawson, Jane. *John Knox.* New Haven, CT: Yale University Press, 2016.

Dechent, Hermann. *Kirchengeschichte von Frankfurt am Main seit der Reformation.* 2 vols. Leipzig and Frankfurt a. M.: Kesselring, 1913–21.

Denis, Philippe. *Les Églises d'étrangers en Pays Rhénans, 1538–1564.* Paris: Les Belles Lettres, 1984.

Dickens, A. G. *The English Reformation.* 2nd ed. University Park: Pennsylvania State University Press, 2005.

Diefendorf, Barbara B. *Beneath the Cross: Catholic and Huguenots in Sixteenth-Century Paris.* New York: Oxford University Press, 1991.

Dienst, Karl. "Die Barfüßerkirche als Frankfurter Hauptkirche." In *Von der Barfüßerkirche zur Paulskirche: Beiträge zur Frankfurter Stadt- und Kirchengeschichte,* edited by Roman Fischer, 123–86. Frankfurt a. M.: Kramer, 2001.

———. "Geschichte des lutherischen Gottesdienstes der Freien Reichstadt Frankfurt am Main." Ph.D. diss., Mainz University, 1955.

Dietz, Alexander. *Frankfurter Bürgerbuch: Geschichtliche Mittheilungen über 600 bekannte frankfurter Familien aus der Zeit vor 1806.* Frankfurt a. M.: August Osterrieth, 1897.

———. *Frankfurter Handelsgeschichte.* 4 vols. Frankfurt a. M.: Hermann Minjon, 1910–25.

———. *Stammbuch der Frankfurter Juden: Geschichtliche Mitteilungen über die Frankfurter jüdischen Familien von 1349–1849.* Frankfurt a. M.: J. St. Goar, 1907.

Dingel, Irene. "Religionssupplikationen der Französisch-Reformierten Gemeinde in Frankfurt am Main." In *Calvin und Calvinismus: Europäische Perspektiven,* edited by Dingel and Herman Selderhuis, 281–96. Göttingen: Vanderhoek and Ruprecht, 2011.

Dingel, Irene, and Herman J. Selderhuis, eds. *Calvin and Calvinismus: Europäische Perspektiven.* Göttingen: Vandenhoek and Ruprecht, 2011.

Dölemeyer, Barbara. *Aspekte zur Rechtsgeschichte des Deutschen Refuge.* Sickte: Verlag des Deutschen Hugenotten-Vereins, 1998.

———. *Die Hugenotten.* Stuttgart: Kohlhammer, 2006.

———. *Hier finde ich meine Zuflucht: Auf den Spuren der Hugenotten und Waldenser im südlichen Hessen.* Bad Karlshafen: Verlag der Deutschen Hugenotten-Gesellschaft, 1999.

Druffel, August von, ed. *Beiträge zur Reichsgeschichte 1546–1555.* 4 vols. Munich: M. Rieger, 1873–96.

Duffy, Eamon. *Fires of Faith: Catholic England under Mary Tudor.* New Haven, CT: Yale University Press, 2009.

Duke, Alastair. *Reformation and Revolt in the Low Countries.* London: Hambledon and London, 2003.

Dülmen, Richard, van. *Theatre of Horror: Crime and Punishment in Early Modern Germany.* Translated by Elisabeth Neu. Cambridge: UK: Polity, 1990.

DuPlessis, Robert. *Lille and the Dutch Revolt: Urban Stability in an Era of Revolution, 1500–1582.* Cambridge: Cambridge University Press, 1991.

Dyer, Thomas Henry. *The Life of John Calvin.* New York, 1850.

Ebrard, Friedrich Clemens. *Die französisch-reformierte Gemeinde in Frankfurt am Main, 1554–1904.* Frankfurt a. M.: Richard Ecklin, 1906.

Edelmayer, Friedrich. "The Duke of Alba in the Holy Roman Empire." In *Alba: General and Servant to the Crown,* edited by Maurits Ebben, Margriet Lacy-Bruijn, and Rolof van Hövel tot Westerflier, 208–25. Rotterdam: Karwansaray, 2013.

Ehrenpreis, Stefan, and Ute Lotz-Heumann. *Reformation und konfessionelles Zeitalter.* Darmstadt: Wissenschaftliche Buchgesellschaft, 2002.

Ehrmantraut, Dominique. "L'Immigration des Hugenots dans le Palatinat entre 1649 et 1685." In *Les États allemands et les Huguenots,* edited by Guido Braun, Susanne Lachenicht, and the Institut Historique Allemand Paris. Munich: Oldenbourg, 2007.

Ehrmantraut, Dominique, and Michael Martin, eds. *Das Protokollbuch der französisch-reformierten Gemeinde zu Frankenthal, 1658–1689.* Leinfelden-Echterdingen: G. Braun Buchverlag, 2009.

Eire, Carlos M. N. "Calvin and Nicodemism: A Reappraisal." *Sixteenth Century Journal* 10 (1979): 45–69.

———. "Calvinism and the Reform of the Reformation." In *The Oxford Illustrated History of the Reformation*, edited by Peter Marshall. Oxford: Oxford University Press, 2015.

———. *Reformations: The Early Modern World, 1450–1650*. New Haven, CT: Yale University Press, 2016.

———. *War against the Idols: The Reformation of Worship from Erasmus to Calvin*. Cambridge: Cambridge University Press, 1986.

Elliott, John. *Imperial Spain, 1469–1716*. London: E. Arnold, 1963.

Ellrich, Hartmut. *Die Wittelsbacher in Bayern und am Rhein*. Petersberg: Michael Imhof, 2014.

Eltis, David. *The Military Revolution in Sixteenth Century Europe*. London: St. Martin's, 1995.

Engammare, Max. "Calvin the Workaholic." Translated by Calvin Tams. In *Calvin and His Influences, 1509–2009*, edited by Irena Backus and Philip Benedict, 67–83. Oxford: Oxford University Press, 2011.

Erichson, Alfred. *Martin Butzer, der elsässische reformator: Zu dessen 400-Jähriger Geburtsfeier den elsässischen Protestanten gewidment*. Strassburg: J. H. E. Heitz, 1891.

Evenden, Elizabeth. "The Michael Wood Mystery: William Cecil and the Lincolnshire Printing of John Day." *Sixteenth Century Journal* 35, no. 2 (2004): 383–94.

Fairfield, Leslie P. "The Mysterious Press of Michael Wood (1553–1554)." *Library* 5, no. 3 (1972): 220–23.

Favresse, Felicien. "Les Débuts de la nouvelle draperie Bruxelloise, appellee aussi draperie légère, fin du XIVe siècle-1443." *Revue belge de philology et d'histoire* 28, no. 2 (1950): 461–77.

Fehler, Timothy G. *Poor Relief and Protestantism: The Evolution of Social Welfare in Sixteenth-Century Emden*. Aldershot, UK: Ashgate, 1999.

Fehler, Timothy G., Charles H. Parker, Greta Grace Kroeker, and Jonathan Ray, eds. *Religious Diaspora in Early Modern Europe*. London: Pickering and Chatto, 2014.

Fischer, Roman. "Die Gründung der Hanauer Neustadt aus Frankfurter Sicht" In *Auswirkungen eines Stadtgründung*, edited by the Magistrat der Stadt Hanau. Hanau, 1997.

———. "Niederländische Glaubensflüchtlinge in Frankfurt am Main." *Archiv Brief: Institut für Stadtgeschichte* (2001): 7–8

Flores, A. A. "Dies wirtschaftlichen Beiträge der niederländischen Einwanderung in Nordwestdeutschland im 16. und 17. Jahrhundert." Diplomarbeit am Sem. für Wirtschafts- und Sozialgeschichte der Universität Köln, 1957–58.

Forster, Marc R. *Catholic Germany from the Reformation to the Enlightenment*. Houndmills, UK: Palgrave Macmillan, 2007.

François, Etienne, ed. *Immigration et société urbaine en Europe occidentale, XVIe–XXe siècles*. Paris: Éditions Recherche sur les civilisations, 1985.

Frankfurter Historischen Kommission, ed. *Frankfurt am Main: Die Geschichte der Stadt in neun Beiträgen*. Sigmaringen: Jan Thorbecke, 1991.

Franz, Georg. *Aus der Geschichte der Stadt Frankenthal*. Frankenthal: Ernst René Grosser, 1912.

Freudenberg Matthias, and Aleida Siller, eds. *Emder Synode 1571: Wesen und Wirkungen eines Grundtextes der Moderne*. Göttingen: Vandenhoeck and Ruprecht, 2020.

Friedrichs, Christopher R. *The Early Modern City, 1450–1750*. London: Longman, 1995.

———. "German Town Revolts and the Seventeenth-Century Crisis." *Renaissance and Modern Studies* 16 (1982): 27–51.

———. "Politics of Pogrom? The Fettmilch Uprising in German and Jewish History." *Central European History* 19, no. 2 (June 1986): 186–228.

———. "Urban Conflicts and the Imperial Constitution in Seventeenth-Century Germany." *Journal of Modern History* 58 suppl. (1986): 98–125.

Fuchs, Thomas. *Traditionsstiftung und Erinnerungspolitik: Geschichtsschreibung in Hessen in der Frühen Neuzeit*. Kassel: Verein für hessische Geschichte und Landeskunde, 2002.

Führ, Christoph, und Jürgen Telschow, eds. *Die Evangelische Kirche von Frankfurt am Main in Geschichte und Gegenwart*. Frankfurt a. M.: Evangelischer Regionalverband, 1978.

Garrett, Christina Hallowell. *The Marian Exiles: A Study in the Origins of Elizabethan Puritanism*. Cambridge: Cambridge University Press, 1938.

Gatrell, Peter. *The Making of the Modern Refugee*. Oxford: Oxford University Press, 2013.

Gelderblom, Arie-Jan, Jan L. de Jong, and Marc van Vaeck, eds. *The Low Countries as a Crossroads of Religious Beliefs*. Leiden: Brill, 2004.

Gerhard, Ernst Georg. "Geschichte der Säkularisation in Frankfurt a. M." Ph.D. diss., Johann-Wolfgang-Goethe Universität Frankfurt, 1933.

Gerteis, Klaus. *Die deutschen Städte in der Frühen Neuzeit: Zur Vorgeschichte der "bürgerlichen Welt."* Darmstadt: Wissenschaftliche Buchgesellschaft, 1986.

Görcke, Ernst. "Das Bauen der evangelischen Kirche von 1900 bis 1975 in der Stadt Frankfurt a. M." In *Die evangelische Kirche von Frankfurt am Main in Geschichte und Gegenwart*, edited by Christoph Führ and Jürgen Telschow, 246–51. Frankfurt a. M.: Evangelischer Regionalverband, 1980.

Gordon, Bruce. *Calvin*. New Haven, CT: Yale University Press, 2011.

———. *The Swiss Reformation*. Manchester: Manchester University Press, 2002.

Gotthard, Axel. *Der Augsburger Religionsfrieden*. Münster: Aschendorff, 2004.

Götz, Johann Baptist. *Die erste Einführung des Kalvinismus in der Oberpfalz, 1559–1576*. Münster i. W.: Aschendorff, 1933.

Grabau, Richard, ed. *Das evangelisch-lutherische Predigerministerium der Stadt Frankfurt a. M.* Frankfurt a. M.: Kesselringschen Hofbuchhandlung-Verlag, 1913.

Gregory, Brad S. *Salvation at Stake: Christian Martyrdom in Early Modern Europe.* Cambridge, MA: Harvard University Press, 1999.

Grell, Ole Peter. *Brethren in Christ: A Calvinist Network in Reformation Europe.* Cambridge: Cambridge University Press, 2011.

———. *Calvinist Exiles in Tudor and Stuart England.* Brookfield, VT: Ashgate, 1996.

———. "Merchants and Ministers: The Foundation of International Calvinism." In *Calvinism in Europe, 1540–1620,* edited by Andrew Pettegree, Alastair Duke, and Gillian Lewis, 254–73. Cambridge: Cambridge University Press, 1994.

Grell, Ole Peter, and Bob Scribner, eds. *Tolerance and Intolerance in the European Reformation.* Cambridge: Cambridge University Press, 1996.

Grigg, D. B. "E. G. Ravenstein and the 'Laws of Migration.'" *Journal of Historical Geography* 3, no. 1 (1977): 41–54.

Grotefend, Hermann. *Christian Egenolff, der erste ständige Buchdrucker zu Frankfurt, und seine Vorläufer.* Frankfurt a. M.: Völcker, 1881.

———, ed. *Taschenbuch der Zeitrechnung des deutschen Mittelalters und der Neuzeit.* 8th ed. Hannover: Hahn, 1941.

Guilday, Peter. *The English Catholic Refugees on the Continent 1558–1795.* Vol. 1: *The English Colleges and Convents in the Catholic Low Countries, 1558–1795.* London: Longmans, Green, 1914.

Gunther, Karl. *Reformation Unbound: Protestant Visions of Reform in England, 1525–1590.* Cambridge: Cambridge University Press, 2017.

Haas, Irene. *Reformation, Konfession, Tradition: Frankfurt am Main im Schmalkaldischen Bund, 1536–1547.* Frankfurt a. M.: Waldemar Kramer, 1991.

Hamm, Berndt. "Farewell to Epochs in Reformation History: A Plea." *Reformation and Renaissance Review* 16, no. 3 (November 2014): 211–45.

Hardy, Duncan. *Associative Political Culture in the Holy Roman Empire: Upper Germany, 1346–1521.* Oxford: Oxford University Press, 2018.

Harkrider, Melissa Franklin. *Women, Reform and Community in Early Modern England: Katherine Willoughby, Duchess of Suffolk, and Lincolnshire's Godly Aristocracy, 1519–1580.* Woodbridge, UK: Boydell, 2008.

Harrington, Joel F., and Helmut Walser Smith. "Confessionalizatoin, Community, and State Building in Germany, 1555–1870." *Journal of Modern History* 69 (March 1997): 77–101.

Harte, Negley B., ed. *The New Draperies in the Low Countries and England, 1300—1800.* Pasold Studies in Textile History no. 10. Oxford: Oxford University Press, 1997.

Hartweg, Frédéric. *Die Hugenotten und das Refuge: Deutschland und Europa: Beiträge zu einer Tagung.* Berlin: Colloquium Verlag, 1990.

Haug-Mortiz, Gabriele. *Der Schmalkaldische Bund, 1530–1541/2: Eine Studie zu den genossenschaftlichen Strukturelementen der politischen Ordnung des Heiligen Römischen Reiches Deutscher Nation.* Leinfelden-Echterdingen: DRW, 2002.

Hein, Gerhard. "Anabaptists in Frankfort on the Main." *Mennonite Quarterly Review* 33, no. 1 (1959): 69–72.

Herr, Jakob. "Die Stifter Klöster und Kirchen Frankfurts im Mittelalter." In *Bilder aus dem katholischen Leben der Stadt Frankfurt a. M.* Frankfurt a. M.: Herder, 1939.

Herrmann, Hans-Walter, and Deutscher Hugenottentag. *Vom Werden und Vergehen Französisch-Reformierter Gemeinden im Pfälzisch-Lothringischen Grenzbereich: Erweiterte Fassung eines Vortrages auf Dem 35. Deutschen Hugenottentag in Zweibrücken am 24. April 1987.* Sickte: Verlag des Deutschen Hugenotten-Vereins.

Hils-Brockhoff, Evelyn, ed. *Das Karmeliterkloster in Frankfurt am Main: Geschichte und Kunstdenkmäler.* Frankfurt a. M.: n.p., 1999.

Historisches Museum Frankfurt am Main. *Frankfurt um 1600.* Frankfurt a. M.: Historisches Museum Frankfurt a. M., 1976.

Holborn, Hajo. *A History of Modern Germany.* Vol. 1: *The Reformation.* New York: Knopf, 1959.

Holder, R. Ward. *Crisis and Renewal: The Era of the Reformations.* Louisville, KY: Westminster John Knox, 2009.

Horie, Hirofumi. "The Lutheran Influence on the Elizabethan Settlement, 1558–1563." *Historical Journal* 34, no. 3 (September 1991): 519–37.

Horowitz, Markus. *Frankfurter Rabbinen: Ein Beitrag zur Geschichte der israelitischen Gemeinde in Frankfurt a. M.* Vols. 1–2 (1200–1740). Frankfurt a. M.: Commissions Verlag der Jaegerschen Buchhandlung, 1882–83.

Hovda, Bjorn Ole. *The Controversy over the Lord's Supper in Danzig 1561–1567: Presence and Practice—Theology and Confessional Policy.* Göttingen: Vandenhoeck and Ruprecht, 2019.

Hsia, R. Po-chia. *Society and Religion in Münster, 1535–1618.* New Haven, CT: Yale University Press, 1984.

Hürkey, Edgar, ed. *Kunst, Kommerz, Glaubenskampf: Frankenthal um 1600.* Worms: Wernersche Verlagsgesellschaft, 1995.

Isenmann, Eberhard. *Die deutsche Stadt im Mittelalter, 1150–1550: Stadtgestalt, Recht, Verfassung, Stadtregiment, Kirche, Gesellschaft, Wirtschaft.* Cologne: Böhlau, 2014.

———. "Reichsfinanzen und Reichssteuern im 15. Jahrhundert." *Zeitschrift für Historische Forschung* 7 (1980): 1–76, 129–218.

Israel, Jonathan I. *Diasporas within a Diaspora: Jews, Crypto-Jews, and the World of Maritime Empires, 1540–1740.* Leiden: Brill, 2002.

———. *The Dutch Republic: Its Rise, Greatness and Fall, 1477–1806.* Oxford: Oxford University Press, 1995.

Jahns, Sigrid. "Frankfurt am Main im Zeitalter der Reformation (um 1500–1555)." In *Frankfurt am Main: Die Geschichte der Stadt in neun Beiträgen*, edited by Frankfurter Historischen Kommission, 151–204. Sigmaringen: Jan Thorbecke, 1994.

———. *Frankfurt, Reformation und Schmalkaldischer Bund: Die Reformations-, Reichs- und Bündnispolitik der Reichsstadt Frankfurt am Main 1525–1536.* Frankfurt a. M.: Waldemar Kramer, 1976.

Janssens, Geert. *Brabant in Verweer: Loyale oppositie tegen Spanje's bewind in de Nederlanden van Alva tot Farnese, 1567–1578.* Kortrijk: UGA, 1989.

———. "The Legacy of Exile and the Rise of Humanitarianism." In *Remembering the Reformation*, edited by B. Cummings, C. Law, K. Riley, and A. Walsham, 226–42. London: Routledge, 2020.

———. "The Republic of Refugees: Early Modern Migrations and the Dutch Experience." *Historical Journal* 60, no. 1 (March 2017): 233–52.

Johann, Anja. *Kontrolle mit Konsens: Sozialdiszipilierung in der Reichsstadt Frankfurt am Main im 16. Jahrhundert.* Frankfurt a. M.: Waldemar Kramer, 2001.

Jung, Rudolf. *Die englische Flüchtlings-Gemeinde in Frankfurt am Main, 1554–1559.* Frankfurt a. M.: Joseph Baer, 1910.

———. "Zur Entstehung der Frankfurter Artikel von 1525." *AFGK*, Dritte Folge, vol. 2 (1889): 198–208.

Jürgens, Henning. "Benedict Morgenstern." In *Calvin and Luther: The Continuing Relationship*, edited by R. Ward Holder, 143–64. Göttingen: Vandenhoeck and Ruprecht, 2013.

Kaller, Gerhard. "Die Anfänge der kurpfälzischen Exulantengemeinden Frankenthal, Schönau, Heidelberg und Otterberg, 1562–1590." *Zeitschrift für die Geschichte des Oberrheins* 147 (1999): 393–403.

———. "Wallonische und niederländische Exulantensiedlungen in der Pfalz im 16. Jahrhundert." In *Oberrheinische Studien* 3, Festschrift für Günther Haselier, edited by Alfons Schäfer, 327–51. Karlsruhe: Braun, 1975.

Kamen, Henry. *The Duke of Alba.* New Haven, CT: Yale University Press, 2004.

———. *The Rise of Toleration.* London: Weidenfeld and Nicolson, 1967.

Kamp, Jan van de. "Ein frühes reformiert-pietistisches Netzwerk in der Kurpfalz in der ersten Hälfte des 17. Jahrhunderts." *Archiv für Reformationsgeschichte* 103, no. 1 (October 2012): 182–208.

Kaplan, Benjamin J. *Calvinists and Libertines: Confession and Community in Utrecht, 1578–1620.* Oxford: Clarendon, 1995.

———. *Divided by Faith: Religious Conflict and the Practice of Toleration in Early Modern Europe.* Cambridge, MA: Harvard University Press, 2007.

———. "Dutch Particularism and the Calvinist Quest for 'Holy Uniformity.'" *Archiv für Reformationsgeschichte* 82 (1991): 239–56.

———. "The Legal Rights of Religious Refugees in the 'Refugee-Cities' of Early Modern Germany." *Journal of Refugee Studies* 32, no. 1 (March 2019): 86–105.

Karant-Nunn, Susan. *Reformation and Ritual: An Interpretation of Early Modern Germany*. London: Routledge, 1996.

Kasper-Holtkotte, Cilli. *Die jüdische Gemeinde von Frankfurt/Main in der Frühen Neuzeit: Familien, Netzwerke und Konflikte eines jüdischen Zentrums*. Berlin: De Gruyter, 2010.

Kelley, Donald. *The Beginning of Ideology: Consciousness and Society in the French Reformation*. New York: Cambridge University Press, 1981.

Kinder, Arthur Gordon. *Casiodoro de Reina: Spanish Reformer of the Sixteenth Century*. London: Tamesis, 1975.

———. "Juan Morilo: Catholic Theologian at Trent, Calvinist Elder in Frankfurt." *Bibliothèque d'humanisme et renaissance: Travaux et documents* 38 (1976): 345–50.

King, John N. "John Day: Master Printer of the English Reformation." In *The Beginnings of English Protestantism*, edited by Peter Marshall and Alec Ryrie, 180–208. Cambridge: Cambridge University Press, 2002.

Kingdon, Robert McCune. *Adultery and Divorce in Calvin's Geneva*. Cambridge, MA: Harvard University Press, 1995.

Kirchner, Anton. *Geschichte der Stadt Frankfurt am Main*. 2 vols. Frankfurt a. M.: Jäger and Eichenberg, 1807–10.

Kirchner, Thomas. *Katholiken, Lutheraner und Reformierte in Aachen, 1555–1618*. Tübingen: Mohr-Siebeck, 2015.

Kittelson, James M. "The Confessional Age: The Late Reformation in Germany." In *Reformation Europe: A Guide to Research*, edited by Steven Ozment, 361–81. St. Louis, MO: Center for Reformation Research, 1982.

Kleinschmidt, Harald. *Charles V: The World Emperor*. Stroud, UK: Sutton, 2004.

Klötzer, Wolfgang. "Frankfurt am Main von der Französischen Revolution bis zur preußischen Okkupation." In *Frankfurt am Main: Die Geschichte der Stadt in neun Beiträgen*, edited by Frankfurter Historischen Kommission, 303–48. Sigmaringen: Jan Thorbecke, 1994.

———, ed. *Frankfurter Biographie: Persongeschichtliches Lexikon*, 2 vols. Frankfurt a. M.: Waldemar Kramer, 1994.

Kluckhohn, August. "Wie ist Kurfürst Friedrich III von der Pfalz Calvinist geworden?" *Münchner Historisches Jahrbuch* (1866): 421–520.

Koch, Ernst, and Herbert J. A. Bouman. "Striving for the Union of Lutheran Churches: The Church-Historical Background of the Work Done on the Formula of Concord at Magdeburg." *Sixteenth Century Journal* 8, no. 4 (December 1977): 105–22.

Kohler, Alfred. *Karl V: 1500–1558: Eine Biographie*. Munich: C. H. Beck, 2014.

Kooi, Christine. *Liberty and Religion: Church and State in Leiden's Reformation, 1572–1620*. Leiden: Brill, 2000.

Körner, Hans. *Frankfurter Patrizier: Historisch-Genealogisches Handbuch der Adeligen Ganerbschaft des Hauses Alten-Limpurg zu Frankfurt am Main*. Munich: Ernst Vögel, 1971.

Kracauer, Hedwig. "Das Frankfurter Hochgericht und seine Wiederherstellung in den Jahren 1561, 1652 und 1720." In *Alt-Frankfurt a. M.: Zeitschrift [. . .]*. February 1929. 2. Jahrgang, Nr. 2.

Kracauer, Isidor. *Die Geschichte der Judengasse in Frankfurt am Main.* Frankfurt a. M.: Kauffmann, 1906.

———. "Die Juden Frankfurts im Fettmilch'schen Aufstand, 1612–1618." *Zeitschrift für die Geschichte der Juden in Deutschland* 4 (1890): 127–69, 319–65; 5 (1892): 1–26.

———. *Geschichte der Juden in Frankfurt a. M.: 1150–1824.* 2 vols. Frankfurt a. M: I. Kauffmann, 1925, 1927.

———. "Ein Versuch Ferdinands II., die Jesuiten in Frankfurt am Main einzuführen. (1628)." *Archiv zu Frankfurts Geschichte und Kunst* 3, no. 2 (1889): 260–89.

Kriegk, Georg Ludwig. *Deutsches Bürgerthum im Mittelalter.* 2 vols. 1868. Reprint, Frankfurt a. M.: Sauer and Auvermann, 1969.

———. *Frankufter Bürgerzwiste und Zustände im Mittelalter.* Frankfurt a. M.: J. D. Sauerländer, 1862.

———. *Geschichte von Frankfurt am Main in ausgewählten Darstellungen nach Urkunden und Acten.* Frankfurt a. M.: Heyder & Zimmer, 1871.

Kroll, Frank-Lothar, and Rüdiger von Voss, eds. *Schrifsteller und Widerstand: Facetten und Probleme der "Inneren" Emigration.* Göttingen: Wallstein, 2012.

Kröner, Hans, and Andreas Hansert. *Frankfurter Patrizier: Historisch-Genealogisches Handbuch der Adeligen Ganerbschaft des Hauses Alten-Limpurg zur Frankfurt am Main.* Neustadt: Degener, 2003.

Kuby, Alfred Hans. "Gründe, Wege und Folgen der Kirchenreformation in Kurpfalz unter besonderer Berücksichtigung von Frankenthal." In *Kunst, Kommerz, Glaubenskampf: Frankenthal um 1600,* edited by Edgar Hürkey, 22–28. Worms: Wernersche Verlagsgesellschaft, 1995.

Kymlicka, Will. *Multicultural Citizenship: A Liberal Theory of Minority Rights.* Oxford: Clarendon, 1995.

Lachenicht, Susanne. "Refugees and Refugee Protection in the Early Modern Period." *Journal of Refugee Studies* 30, no. 2 (June 2017): 261–81.

Laurentiis, Elena de. "La collezione di 'Italian illuminated cuttings' della British Library: Nuove miniature di Simonzio Lupi da Bergamo, Giovanni Battista Castello il Genovese e Sante Avanzini." In *Il codice miniato in Europa: Libri per la chiesa, per la città, per la corte: Atti del Convegno di studi,* edited by Giordana Mariani Canova and Alessandra Perriccioli Saggese, 673–95. Padua: Il Poligrafo, 2014.

Laursen, John Christian, and Cary Nederman, eds. *Beyond the Persecuting Society: Religious Toleration before the Enlightenment.* Philadelphia: University of Pennsylvania Press, 1998.

Leaman, Hans. "'Count Every Step in My Flight': Rhegius's and Luther's Consolations for Evangelical Exiles, 1531–3." In *Exile and Religious Identity,*

*1500–1800*, edited by Jesse Spohnholz and Gary K. Waite, 9–24. London: Pickering and Chatto, 2014.

Leaver, Robin A., ed. *The Liturgy of the Frankfurt Exiles, 1555.* Bramcote Grove, 1984.

Lecler, Joseph. *Toleration and the Reformation.* Translated by T. L. Westow. New York: Association Press, 1960.

Leeb, Josef. *Der Kurfürstentag zu Frankfurt 1558 und der Reichstag zu Augsburg 1559.* Göttingen: Vandenhoeck and Ruprecht, 1999.

Lehnemann, Johannes. *Historische Nachricht von der vormals im 16. Jahrhundert berühmten evangelisch lutherischen Kirche in Antorff und der daraus entstandenen niderländischen Gemeinde A. C. in Frankfurt a. M.* Frankfurt a. M., 1725.

Lerner, Franz. *Die Frankfurt Patriziergesellschaft Alten-Limpurg und ihre Stiftungen.* Frankfurt a. M.: Waldemar Kramer, 1952.

Lersner, Achilles August von. *Der Weit-berühmten Freyen Reichs-, Wahl- und Handels Stadt.* 2 vols. Frankfurt a. M., 1706 and 1734.

Lilienthal, Saul. *Jüdische Wanderungen in Frankfurt am Main, Hessen, Hessen-Nassau.* Frankfurt a. M.: J. Kauffmann, 1938.

Lim, Paul Chang-Ha. *In Pursuit of Purity, Unity, and Liberty: Richard Baxter's Puritan Ecclesiology in Its Seventeenth-Century Context.* Leiden: Brill, 2004.

Lindberg, Carter. *The European Reformations.* 2nd ed. Malden, MA: Wiley Blackwell, 2010.

Lotz-Heumann, Ute. "Confessionalization." In *Reformation and Early Modern Europe: A Guide to Research*, edited by David M. Whitford, 136–57. Kirksville, MO: Truman State University, 2008.

Luebke, David. *Hometown Religion: Regimes of Coexistence in Early Modern Westphalia.* Charlottesville: University of Virginia Press, 2016.

Lühe, Wilhelm. "Die Ablösung der ewigen Zinsen in Frankfurt a. M. in den Jahren 1522–1562." *Westdeutsche Zeitschrift für Geschichte und Kunst* 23 (1904): 236–69.

Luria, Keith. *Sacred Boundaries: Religious Coexistence and Conflict in Early-Modern France.* Washington, DC: Catholic University of America Press, 2005.

Magdelaine, Michelle. "Francfort-sur-le-Main et les Réfugiés Huguenots." In *Les États allemands et les Huguenots*, edited by Guido Braun and Susanne Lachenicht. Munich: Oldenbourg, 2007.

———. "Frankfurt am Main: Drehscheibe des Refuge." In *Die Hugenotten, 1685–1985*, edited by Rudolf von Thadden and Magdelaine, 26–37. Munich: C. H. Beck, 1986.

Malkii, Liisa. "Speechless Emissaries: Refugees, Humanitarianism, and Dehistoricization." *Cultural Anthropology* 11, no. 3 (August 1996): 377–404.

Manetsch, Scott M. "Calvin's Company of Pastors: Pastoral Care and the Emerging Reformed Church, 1536–1609." Oxford: Oxford Univeristy Press, 2012

Mangon, Abraham. *Kurze doch wahrhafftige Beschreibung der Geschichte der Reformierten in Frankfurt 1554–1712.* Edited by Irene Dingel. Leipzig: Evangelische Verlagsanstalt, 2004.

Marnef, Guido. *Antwerp in the Age of Reformation: Underground Protestantism in a Commercial Metropolis, 1550–1577.* Johns Hopkins University Studies in Historical and Political Science. Baltimore: Johns Hopkins University Press, 1996.

————. "Protestant Conversions in an Age of Catholic Reformation: The Case of Sixteenth-Century Antwerp." In *The Low Countries as a Crossroads of Religious Beliefs,* edited by Arie-Jan Gelderblom, Jan L. de Jong, and Marc van Vaeck. Leiden: Brill, 2004.

Mason, Roger. *John Knox and the British Reformations.* Aldershot, UK: Ashgate, 1998.

Matthäus, Michael. *Hamman von Holzhausen (1467–1536): Ein Frankfurter Patrizier im Zeitalter der Reformation.* Frankfurt a. M.: Waldemar Kramer, 2002.

Mauer, Anton. *Der Übergang der Stadt Konstanz an das Haus Österreich nach dem Schmalkaldischen Kriege.* Frauenfeld: Druck von Huber, 1904.

Mauersberg, Hans. *Wirtschafts- und Sozialgeschichte zentraleuropäischer Städte in neuerer Zeit: Dargestellt an den Beispielen von Basel, Frankfurt a M., Hamburg, Hannover und München.* Göttingen: Vandenhoeck and Ruprecht, 1960.

Maus, Anna, ed. *Die Geschichte der Stadt Frankenthal und ihrer Vororte.* Speyer: Pilger Druckerei, 1969.

Mayer, Eugen, *The Jews of Frankfurt a. M.: Glimpses of the Past.* Translated by Israel Meir. Frankfurt a. M.: Waldemar Kramer, 1990.

McGrath, Alister E. *Reformation Thought.* 3rd ed. Malden, MA: Blackwell, 1999.

Meinert, Hermann. Introduction to *Die Eingliederung der Niederländischen Glaubensflüchtlinge in die Frankfurter Bürgerschaft, 1554–1696: Auszüge aus den Frankfurter Ratsprotokollen* Frankfurt a. M.: Waldemar Kramer, 1981.

Meinert, Hermann, and Wolfram Dahmer. Introduction to *Das Protokollbuch der Niederländischen Reformierten Gemeinde zu Frankfurt am Main, 1570–1581.* Edited by Meinert and Dahmer. Frankfurt a. M.: Waldemar Kramer, 1977.

Mentgen, Gerd. "Juden Zwischen Koexistenz und Pogrom." In *Randgruppen der spätmittelalterlichen Gesellschaft,* edited by Bernd-Ulrich Hergemöller, 333–87. Warendorf: Fahlbusch, 2001.

Mentzer, Raymond A. "Disciplina nervus ecclesiae: The Calvinist Reform of Morals at Nimes." *Sixteenth Century Journal* 18, no. 1 (1987): 89–115.

Mentzer, Raymond A., and Andrew Spicer, eds. *Society and Culture in the Huguenot World, 1559–1685.* Cambridge: Cambridge University Press, 2002.

Meyn, Matthias. *Die Reichstadt Frankfurt vor dem Bürgeraufstand von 1612 bis 1614: Struktur und Krise.* Frankfurt a. M.: Waldemar Kramer, 1980.

Moch, Leslie Page. *Moving Europeans: Migration in Western Europe since 1650.* Bloomington: Indiana University Press, 2003.

Moeller, Bernd. *Imperial Cities and the Reformation: Three Essays.* Edited and translated by H. C. Erik Midelfort and Mark U. Edwards. Durham, NC: Labyrinth, 1982.

———. *Reichsstadt und Reformation.* Gütersloh: Gerd Mohn, 1962.

———. "Religious Life in Germany on the Eve of the Reformation." In *Pre-Reformation Germany*, edited by Gerald Strauss, 13–35. London: Macmillan, 1972.

———. *Spätmittelalter.* Göttingen: Vandenhoeck and Ruprecht, 1966.

———. "Was wurde in der Frühzeit der Reformation in den deutschen Städten gepredigt?" *ARG* 75 (1984): 176–93.

Moger, Jourden Travis. "Wolfgang Königstein and the Reformation in Frankfurt am Main, 1520–1533." PhD diss., University of California, Santa Barbara, 2011.

———. *Priestly Resistance to the Early Reformation in Germany.* London: Pickering and Chatto, 2014.

Molen, Ronald Vander. "Anglican against Puritan: Ideological Origins during the Marian Exile." *Church History* 42, no. 1 (1973): 45–57.

Monnard, H. "La foundation de l'église réformée français de Francfort s. M." *Der deutsche Hugenott* 17 (1953): 66–87, 108–28.

Monnet, Pierre. *Führungseliten und Bewußtsein sozialer Distinktion in Frankfurt am Main, mit Exkurs Das Melemsche Hausbuch: Eine Quelle für die Geschichte der Frankfurter Stadteliten im 15. und 16. Jahrhundert.* 1997. Discussion in *AFGK*, no. 66 (2000): 12–77.

Moreau, Gérard. *Histoire du Protestantisme à Tournai jusqu'à la veille de la Révolution des Pays-Bas.* Paris: Société d'édition Les belles lettres, 1962.

Morgan, Edmund. *The Puritan Dilemma: The Story of John Winthrop.* New York: Longman, 1999.

Mortiz, Johann Anton. *Versuch einer Enleitung in die Staatsverfassung derer oberrheinischen Reichsstädte.* Vol. 1: *Reichsstadt Frankfurt*, 206–7. Frankfurt a. M., 1785.

Müller, Johannes. *Exile Memories and the Dutch Revolt: The Narrated Diaspora, 1550–1750.* Leiden: Brill, 2016.

Murdock, Graeme. *Calvinism on the Frontier, 1600–1660: International Calvinism and the Reformed Church in Hungary and Transylvania.* Oxford: Clarendon; Oxford University Press, 2000.

Niggemann, Ulrich. *Immigrationspolitik zwischen Konflikt und Konsens: Die Hugenottenansiedlung in Deutschland und England (1681–1697).* Cologne: Böhlau, 2008.

Ninness, Richard. *Between Opposition and Collaboration: Nobles, Bishops, and the German Reformations in the Prince-Bishopric of Bamberg, 1555–1619.* Leiden: Brill, 2011.

Nirenberg, David. *Communities of Violence: Persecution of Minorities in the Middle Ages.* Princeton, NJ: Princeton University Press, 1996.

Nischan, Bodo. *Lutherans and Calvinists in the Age of Confessionalism.* Aldershot, UK: Ashgate, 1999.

———. *Prince, People and Confession: The Second Reformation in Brandenburg.* Philadelphia: University of Pennsylvania Press, 1994.

Norwood, Frederick Abbott. "The London Dutch Refugees in Search of a Home, 1553–1554." *American Historical Review* 58 (1952): 64–72.

———. *The Reformation Refugees as an Economic Force.* American Society of Church History. Chicago: American Society of Church History, 1942.

———. *Strangers and Exiles: A History of Religious Refugees.* Nashville, TN: Abingdon, 1969.

Oberman, Heiko, A. *John Calvin and the Reformation of the Refugees.* Geneva: Librairie Droz, 2009.

Odmalm, Pontus. *Migration Policies and Political Participation: Inclusion or Intrusion in Western Europe?* Houndsmills, UK: Macmillan, 2005.

Orth, Johann Philipp. *Nöthig- und nützlich-erachteter Anmerkungen über die so genannte erneuerte Reformation der Stadt Frankfurt am Main.* 4 vols. Frankfurt a. M., 1731–57.

———. *Samlung merkwürdiger Rechtshändel samt ihren Zweifels- und Entscheidungsgrüngen.* 5 vols. Frankfurt a. M.: Brönner, 1763–69.

Ozment, Steven E. *The Age of Reform, 1250–1550: An Intellectual and Religious History of Late Medieval and Reformation Europe.* New Haven, CT: Yale University Press, 1980.

———. *The Reformation in the Cities: The Appeal of Protestantism to Sixteenth-Century Germany and Switzerland.* New Haven, CT: Yale University Press, 1975.

Parker, Charles. "The Moral Agency and Moral Autonomy of Church Folk in the Dutch Reformed Church of Delft, 1580–1620." *Journal of Ecclesiastical History* 48, no. 1 (January 1997): 44–70.

Parker, Geoffrey. *The Army of Flanders and the Spanish Road, 1567–1659: The Logistics of Spanish Victory and Defeat in the Low Countries' Wars.* Cambridge: Cambridge University Press, 1972.

———. *The Dutch Revolt.* Ithaca, NY: Cornell University Press, 1977.

———. *Emperor: A New Life of Charles V.* New Haven, CT: Yale University Press, 2019.

———. *The Grand Strategy of Philip II.* New Haven, CT: Yale University Press, 1998.

———. *The Military Revolution: Military Innovation and the Rise of the West, 1500–1800,* 2nd ed. Cambridge: Cambridge University Press, 1996.

Pettegree, Andrew. *Emden and the Dutch Revolt: Exile and the Development of Reformed Protestantism.* Oxford: Clarendon, 1992.

———. *Foreign Protestant Communities in Sixteenth-Century London.* Oxford: Clarendon, 1986.

———. "The London Exile Community and the Second Sacramentarian Controversy, 1553–1560." *Archive for Reformation History* 78 (1987): 223–51.

———. *Marian Protestantism: Six Studies.* Aldershot, UK: Scolar, 1996.

Pettegree, Andrew, Alastair Duke, and Gillian Lewis, eds. *Calvinism in Europe, 1540–1620.* Cambridge: Cambridge University Press, 1994.

Pietsch, Andreas, and Barbara Stollberg-Rilinger, eds. *Konfessionelle Ambiguität: Uneindeutigkeit und Verstellung als religiose Praxis in der Frühen Neuzeit.* Gütersloh: Gütersloh Verlaghaus, 2013.

Pirenne, Henri. *Economic and Social History of Medieval Europe.* Translated by. I. E. Clegg. New York: Harcourt, Brace, 1937.

———. *A History of Europe.* 2 vols. Translated by Bernard Miall. Garden City, NY: Doubleday, 1956.

Pohl, Hans. "Die ständische Gesellschaft." In *Deutsche Verwaltungsgeschichte,* vol. 1: *Vom Spätmittelalter bis zum Ende des Reiches.* Stuttgart: Deutsche Verlags-Anstalt, 1983.

Pollman, Judith. "Off the Record: Problems in the Quantification of Calvinist Church Discipline." *Sixteenth Century Journal* 33, no. 2 (Summer 2002): 423–38.

Press, Volker. *Calvinismus und Territorialstaat: Regierung und Zentralbehörden der Kurpfalz 1559–1619.* Stuttgart: Ernst Klet, 1970.

Prestwich, Menna, ed. *International Calvinism, 1541–1715.* Oxford: Clarendon, 1985.

Procter, Francis. *A History of the Book of Common Prayer.* London: Macmillan, 1898.

Proescholdt, Joachim, ed. *Minderheiten in Frankfurt am Main: Vom Umgang mit Andersdenkenden–Andersglaubenden–Anderslebenden.* Frankfurt a. M.: Evanglischer Regionalverband, 2000.

Raitt, Jill. *The Colloquy of Montbéliard: Religion and Politics in the Sixteenth Century.* New York: Oxford University Press, 1993.

Reinhard, Wolfgang. "Reformation, Counter-Reformation, and the Early Modern State, a Reassessment." *Catholic Historical Review* 75, no. 3 (July 1989): 383–404.

Remer, Gary. *Humanism and the Rhetoric of Toleration.* University Park: Pennsylvania State University Press, 1996.

Remling, F. X. *Der Retscher in Speyer, urkundlich erläutert.* Vol. 3. Speyer: Verlag von A. Wappler Buchhandlung, 1859.

Reston, James, Jr. *Defenders of the Faith: Charles V, Suleyman the Magnificent, and the Battle for Europe, 1520–1536.* New York: Penguin, 2009.

Reuss, Rodolphe. *Notes pour server à l'histoire de l'Égglise française de Strasbourg, 1538–1794.* Strasbourg, 1880.

Ritter, Johann Balthasar. *Evangelisches Denckmahl der Stadt Frankfurth am Mayn.* Frankfurt a. M.: Johann Friedrich Fleischer, 1726.

Rodgers, Dirk. *John a Lasco in England.* New York: Peter Lang, 1994.

Roeck, Bernd. *Außenseiter, Randgruppen, Minderheiten: Fremde im Deustchland der frühen Neuzeit.* Göttingen: Vandenhoeck and Ruprecht, 1993.

———. *Civic Culture and Everyday Life in Early Modern Germany.* Leiden: Brill, 2006.

————. *Eine Stadt in Krieg und Frieden: Studien zur Geschichte der Reichsstadt Augsburg.* 2 vols. Göttingen: Vandenhoeck and Ruprecht, 1989.

Römer-Büchner, B. J. *Die Entwicklung der Stadtverfassung und die Bürgervereine der Stadt Frankfurt am Main.* Frankfurt a. M., 1855.

Roosbroeck, Robert van. *Emigranten: Nederlandsche Vluchtelingen in Duitsland, 1550–1600.* Leuven: Davidsfonds, 1968.

————. "Die niederländischen Glaubensflüchtlinge in Deutschland und die Anfänge der Stadt Frankenthal." *Blätte für Pfälzische Kirchengeschichte und religiose Volkskunde* 30 (1963): 11–15.

Rosseaux, Ulrich. *Städte in der Frühen Neuzeit.* Darmstadt: Wissenschaftliche Buchgesellschaft, 2006.

Ruppersberg, Otto. "Der Aufbau des reichsstädtischen Behörden." In *Die Stadt Goethes,* edited by H. Voelcker. Frankfurt a. M.: Hauserpresse, 1932.

Ruymbeke, Bertrand Van, and Randy J. Sparks, eds. *Memory and Identity: The Huguenots in France and the Atlantic Diaspora.* Columbia: University of South Carolina Press, 2003.

Sandl, Marcus. "'Here I Stand': Face-to-Face Communication and Print Media in the Early Reformation." In *Cultures of Communication: Theologies of Media in Early Modern Europe and Beyond,* edited by Helmut Puff, Ulrike Strasser, and Christopher Wild, 77–98. Toronto: University of Toronto Press, 2017.

Schäfer, Alfons. "Wallonische und niederländische Exulantensiedlugnen." In *Oberrheinische Studien Band III: Festschrift für Günther Haselier aus Anlass seines 60. Geburtstages am 19. April 1974,* edited by Schäfer. Karlsruhe: Braun-Verlag, 1975.

Schäfer, Ernst. *Die Kirche in Frankfurt am Main im Wandel der Zeitgeschichte: Von Anfängen bis zur Reformation.* Frankfurt a. M.: Hausdruckerei des Evangelischen Regionalverbandes, 1987.

Scharff, Friedrich. "Die Niederländische und die Französische Gemeinde Frankfurt a. M." *Archiv für Frankfurts Geschichte und Kunst,* Neue Folge, 2 (1862): 245–318.

Schätz, Harald. *Die Aufnahmeprivilegien für Waldenser und Hugenotten in Herzogtum Württemberg: Eine rechtsgeschichtliche Studie zum deutschen Refuge.* Stuttgart: Kohlhammer, 2010.

Scheible, Heinz. *Kurfürst Ottheinrich, ein Mann des Kairos.* Ludwigshafen: Dr. Frank Hennecke, 2007.

Schelven, Aart Arnout van. *De Nederduitsche vluchtelingenkerken der XVIe eeuw in Engeland en Duitschland in hunne beteekenis voor de Reformatie in de Nederlanden.* 's-Gravenhage: M. Nijhoff, 1909.

Schembs, Hans-Otto. "Die Alte Brücke und ihre Erneuerung im Laufe der Jahrhunderte." *AFGK* 70 (2004): 185–221.

Schilling, Heinz. *Ausgewählte Abhandlungen zur europäischen Reformations- und Konfessionsgeschichte.* Edited by Luise Schorn-Schütte. Berlin: Duncker and Humbolt, 2002.

———. *Civic Calvinism in Northwestern Germany and the Netherlands: Sixteenth to Nineteenth Centuries.* Kirksville, MO: Sixteenth Century Journal, 1991.

———. *Early Modern European Civilization and Its Political and Cultural Dynamism.* Hanover, NH: University Press of New England, 2008.

———. *Konfessionskonflikt und Staatsbildung: Eine Fallstudie über das Verhältnis von religiösem und sozialem Wandel in der Frühneuzeit am Beispiel der Grafschaft Lippe.* Gütersloh: Gerd Mohn, 1981.

———. *Niederländische Exulanten im 16. Jahrhundert: Ihre Stellung im Sozialgefüge und im religiösen Leben deutscher und englischer Städte.* Gütersloh: Gerd Mohn, 1972.

———, ed. *Die reformierte Konfessionalisierung in Deutschland: Das Problem der "Zweiten Reformation": Wissenschaftliches Symposion des Vereins für Reformationsgeschichte 1985.* Gütersloh: Gerd Mohn, 1986.

———. "Religion, Politik und Kommerz: Die europäische Konfessionsmigration des 16. Jahrhunderts und ihre Folgen." In *Kunst, Kommerz, Glaubenskampf: Frankenthal um 1600,* edited by Edgar Hürkey, 29–36. Worms: Wernersche Verlagsgesellschaft, 1995,

Schmidt, Benno, ed. *Frankfurter Zunfturkunden bis zum Jahre 1612.* 2 vols. Frankfurt a. M.: Baer, 1914.

Schmidt, Heinrich R. *Reichsstädte, Reich und Reformation: Korporative Religionspolitik, 1521–1529.* Stuttgart: F. Steiner Verlag Wiesbaden, 1986.

Schnabel, Werner Wilhelm. *Österreichische Exulanten in Oberdeutschen Reichstädten: Zur Migration von Führungsschichte im 17. Jahrhundert.* Munich: C. H. Beck, 1992.

Schnapper-Arndt, Gottlieb. *Studien zur Geschichte der Lebenshaltung in Frankfurt a. M. während des 17. und 18. Jahrhunderts.* Edited by Karl Bräuer. 2 vols. Frankfurt a. M.: Baer, 1915.

Schofield, John. *Philip Melanchthon and the English Reformation.* Aldershot, UK: Ashgate, 2006.

Scholz, Bettina R. *The Cosmopolitan Potential of Exclusive Associations: Criteria for Assessing the Advancement of Cosmopolitan Norms.* Lanham, MD: Lexington, 2015.

Scholz, Maximilian Miguel. "Religious Refugees and the Search for Public Worship in Frankfurt, 1554–1608." *Sixteenth Century Journal* 50, no. 3 (Fall 2019): 765–82.

Schorn-Schütte, Luise. *Geschichte Europas in der Frühen Neuzeit: Studienhandbuch 1500–1789.* Paderborn: Ferdinand Schöningh, 2009.

———, ed. *Das Interim 1548/50: Herrschaftskrise und Glaubenskonflikt.* Gütersloh: Gütersloher Verlagshaus, 2005.

———. *Karl V.: Kaiser zwischen Mittelalter und Neuzeit.* Munich: C. H. Beck, 2000.

———. *Konfessionskriege und europäische Expansion: Europa 1500–1648.* Munich: C. H. Beck, 2010.

Schroeder, F. C. *Troisième Jubilé Séculaire de la Fondation de L'Église Réformée Française de Francfort s/M: Discours prononcés a cette occasion, le 18 Mars 1854 par les pasteurs de cette église.* Frankfurt a. M., 1854.

Schudt, Johann Jacob. *Jüdische Merckwürdigkeiten.* 4 vols. Frankfurt, 1714–18.

Schulze, Hans K. *Grundstrukturen der Verfassung im Mittelalter.* Vol. 3: *Kaiser und Reich.* Stuttgart: W. Kohlhammer, 1998.

Schunka, Alexander. "Migrationsgeschichte." In *Historische Schlesienforschung: Methoden, Themen und Perspektiven zwischen traditioneller Landesgeschichtsschreibung und moderner Kulturwissenschaft,* edited by Joachim Bahlcke. Cologne: Böhlau, 2005.

Schwartz, Stuart. *All Can Be Saved: Religious Tolerance and Salvation in the Iberian Atlantic World.* New Haven, CT: Yale University Press, 2008.

Schwarzlose, Karl. "Hartmann Ibach und die Reformation in Frankfurt a. M." In *Frankfurter Kirchenkalendar* (1922), reprinted in *Die evangelische Kirche von Frankfurt am Main in Geschichte und Gegenwart,* edited by Christoph Führ and Jürgen Telschow, 83–86. Frankfurt a. M.: Evangelischer Regionalverband, 1980.

Schwemer, Richar. *Geschichte der freien Stadt Frankfurt a. m. (1814–1866).* Frankfurt a. M.: Baer, 1910.

Scott, Tom. *The City-State in Europe 1000–1600: Hinterland, Territory, Region.* Oxford: Oxford University Press, 2012.

———. *Society and Economy in Germany, 1300–1600.* Houndsmill, UK: Palgrave, 2002.

Seuffert, Ralk. *Konstanz: 2000 Jahre Geschichte.* Konstanz: UVK Verlagsgesellschaft, 2003.

Shachar, Ayelet. *Multicultural Jurisdictions: Cultural Differences and Women's Rights.* Cambridge: Cambridge University Press, 2001.

Simon, G. *Die Geschichte des reichsständischen Hauses Ysenburg und Büdigen.* 3 vols. Frankfurt, 1865.

Smid, Menno. "Reisen und Aufenthaltsorte a Lascos." In *Johannes a Lasco, 1499–1560: Polnischer Baron, Humanist und europäischer Reformator,* edited by Christoph Strohm, 187–98. Tübingen: J. C. B. Mohr Dieback, 2000.

Soen, Violet. *Geen pardon zonder Paus! Studie over de complementariteit van het koninklijk en pauselijk general pardon (1570–1574) en over inquisiteur-generaal Michael Baius (1560–1576).* Brussels: Koninklijke Vlaamse Academie van België voor Wetenschappen en Kunsten, 2007.

Soliday, Gerald Lyman. *A Community in Conflict: Frankfurt Society in the Seventeenth and Early Eighteenth Centuries.* Hanover, NH: Brandeis University Press, 1974.

Spijker, W. van 't. *The Ecclesiastical Offices in the Thought of Martin Bucer.* Leiden: Brill, 1996.

Spohnholz, Jesse. *The Convent of Wesel: The Event That Never Was and the Invention of Tradition.* Cambridge: Cambridge University Press, 2017.

———. "Multiconfessional Celebration of the Eucharist in Sixteenth-Century Wesel." *Sixteenth Century Journal* 39 (2008): 705–30.

———. *The Tactics of Toleration: A Refugee Community in the Age of Religious Wars.* Newark: University of Delaware Press, 2011.

Spohnholz, Jesse, and Gary K. Waite, eds. *Exile and Religious Identity, 1500–1800.* London: Pickering and Chatto, 2014.

Springer, Michael S. *Restoring Christ's Church: John a Lasco and the Forma ac ratio.* Aldershot, UK: Ashgate, 2007.

Steitz, Georg Eduard. "Der Antoniterhof in Frankfurt." *AFGK* 6 (1854): 114–53.

———. "Dr. Gerhard Westerburg: Der Leiter des Bürgeraufstandes zu Frankfurt a. M. im Jahre 1525." *AFGK,* n.s., 5 (1872): 1–215.

———. "Der Humanist Wilhelm Nesen, der Begründer des Gymnasiums und erste Anreger der Reformation in der alten Reichsstadt Frankfurt a. M." *AFGK,* n.s., 6 (1877): 36–160.

———. *Der Lutherische Prädicant Hartmann Beyer: Ein Zeitbild aus Frankfurts Kirchengeschichte im Jahrhundert der Reformation.* Frankfurt a. M.: 1852.

———. "Luthers Warnungsschrift an Rath und Gemeinde zu Frankfurt 1533 und Dionysius Melande's Abschied von seinem Amte 1535: Zwei urkundliche Beiträge zu Frankfurts Reformationsgeschichte." *AFGK,* n.s., 5 (1872): 257–81.

———. *M. Johannes Cnipius Andronicus, Schulmeister zu d. Barfüssern 1550–1562, der theologische Vertreter des Melanchthonianismus in Frankfurt.* Frankfurt, 1860.

———. "Die Melanchthons- und Lutherherbergen zu Frankfurt am Main." *Neujahrs-Blatt, des Vereins für Geschichte und Altertumskunde zu Frankfurt am Main 1861* (1861): 14–44.

———. "Des Rector Micyllus Abzug von Frankfurt 1533." *AFGK,* n.s., 5 (1872): 216–56.

———. "Reformatorische Persönlichkeiten, Einflüsse und Vorgänge in der Reichsstadt Frankfurt a. M. von 1519–1522." *AFGK,* n.s., 4 (1869): 57–174.

———, ed. *Tagebuch des Canonicus Wolfgang Königstein am Liebfrauenstifte über die Vorgänge seines Capitels und die Ereignisse der Reichsstadt Frankfurt am Main in den Jahren 1520 bis 1548.* Frankfurt a. M.: Selbstverlag des Vereins für Geschichte Altertumskunde, 1876.

Steitz, Georg Eduard, und H. Dechent. *Geschichte der Antwerpen nach Frankfurt a. M. verpflanzten Niederländischen Gemeinde Augsburger Confession.* Frankfurt a. M., 1885.

Stensland, Monica. *Habsburg Communication in the Dutch Revolt.* Amsterdam: Amsterdam University Press, 2012.

Stollberg-Rilinger, Barbara. *Das Heilige Römische Reich Deutscher Nation: Vom Ende des Mittelalters bis 1806.* 2nd ed. Munich: C. H. Beck, 2006.

———. *The Holy Roman Empire: A Short History.* Translated by Yair Mintzker. Princeton, NJ: Princeton University Press, 2018.

Strohm, Christoph. *Johannes Calvin: Leben und Werk des Reformators.* Munich: C. H. Beck, 2009.

———, ed. *Profil und Wirkung des Heidelberger Katechismus: Neue Forschungsbeiträge anlässlich des 450jährigen Jubiläums.* Gütersloh: Gütersloher Verlagshaus, 2015.

Te Brake, Wayne. *Religious War and Religious Peace in Early Modern Europe.* Cambridge: Cambridge University Press, 2017.

Telschow, Jürgen. *Die alte Frankfurter Kirche: Recht und Organisation der früheren evangelischen Kirche in Frankfurt.* Frankfurt a. M.: Evangelischer Regionalverband, 1979.

———. *Ringen um den rechten Weg: Die evangelische Kirche in Frankfurt am Main zwischen 1933 und 1945.* Darmstadt: Verlag der Hessischen Kirchengeschichtlichen Vereinigung, 2003.

Telschow, Jürgen, and Elisabeth Reiter. *Die evangelischen Pfarrer von Frnakfurt am Main.* Frankfurt a. M.: Evangelischer Regionalverband, 1985.

Terpstra, Nicholas. *Religious Refugees in the Early Modern World: An Alternative History of the Reformation.* Cambridge: Cambridge University Press, 2015.

Thevet, André. *Le Brésil d'André Thevet: Les Singularités de la France Antarctique.* Reprint, Paris: Chandeigne, 1997.

Thomas, Andrew L. *A House Divided: Wittelsbach Confessional Court Cultures in the Holy Roman Empire, c. 1550–1650.* Leiden: Brill, 2010.

Tilly, Charles. "What Good Is Urban History?" *Journal of Urban History* 22 (1996): 702–19.

Toch, Michael. "Wirtschaft und Geldwesen den Juden Frankfurts im Spätmittelalter und in der Frühen Neuzeit." In *Jüdische Kultur in Frankfurt am Main von den Anfängen bis zur Gegenwart,* edited by Karl E. Grözinger, 25–46. Wiesbaden: Harrassowitz, 1997.

Tol, Jonas van. *Germany and the French Wars of Religion, 1560–1572.* Leiden: Brill, 2019.

Toussaert, Jacques. *Le sentiment religieux en Flandre à la fin du Moyen-Age.* Paris: Plon, 1963.

Tracy, James. *Holland under Habsburg Rule, 1506–1566: The Formation of a Body Politic.* Berkeley: University of California Press, 1990.

Traut, Hermann. "Dr. Adolf von Glauburg und seine Bibliothek." In *Festgabe für Friedrich Clemens Ebrard.* Frankfurt a. M.: Joseph Baer, 1920.

Trivellato, Francesca. *The Familiarity of Strangers: The Sephardic Diaspora, Livorno, and Cross-Cultural Trade in the Early Modern Period.* New Haven, CT: Yale University Press, 2009.

Turchetti, Mario. "Religious Concord and Political Tolerance in Sixteenth- and Seventeenth-Century France." *Sixteenth Century Journal* 22, no. 1 (Spring 1991): 15–25.

Turniasky, H. "The Events in Frankfurt am Main, 1612–1616." In *Schöpferische Momente des Europäischen Judentums*, edited by M. Graertz, 221–37. Heidelberg: Winter, 2000.

Veen, Mirjam van. "'Wir sind ständig unterwegs . . .': Haben die reformierten Flüchtlinge des 16. Jh sich als Exulanten bezeichnet?" *Archiv für Reformationsgeschiche* 109, no. 1 (September 2018): 442–58.

Veen, Mirjam van, and Jesse Spohnholz. "Calvinists vs. Libertines: A New Look at Religious Exile and the Origins of 'Dutch' Tolerance." In *Calvinism and the Making of the European Mind*, 76–99. Boston: Brill, 2014.

Vogler, Bernard. "Le role des électeurs Palatins dans les Guerres de Religion en France, 1559–1592." *Cahiers d'Histoire* 10 (1965): 51–85.

Volk, Stefan. "Peuplierung und religiose Toleranz: Neuwied von der Mitte des 17. bis zur Mitte des 18. Jahrhunderts." *Rheinische Vierteljahrsblätter* 55 (1991): 205–31.

Waite, Gary K. "Conversos and Spiritualists in Spain and the Netherlands: The Experience of Inner Exile, c. 1540–1620." In *Exile and Religious Identity, 1500–1800*, edited by Jesse Spohnholz and Waite, 157–70. London: Pickering and Chatto, 2014.

Walsham, Alexandra. *Charitable Hatred: Tolerance and Intolerance in England, 1500–1700*. Manchester: Manchester University Press, 2006.

Walzer, Michael. *On Toleration*. New Haven, CT: Yale University Press, 1997.

Wandel, Lee Palmer. *The Eucharist in the Reformation*. Cambridge: Cambridge University Press, 2005.

———. "Fragmentation and Presence: Reformation Debates and Cultural Theory." In *Cultures of Communication: Theologies of Media in Early Modern Europe and Beyond*, edited by Helmut Puff, Ulrike Strasser, and Christopher Wild, 55–76. Toronto: University of Toronto Press, 2017.

Washburn, Daniel. *Banishment in the Later Roman Empire, 284–476 CE*. New York: Routledge, 2012.

Weber, Beda. *Zur Reformationsgeschichte der freien Reichsstadt Frankfurt a. M.* Edited by Johann Diefenbach. Frankfurt a. M.: Foesser, 1895.

Weber, Max. *The Theory of Social and Economic Organization*. Translated by A. M. Henderson and Talcott Parsons. New York: Oxford University Press, 1947.

Weidhass, Peter. *A History of the Frankfurt Book Fair*. Translated and edited by C. M. Gossage and W. A. Wright. Toronto: Dundurn, 2007.

Whaley, Joachim. *Religious Toleration and Social Change in Hamburg, 1529–1819*. Cambridge: Cambridge University Press, 1985.

Wilson, Francesca M. *They Came as Strangers: Tthe Story of Refugees to Great Britain*. London: H. Hamilton, 1959.

Wilson, Peter. "Dynasty, Constitution, and Confession: The Role of Religion in the Thirty Years War." *International History Review* 30, no. 3 (September 2008): 473–514.

———. *Heart of Europe: A History of the Holy Roman Empire.* Cambridge, MA: Harvard University Press, 2016.

Witzel, G. "Gewerbegeschichtliche Studien zur niederländischen Einwanderung in Deutschland im 16. Jahrhundert." *Westdetsche Zeitschrift für Geschichte und Kunst* 29 (1910): 117–81.

Wolfart, Johannes. *Religion, Government and Political Culture in Early Modern Germany: Lindau, 1520–1628.* Houndsmill, UK: Palgrave, 2002.

Wolff, Carl, and Rudolf Jung, eds. *Die Baudenkmäler in Frankfurt am Main.* 3 vols. Frankfurt a. M.: Völcker, 1896–1914.

Woo, Kenneth. "Nicodemism and Libertinism." In *John Calvin in Context,* edited by R. Ward Holder, 287–96. Cambridge: Cambridge University Press, 2020.

Yungblut, Laura Hunt. *Strangers Settled Here amongst Us: Policies, Perceptions and the Presence of Aliens in Elizabethan England.* London: Routledge, 1996.

Zachman, Randall C. *John Calvin as Teacher, Pastor, and Theologian: The Shape of His Writings and Thought.* Grand Rapids, MI: Baker Academic, 2006.

Zagorin, Perez. *Ways of Lying: Dissimulation, Persecution, and Conformity in Early Modern Europe.* Cambridge, MA: Harvard University Press, 1990.

Zeeden, Ernst Walter. *Die Entstehung der Konfessionen: Grundlagen und Formen der Konfessionsbildung im Zeitalter der Glaubenskämpfe.* Munich: R. Oldenbourg, 1965.

———. "Grundlagen und Wege der Konfessionsbildung im Zeitalter der Glaubenskämpfe." *Historische Zeitschrift* 185 (December 1958): 249–99.

Zitter, Miriam. "Ansichten eines Studenten: Der Briefwechsel des Johann Hartmann Beyer, 1563–1625." In *Ars und Scientia im Mittelalter und der frühen Neuzeit: Ergebnisse interdisziplinärer Forschung,* edited by Cora Dietl et al. Tübingen: Francke, 2002.

Zolberg, Aristide R., Astri Suhrke, and Sergio Aguayo. *Escape from Violence: Conflict and Refugee Crisis in the Developing World.* Oxford: Oxford University Press, 1989.

# INDEX

*Page numbers in italics refer to illustrations.*

# Studies in Early Modern German History

*The German Discovery of the World: Renaissance Encounters*
*with the Strange and Marvelous*
Christine R. Johnson

*Cautio Criminalis, or a Book on Witch Trials*
Friedrich Spee von Langenfeld, translated by Marcus Hellyer

*Bacchus and Civic Order: The Culture of Drink in Early Modern Germany*
B. Ann Tlusty

*Shaman of Oberstdorf: Chonrad Stoeckhlin and the Phantoms of the Night*
Wolfgang Behringer , translated by H. C. Erik Midelfort

*Obedient Germans? A Rebuttal: A New View of German History*
Peter Blickle, translated by Thomas A. Brady Jr.

*Lost Worlds: How Our European Ancestors Coped with Everyday Life*
*and Why Life Is So Hard Today*
Arthur E. Imhof, translated by Thomas Robisheaux

*Mad Princes of Renaissance Germany*
H. C. Erik Midelfort